P9-DVQ-793

WHAT MEN OR GODS ARE THESE ?

A Genealogical Approach to Classical Mythology

BY FRED AND JEANETTA BOSWELL

CORBAN UNIVERSITY
LIBRARY
5000 Deer Park Drive SE
Salem, OR 97317-9392

The Scarecrow Press, Inc. • Metuchen, N.J., & London • 1980

Library of Congress Cataloging in Publication Data

Boswell, Fred.
    What men or gods are these?

    Bibliography: p.
    Includes index.
    1. Mythology, Greek--Handbooks, manuals, etc.
I. Boswell, Jeanetta, 1922-   joint author.
II. Title.
BL782.B6   292'.13   80-13780
ISBN 0-8108-1314-9

Copyright © 1980 by Jeanetta Boswell
Manufactured in the United States of America

46863

This work is sincerely
dedicated to my student and
faithful assistant, Sarah--
and to Christopher, the son
of Sarah.

PREFACE

"What men or gods are these?" Keats asked when he was describing the figures on his Grecian Urn; and now, once again, we ask the question, and attempt to supply another answer. This is not, however, another book of mythological stories. Students may take their choice in this field, and are urged to do so: Edith Hamilton, Mythology; Michael Grant, Myths of the Greeks and Romans; Bulfinch, The Age of Fable; Gayley, The Classic Myths in English Literature; H. J. Rose, A Handbook of Greek Mythology; and the Larousse Encyclopedia of Mythology, a large-format volume containing mythology from all nations and hundreds of valuable illustrations.

Nor is this present work primarily another dictionary of mythology. There are already enough good works in this category: The Oxford Classical Dictionary, a large volume and not readily obtainable for the average student's purse, but by far the most complete and authoritative of its kind; Lemprière, Classical Dictionary of Popular Names, first published in 1788 and recently issued in a new edition by an American publisher; Edward Tripp, Crowell's Handbook of Classical Mythology; Richmond Y. Hathorn, Crowell's Handbook of Classical Drama; Lillian Feder, Crowell's Handbook of Classical Literature; and J. E. Zimmerman, Dictionary of Classical Mythology, available in a pocket-size, quick-reference format.

This present work is primarily a study of genealogy, and thus shares the characteristics of the book of mythological stories and the dictionary. It is arranged according to family relationships, some forty of them, including the gods beginning with Gaea and Uranus. In addition to the family charts, there are four major lists of heroes who participated in (1) the voyage of the Argo, (2) the Calydonian Boar Hunt, (3) the Wars against Thebes, and (4) the Trojan War. The lineage of both mother and father have been given when at all possible, and this is indicated by cross-referencing in parentheses. Each chart is accompanied by a series of notes in which familiar material about the character is summarized, and there is an Index to the Charts in which all names have been listed. In addition, there is a Subject Index, in which all the gods and demigods are given in an alphabetical listing according to their functions; an Index to the genealogy charts; and ample bibliographical material to engage the undergraduate student for some time.

Our work has led to an increased awareness of the reality of these mythological creations, both human and divine. In the bare context of their family relationships, they become remarkably alive, and their problems do not seem very alien to our own: some lived to be very old and died leaving many sons and daughters to continue their line; others died childless. Some died young before their lives had hardly begun; others lived to see their children slaughtered before their very eyes. Most women were faithful to their husbands; some were wayward and went looking elsewhere. Some daughters made good marriages to great heroes and were the mothers of great sons; other daughters were married to great criminals. Sons were mostly obedient to their fathers, but sometimes they were not; and on a few sad occasions sons murdered their mothers, the most hideous of crimes.

Fred and Jeanetta Boswell
Arlington, Texas
August, 1976

References and quotations are based on translations in the Loeb Library.

ACKNOWLEDGMENTS

Special thanks are extended to the following:

Bobbs-Merrill, for permission to quote from the Frank O. Copley translation of the Aeneid.

W. W. Norton, for permission to quote from the Albert Cook translation of the Odyssey.

Grover Grubb, professor of engineering at the University of Texas at Arlington, and David Manning for the artwork on the charts.

Bantam Books, for permission to quote from Euripides, Ten Plays, translated by Moses Hadas and John McLean, copyright © 1960 Bantam Books Inc. By permission of Bantam Books. All rights reserved.

The extract from Apollodorus' The Library, translated by J. G. Frazer, is reprinted by permission of Harvard University Press and the Loeb Classical Library.

TABLE OF CONTENTS

Principal Figures:

WHAT MEN OR GODS ARE THESE?

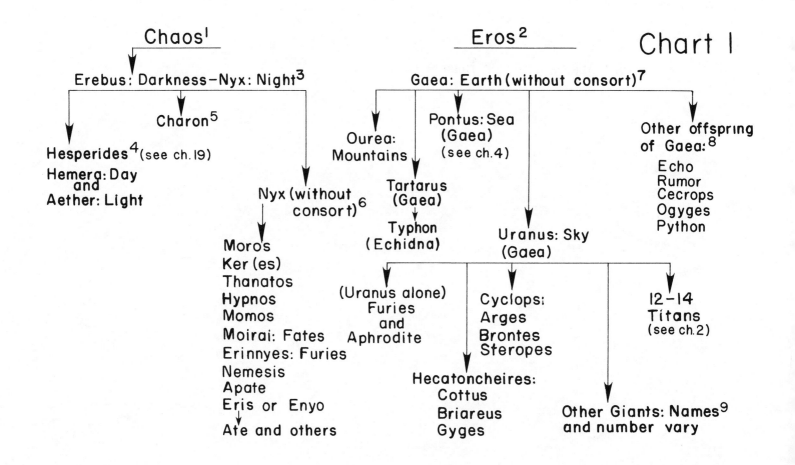

Chaos[1]

Eros[2]

Chart I

Erebus: Darkness—Nyx: Night[3]

Charon[5]

Hesperides[4](see ch.19)

Hemera: Day
and
Aether: Light

Nyx (without
consort)[6]

Moros
Ker (es)
Thanatos
Hypnos
Momos
Moirai: Fates
Erinnyes: Furies
Nemesis
Apate
Eris or Enyo

Ate and others

Gaea: Earth (without consort)[7]

Ourea:
Mountains

Pontus: Sea
(Gaea)
(see ch.4)

Tartarus
(Gaea)

Typhon
(Echidna)

Uranus: Sky
(Gaea)

Other offspring
of Gaea:[8]

Echo
Rumor
Cecrops
Ogyges
Python

(Uranus alone)
Furies
and
Aphrodite

Cyclops:
Arges
Brontes
Steropes

Hecatoncheires:
Cottus
Briareus
Gyges

12–14
Titans
(see ch.2)

Other Giants: Names[9]
and number vary

NOTES FOR CHART 1

[1]Chaos came first, according to Hesiod, but did not beget the other primeval gods. Apollodorus does not begin with Chaos, but says, "Sky was the first who ruled over the whole earth," and then wedded Earth. Ovid begins the Metamorphoses with the following observation:

> Before the seas, and this terrestrial ball,
> And Heav'n's high canopy that covers all,
> One was the face of Nature; if a face:
> Rather a rude and indigested Mass:
> A lifeless lump, unfashioned and unfram'd,
> Of jarring seeds; and justly Chaos named.

Ovid continues by saying that from Chaos came Earth, then Sky, Stars, Winds, and the gods.

[2]Eros not to be confused with the son of Aphrodite and Ares, who is more familiarly known as the Roman god Cupid. Hesiod says that after Chaos, came Earth, Gaea, "broad-bosomed ... the solid and eternal home of all," and then Eros, "the most beautiful of the immortal gods," an influence or force that would thenceforth preside over the ordering of things and beings.

[3]Erebus-Nyx Hesiod does not say that Gaea came from Chaos, but that "out of Chaos came Erebus (Darkness) and black Nyx (Night)," and they united and produced Hemera (Day) and Aether (Light). The respect with which Nyx was regarded and feared is well illustrated in Book VII of the Iliad, in which Ajax, son of Telamon, and Hector fight all day, but when "Night darkens" they put down their arms and exchange gifts with each other. Also in the Iliad, Book XIV, the story is told that even Zeus, angry with Sleep, a son of Nyx, refrained from doing anything "displeasing to swift Night."

[4]Hesperides whom Hesiod calls daughters of Erebus and Nyx. Another myth makes them descendants of Hyperion and Thea, through Eos (Dawn) and her son Hesperus. A similar myth makes Hesperus, the Evening Star, a son of Iapetus and Clymene, and has his daughter Hesperis married to Atlas, her father's brother. The least familiar genealogy makes the Hesperides daughters of Phorcys and Ceto, brother and sister monster offspring of Pontus and Gaea. Regardless of genealogy, however, the Hesperides are uniformly associated with the Garden of Golden Apples owned by Atlas. Their names and number vary: Aigle, Erytheia, Arethusa, Hespere, Hesperethusa. They, with a dragon named Ladon, guarded the apples until Heracles in his Eleventh Labor, killed the dragon, tricked Atlas, and stole the golden fruit.

[5]Charon son of Erebus and Nyx, who for a fee piloted

dead souls across Styx and Acheron in the Underworld. In the Aeneid, Charon is described as a "ragged horror, whose thick white beard lies matted upon his chin. His eyes are flames, and knotted rags hang filthy from his frame." It should be noted that Charon piloted only those souls whose bodies had been buried. Those who had not found a resting place in the earth fluttered aimlessly about for a hundred years, according to Virgil. The reader may be prompted to agree with Aeneas, who was "puzzled and grieved at death's inequities."

[6]Nyx (Without Consort)   Hesiod says, "All these the dark goddess Night bore without sleeping with any male," and lists the following:

Destruction (Moros)
Specter (Ker)
Death (Thanatos)
Sleep, called "brother of Death" by Homer (Hypnos)
Dreams (Oneiroi)
Blame "carping criticism" (Momos)
Grief (Oizys)
Fates (Moirai, or the Roman Parcae):
    Clotho, spinner of the thread of life
    Lachesis, measures the length of life
    Atropos, carries the shears and cuts the thread of life
Specters of Vengeance, violent death (Keres, Erinnyes, Furies, or the Roman Dirae):
    Alecto
    Tisiphone
    Megaera

Several variations in the genealogy of the Fates and Furies exist: Apollodorus calls the Fates daughters of Zeus and Themis, and the Furies are called the daughters of Acheron and Nyx, instead of Nyx alone; Hades and Persephone, and Chaos and Gaea are also given as the parents of the Furies. Both Hesiod and Apollodorus say the Furies sprang from the drops of blood shed by Uranus when he was castrated by his son Cronus. Also in this same story, Hesiod says that Aphrodite emerged from the foam when the genital parts of Uranus were cast upon the sea. In Oedipus at Colonus, Sophocles calls the Furies "dread Goddesses, daughters of the Earth and Gloom." The Furies, who later become identified with the Eumenides, and thus assume a character of benevolence, are best studied in the great Aeschylean trilogy Oresteia.

Hesiod concludes his list of offspring of Nyx with:

Retribution (Nemesis)
Deceit (Apate)
Love, deceitful (Philotes)
Old Age (Geras)
Strife, Discord (Eris)

Eris, Strife or Discord, is also called the sister of Ares, son of Zeus, and god of brutality in warfare. Homer calls this goddess Enyo in the Iliad. Eris is also associated with the familiar story of the Apple of Discord, which is said to have caused the Trojan War. This event is basic to Homer's version of the war, and is also incorporated into Helen's defense of herself at war's end when Menelaus is threatening to put her to death in Euripides' The Trojan Women.

It is interesting to note that Eris is the only child of Nyx who bore further offspring: "Hateful Strife gave birth," says Hesiod and names the following:

Distress (Ponos)
Distraction (Lethe)

Chart 1   5

Famine (Limos)
Sorrow (Alyea)
Wars (Hysminae)
Battles (Machai)
Murders (Phonsi)
Slaughters (Androktasiai)
Feuds (Neika)
Lying Words (Logoi)
Angry Words (Amphilogiai)
Lawlessness (Dysnomia)
Madness, Delusion (Ate)
Oath (Horkos)

<u>Ate</u>, the most familiar of this malevolent brood, is described by Agamemnon in the <u>Iliad</u>. In this passage, Agamemnon is agonizing over the quarrel with Achilles that was provoked at the outset of the story; he says, in effect, that he was "misled": "Delusion ... the elder daughter of Zeus, the accursed who deludes all" was once a goddess on Olympus, but now walks among men. Another catalog of horrors, similar to Hesiod's, but not called the offspring of Eris, is enumerated by Virgil as the hero Aeneas enters the Underworld:

Right at the entrance, where hell's throat begins,
Sorrow, Vengeance, and Care have pitched their
    tents;
there live Diseases pale, and grim Old Age,
Fear, evil-counseling Hunger, shameful Want--
shapes terrible to see--and Death and Toil,
and Death's blood brother, Sleep, and Pleasures
    vile
even in thought. War, dealer of death, stands
    watch,
and Furies chambered in steel, while mad Sedi-
    tion
leers through her bedlam braids of snakes and
    blood.

[7]<u>Gaea</u>: <u>Earth</u>   called the Great Mother; Cybele, the Phrygian Earth goddess, is very similar; also called Lellus Mater by the Romans. Hesiod says that Gaea first, without consort, produced Sky (Uranus; Coelus, Roman), then Mountains (Ourea) and "gloomy Tartarus," and "also gave birth to the barren waters, Sea [Pontus]." After this Gaea united with Uranus, her son, but there are two versions as to which of their offspring came first. Hesiod says that first Gaea gave birth to the Titans and then "to the violent Cyclops--Thunderer [Brontes], Lightner [Steropes], and bold Flash [Arges], who made and gave to Zeus the thunder and the lightening-bolt." The Cyclops were like gods except that a single eye was placed in their foreheads, and their great strength was in their hands. Furthermore, unlike gods, they were subject to death, which they eventually met at the hands of Apollo.

Next, Hesiod says, there were three more children, "big, strong, and horrible, Cottus and Briareus and Gyges [Gyes], the Hecatoncheires, the Hundred-Handed. This unruly brood had a hundred monstrous hands sprouting from their shoulders, and fifty heads on top of their shoulders." Apollodorus says Uranus "begat first the Hundred-Handed as they are named: Briareus, Gyes, Cottus, who were unsurpassed in size and might, each of them having a hundred hands and fifty heads. After these, Earth bore him the Cyclops, to wit, Arges, Steropes, Brontes, of whom each had one eye on his forehead. But them Sky bound and cast into Tartarus, a gloomy place in Hades as far distant from the earth as earth is distant from the sky. And again he begat children by Earth, to wit, the Titans...."

A more familiar reference to the one-eyed Cyclops is the story recounted by Odysseus of his adventure with Polyphemus, the cyclops. In this episode from the <u>Odyssey</u> is also mentioned the Seer-Cyclops Telemus, both of whom claim Poseidon as their father.

Apollodorus also says that these Cyclops are sons of Poseidon and the nymph Thoosa.

In addition to uniting with Uranus, Gaea also mated with Pontus (Sea) and brought forth a notable line of progeny. And finally, according to both Hesiod and Apollodorus, Earth united with Tartarus and produced the most horrible monster of all: Hesiod called him Typhoeus; Apollodorus calls him Typhon, "a hybrid between man and beast." He was finally hurled into Tartarus, but not before he had tried to assault the gods on Olympus, and not before he had lain with Echidna and given birth to his own line of monsters.

8Other Offspring of Gaea   (a) Echo: Ovid gives the most familiar account of Echo, in which she is hopelessly in love with Narcissus. She grieves herself to death, and is finally nothing but bones and a voice. (b) Rumor: According to Virgil, "Men say the Earth, in fury at the gods, bore this last child, a sister to the Giants." (c) Cecrops: Named by Apollodorus as "a son of the soil, with a body compounded of man and serpent, was the first king of Attica." (d) Ogyges: Identified as the most ancient of those who reigned in Greece. He was the son of Earth and Poseidon, and married Thebe, a daughter of Zeus or a daughter of the river god Asopus. He reigned in Boetia, which is sometimes called Ogygia. The name of Ogyges also survives in the name of one of the Seven Gates of Thebes, the Ogygian Gate, named by Pausanias and Apollodorus. The Ogygian Gate, however, is not one of those named by Aeschylus in The Seven Against Thebes. (e) Python: Ovid gives an account of this creation. After the Great Flood, Earth created new monsters out of the mud and slime: "So monstrous was his bulk, so large a space did his vast body, and long train embrace."

9Other Giants   According to Hesiod, these giants arose from the drops of blood from the mutilated Uranus, absorbed by Gaea. These are the Giants who figure in the war of the Giants and gods, which is reputed to have taken place after Zeus warred against the Titans and became supreme god himself. Gaea, angry that her offspring, the Titans, had been treated so badly, called forth the Giants to make war against Zeus. The names of these Giants vary, but most of them are named by Apollodorus in his account of the War of the Giants and Gods:

Alcyoneus, killed by Heracles with an arrow.
Porphyrion, smote with a thunderbolt by Zeus and then shot dead by Heracles.
Ephialtes, shot by Apollo with an arrow in his left eye and by Heracles in the right.
Eurytus, killed by Dionysus with a thyrsus.
Clytius, killed by Hecate with torches.
Mimas, killed by Hephaestus with missiles of red-hot metal.
Enceladus, buried alive by Athene with the island of Sicily.
Pallas, flayed alive by Athene who used his skin to shield her own body in the fight.
Polybotes, chased through the sea by Poseidon and then killed with pieces of an island thrown at him.
Hippolytus, slain by Hermes.
Gration, killed by Artemis.
Agrius and Thoas, killed by the Fates with brazen clubs.
All others destroyed by thunderbolts from Zeus and shot dead by Heracles with arrows.

One of the most celebrated of Giants, not named here by Apollodorus, is Tityus, described by both Homer and

Chart 1   7

Virgil, as he spent his eternity of torment in the Underworld.   Homer says in the <u>Odyssey</u>:

> There Tityus large and long, in fetters bound
> O'erspreads nine acres of infernal ground;
> Two ravenous vultures, furious for their food,
> Scream o'er the fiend, and riot in his blood,
> Incessant gore the liver in his breast,
> The immortal liver grows and gives the immortal feast.

Another giant, Aloeus, fathered two sons, Ephialtes and Otus, who became better known than he. Some variation in their parentage is given, but they are generally called the sons of Iphemedia by Poseidon. The mother deserted her husband, Aloeus, and her sons and went with Poseidon.   The sons were reared by Aloeus and their stepmother Eriboea.   Apollodorus tells their familiar story, but constructs a genealogy that is generally unfamiliar:

Deucalion (son of Prometheus, survivor of the Flood)
(Pyrrha)
↓
Hellen: Hellenes
↓
Aeolus
↓
7 sons and 5 daughters, one of which was Canace
(Poseidon)
Aloeus, Triops, Others
↓
Iphemedia
(Aloeus) (Poseidon)
↓
Ephialtes and
Otus

The story of these two giants, who grew an inch each month, and so by nine years were of monstrous size, is the same in Apollodorus, Homer, and Virgil.   When they were nine years old, they aspired to ascend into Olympus and overthrow the gods; they piled mountains one on top of the other in order to make their ascent, but such ambitions were short-lived.   Apollo and Artemis killed them, and Zeus sent them to Tartarus.   It is in the Underworld that both Odysseus and Aeneas see them and relate their story.   Odysseus says:

> ... I saw Iphimedia, the wife
> Of Aloeus, who said she had lain with Poseidon,
> And she had two sons that were born short-lived,
> The godlike Otus and the far-famed Ephialtes,
> Who were the tallest men nourished by the grain-giving earth,
> And by far the handsomest, next to famous Orion,
> For after nine seasons these men were nine cubits
> In breadth, and they were also nine fathoms in height.
> They made threats to the immortals upon Olympus
> That they would start the combat of an impetuous war.
> They strove to put Ossa on Olympus and to put on Ossa
> Leaf-quivering Pelion, so that heaven might be scaled.
> And they would have done it had they reached the measure of their prime;
> But the son of Zeus, whom fair-haired Leto bore, destroyed
> Both of them, before the whiskers beneath their temples
> Had flowered and their chins got thick with blossoming down.

10

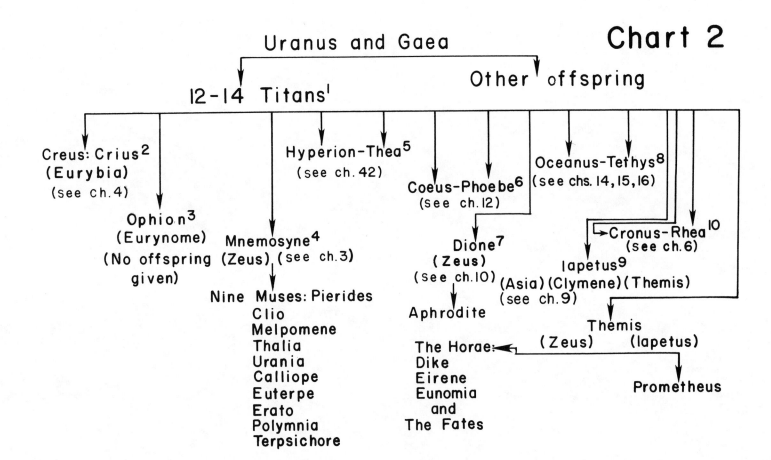

Chart 2

NOTES FOR CHART 2

[1]12-14 Titans   The number of Titans varies: twelve is the basic list. Hesiod names twelve in the following order: Sons--Ocean (the oldest), Coeus, Crius, Hyperion, Iapetus, and Cronus (the youngest); Daughters--Thea, Rhea, Themis, Mnemosyne, Phoebe, and Tethys. Apollodorus names thirteen in the following order: Sons--Ocean, Coeus, Hyperion, Crius, Iapetus, and Cronus (the youngest); Daughters--Tethys, Rhea, Themis, Mnemosyne, Phoebe, Dione, and Thea. Apollodorus adds Dione, mother of Aphrodite by Zeus, as in Homer, but Homer does not refer to the goddess as a Titan. Ophion, not given by either Hesiod or Apollodorus as a Titan, derives from Orphic mythology, and is referred to by Apollonius of Rhodes in the Argonautica.

[2]Crius (or Creus)   married Eurybia, a daughter of Gaea and Pontus. Their offspring were Astraeus, Pallas, and Perses. There are no stories or descriptions of Crius; however, Hesiod called Eurybia a "daughter with a heart of steel."

[3]Ophion and Eurynome   Eurynome is a daughter of Oceanus and Tethys, and the mother by Zeus of the Graces. Ophion and Eurynome are described as the first rulers of Olympus in the Argonautica:

Then too Orpheus lifted up his lyre in his left hand and made essay to sing. He sang how earth, and heaven, and sea, once joined together in unity, were separated, each apart, after a deadly quarrel; and how, forever in heaven, the stars, the moon, and the paths of the sea have their steadfast goal, and how the mountains rose up, and how rivers rushing with their nymphs, and all creeping things came into being. Next he sang how, at the first, Ophion and Eurynome, daughter of Oceanus, held sway o'er snow-capped Olympus, and how the one yielded up his honors to the mighty hands of Cronus, while she gave way to Rhea.

[4]Mnemosyne   means memory. By Zeus, she is the mother of the nine Muses. Sometimes the Muses are called the Pierides, a name derived from their birthplace Pieria, a region near Mount Olympus. Ovid, however, uses this name for the nine daughters of Pierus, the King of Pieria, who competed with the Muses in song, lost the contest, and were changed into chattering magpies. Ovid also tells other stories of the Muses, including that of Pyreneus, a King of Thrace, who offered shelter to the Muses during a shower of rain, and then tried to violate them. They took flight, and he, forgetting that he did not have wings as they did, tried to follow them through an open window, fell from the tower, and was killed. Of their natures and functions, Hesiod says:

These Muses were born in Pieria to Mnemosyne, the Queen of the hills of Eleuther, after her union with Father Zeus the son of Cronus; their nature is forgetfulness of evil and rest from cares. On nine successive nights did Zeus the lord of wisdom unite with her, going to her sacred bed unknown to the rest of the gods; and when the year was up, as the seasons revolved and the months waned and many days had passed, she gave birth to nine daughters all of one mind, all with spirits dedicated to song, all carefree in their hearts.

The individual functions of the Muses, as Clio of history, etc., were not differentiated until late Roman times, according to the Oxford Classical Dictionary; however, Virgil invokes the name of Erato and Calliope in the Aeneid. They are usually represented as young, beautiful virgins, but other traditions attribute many love affairs to them, and their line of progeny is most numerous.

[5]Hyperion-Thea   Titan brother and sister. The name Hyperion refers directly to the Sun as a celestial body, although the name varies with translators, sometimes called Helios or Phoebus. There are no stories of Thea, and references to Hyperion are rare. The only familiar story is that related in Homer's Odyssey of the men who slaughtered and ate Hyperion's cattle. Justice for this deed was meted out by Zeus when Hyperion complained that if he were not compensated he would take his Sun to Hades and shine in the Underworld. The offspring of Hyperion and Thea were Helios: Sun (Sol, Roman), Selene: Moon (Luna, Roman), and Eos: Dawn (Aurora, Roman).

[6]Coeus-Phoebe   Titan brother and sister, of whom there are no stories. They became

parents of two daughters, Leto (Latona, Roman) and Asteria, both of whom were loved by Zeus. One story has it that Asteria, to escape the advances of Zeus, turned herself into a quail; Ovid, however, says that after enjoying the favors of Zeus for a long time, she fell into disfavor, and he turned her into a quail. In either case, she is always referred to as the mother of Hecate by Perses, the son of Crius and Eurybia. Leto was the much-loved daughter of Coeus and Phoebe, and became by Zeus the mother of two of the most famous Olympians--Apollo and Artemis. These two she bore, however, at great pains because Hera, in jealousy and spite, held back the Ilithyias, goddesses of childbirth, and would not allow them to deliver Leto for nine days and nights. Apollo and Artemis were born on the Island of Delos.

[7]Dione   named by Apollodorus as one of the Titans. In Homer, she is the mother, by Zeus, of "laughter-loving" Aphrodite. In the Iliad, it is Dione, "the fair-goddess," who comforts Aphrodite when she is bitterly wounded in battle by the warrior Diomedes. Dione tells her daughter that gods have to bear a great deal at the hands of mortals, but that mortals who wound gods are fools and have not long to live. She warns that the wife of Diomedes may soon awake and find herself a widow. Other than this episode in Homer, there are no familiar stories of Dione, and Aphrodite is the only offspring assigned to her.

[8]Oceanus-Tethys   Titan brother and sister who are said to have born three thousand sons, the river gods, and three thousand daughters, the nymphs and Oceanids. There are few stories or references to this pair, but numerous tales of their many offspring. In the Iliad, when Hera is planning to seduce Zeus and thus deprive the Trojans of the god's help, she pretends

Chart 2   13

that she is going to visit Oceanus and Tethys, who have quarrelled. Hera says:

> For I am faring to visit the limits of the all
> nurturing earth, and Oceanus, from whom the
> gods are sprung, and mother Tethys, even them
> that lovingly nursed and cherished me in their
> halls, when they had taken me from Rhea, that
> time Zeus, whose voice is borne afar, thrust
> Cronus down to dwell beneath earth and the un-
> resting sea.

In the war of the gods and Titans, here referred to by Hera, Oceanus took no part, and thus escaped the fate of those who had warred against Zeus. In Aeschylus' Prometheus Bound, Oceanus is also represented as friendly to Zeus when he visits Prometheus and assures the chained Titan that Zeus will forgive him if he asks.

9Iapetus-Themis   Iapetus' wife is generally given as Clymene, a daughter of Oceanus, by whom Hesiod says he had four sons: Menoetius, Atlas, Prometheus, and Epimetheus. Aeschylus is alone in calling Prometheus the "high-souled son of Themis." Originally an earth goddess, Themis finally became identified with law, physical and moral order. She is represented as residing on Olympus in the Iliad, and is responsible for law and order among the gods. By Zeus, Themis is the mother of the Horae (the Seasons), whose names and numbers vary from three to eleven. Ordinarily they are identified as three sisters, named by Hesiod, Irene: Eirene (Peace); Dike (Justice: As-traea, Roman), a young girl with a pair of scales in one hand and a scarf bound over her eyes; and Eunomia (Order: Legislation), who "hourly attend the labors of mankind." Other young goddesses sometimes related to the Horae are Carpo (Pomona and Vertumnus, Roman,

deities of the Spring and fruit trees); and Thallo (Flora, Roman, goddess of Spring and flowers). The Fates (Moerae) are sometimes assigned to Themis and Zeus, but more often are called daughters of Nyx.

Two well-known stories are told of Themis. After the Great Flood, it was she who advised Deucalion, the son of Prometheus, and Pyrrha, Deucalion's wife, daughter of Epimetheus, to "throw the bones of their mother over their shoulders," and thus repopulate the Earth. The "bones"--rocks--became the men and women of a new race of mortals, according to Ovid's telling of the story. The other story involving Themis is the prophecy that Zeus would take a wife whose son would overthrow the father. Themis revealed this oracle to her son Prometheus, who used the secret to bargain for his freedom from Zeus's punishment. The wife referred to is Thetis, daughter of Nereus and Doris, who, when Zeus and Poseidon learned her name, was hurriedly married to the mortal Peleus and became the mother of Achilles.

10Cronus-Rhea   are the parents of the gods, the six Olympians: Poseidon, Hades, and Zeus; Hestia, Demeter, and Hera. The story is familiar that Cronus led a revolt against his father Uranus, and was in turn revolted against by his son Zeus. In an at-tempt to forestall his fate, Cronus swallowed his children as they were born, except for Zeus, who was hidden away in Crete where he grew to maturity. Instead of the babe, Rhea had given Cronus a stone wrapped in a blanket. Hesiod calls Zeus the youngest of the gods; however, in two references in the Iliad, Homer refers to Zeus as older than Poseidon.

Uranus and Gaea

Chart 3

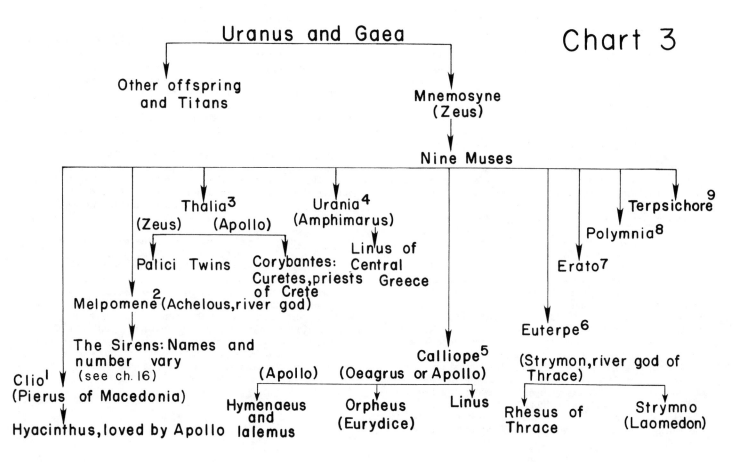

Other offspring and Titans

Mnemosyne (Zeus)

Nine Muses

Thalia[3]

(Zeus) (Apollo)

Urania[4] (Amphimarus)

Terpsichore[9]

Polymnia[8]

Palici Twins

Corybantes: Curetes, priests of Crete

Linus of Central Greece

Erato[7]

Melpomene[2] (Achelous, river god)

Euterpe[6]

The Sirens: Names and number vary (see ch. 16)

Calliope[5]

Clio[1] (Pierus of Macedonia)

(Apollo) (Oeagrus or Apollo)

(Strymon, river god of Thrace)

Linus

Hyacinthus, loved by Apollo

Hymenaeus and Ialemus

Orpheus (Eurydice)

Rhesus of Thrace

Strymno (Laomedon)

NOTES FOR CHART 3

[1]Clio   Muse of History, is represented holding a trum-
          pet in one hand and a book in the other; it was
her duty to record, or celebrate, the deeds of brave
and courageous heroes.   There are many versions of
Clio's offspring, but some figures are given rather consistently.   By Pierus, a son of Magnes, Apollodorus
says she became the mother of Hyacinthus.   She was
also the mother of Hymenaeus, the god of marriage,
and Ialemus, a singer, although these two are also called
the sons of Apollo and Calliope, or the sons of Dionysus
and Aphrodite.   Hyacinthus is sometimes called the son
of Amyclas, son of Lacedaemon and Sparta, and Diomede.   Whatever genealogy is adopted, the story of
Hyacinthus is the same.   In Ovid, the story is told of
the beautiful youth loved by Apollo, who accidentally
killed him in a game of quoits.   Unable to restore the
mortal youth to life, the god created from his blood the
flower that bears his name, Hyacinth.

[2]Melpomene   Muse of Tragedy, is represented as wear-
              ing the tragic mask and holding a dagger
in one hand and a scepter and crown in the other.   She
is sometimes said to be the mother, by the river god
Achelous, of the Sirens.   Calliope and Terpsichore are
also called the mother of the Sirens, and, rarely, the
Sirens are called the daughters of Phorcys and Ceto.
The names and number of the Sirens vary from the usual
three to seven.

[3]Thalia   Muse of Comedy and Pastoral Poetry, is
          represented as holding a comic mask in one
hand and a shepherd's staff in the other.   She wears a
short shepherd's dress with few ornaments.   Thalia is
sometimes called the mother by Apollo of the Corybantes,
priests of Rhea or Cybele, in Crete called the Curetes.
This genealogy is given according to Apollodorus; however, many other accounts of the parents of the Corybantes are given.   The Palici Twins are also called sons
of Thalia and Zeus, but this Thalia may be "a local
nymph" of Sicily, near the mountain Aetna.   The nymph
herself is sometimes called "Aetna."

[4]Urania   Muse of Astronomy, is represented as dressed
          in a blue robe, crowned with stars and holding
a globe in her hands.   Linus, the son of Urania, is a
name attributed to several figures, all of whom died in
their youths.   Their traditional parentage depends upon
the locality from which they derive.   (a) Linus of Central Greece is the son of Urania and Amphimarus, a
son of Poseidon.   Pausanias says he was killed by Apollo because he (Linus) boasted that he could sing as well
as the god.   (b) Linus of Argos is the son of Apollo
and a local princess Psamathe.   The mother exposed
him, according to Pausanias, and he was torn to pieces
by dogs.   In anger Apollo plagued the city until retribution was paid.   (c) Another Linus is the son of Calliope, the Muse, and Oeagrus of Thrace, or Apollo.   He

is referred to as a "brother of Orpheus" by Apollodorus. It is this Linus whom Heracles accidentally killed during a music lesson. (d) And finally there is Linus referred to in the Iliad. This passage is part of the long, highly detailed description of the Shield of Achilles, created by the god-smith Hephaestus. Among the many items that are depicted on this marvelous shield is a group of young girls and young men carrying baskets of grapes, and in their midst a youth with a lyre who played and sang "the beautiful song for Linus."

[5]Calliope   Muse of Epic poetry and eloquence, is represented with a trumpet in one hand and books in the other. Her appearance and function resemble Clio, the only distinction being that Calliope takes notice of the great actions of heroes, whereas Clio records them. Virgil calls on Calliope for help in Book IX of the Aeneid. Orpheus, one of the most celebrated of mythological characters, is called the son of "Calliope herself to her Thracian lover Oeagrus" by Apollonius of Rhodes. Stories of Orpheus are far too extensive for total coverage here, and most of his stories are basically familiar. Ovid tells of his marriage to, and subsequent loss of, Eurydice, and of his death. Apollonius of Rhodes includes Orpheus in the crew of the Argo, and relates several incidents involving him. Apollodorus also includes many stories of his life and death, including his burial at Pieria.

   Hymenaeus and Ialemus, shown here as sons of Calliope and Apollo, are also attributed to Clio (see above). Linus as the brother of Orpheus has been discussed under Urania above.

[6]Euterpe   Muse of Music, is represented as crowned with flowers and holding a flute in her hands. By Strymon, the river god of Thrace, Euterpe is the mother of Rhesus of Thrace and the daughter Strymno,

who married Laomedon of Troy, according to Apollodorus. Rhesus is called the son of Eioneus, King of Thrace, and Euterpe by Homer; but in the play Rhesus, which is attributed to Euripides, the parents of Rhesus are Terpsichore and Strymon. Whatever genealogy is given, the story of Rhesus does not vary. He had come from Thrace as an ally of the Trojans; his camp was raided, and he and his men were brutally murdered at night by Odysseus and Diomedes and their men. The main sources of this story are the Iliad and the play Rhesus.

[7]Erato   Muse of Lyric and Love Poetry, is represented as crowned with roses and myrtle, holding in one hand a lyre and a lute in the other. The name Erato refers to several mythological figures, but there is no evidence that the Muse had any children.

[8]Polymnia   Muse of Singing and Rhetoric, is represented as veiled in white, holding a scepter in one hand, and the other hand raised as though about to speak. One myth makes Triptolemus the son of Polymnia, but there are so many accounts of his parentage that nothing is established. He is called the son of Oceanus and Gaea; the son of a priest of Argos; and the son of Celeus, King of Attica, by Neraea or Metanira or Polymnia. Apollodorus relates a lengthy account of Triptolemus and, as is generally the case, associates him with the goddess Demeter, who tried to make him immortal by plunging him into the fire at night when his mother was asleep. Failing to accomplish her purpose because of the mother's hysterical interference, Demeter then taught him agriculture and how to sow and cultivate seed. Triptolemus is said to have established the Eleusinian festival in honor of Demeter.

Chart 3   17

[9]Terpsichore   Muse of Dancing, is represented crowned
                 with laurel and holding in one hand a mu-
sical instrument.   For possible offspring of Terpsichore,
see Melpomene and Euterpe above.

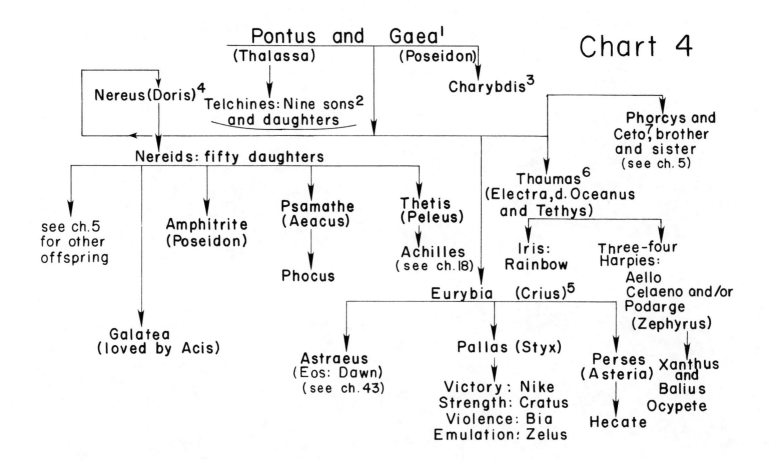

Pontus and Gaea[1]
(Thalassa)   (Poseidon)

Charybdis[3]

Chart 4

Nereus(Doris)[4]

Telchines: Nine sons[2]
and daughters

Phorcys and
Ceto, brother[7]
and sister
(see ch. 5)

Nereids: fifty daughters

Thaumas[6]
(Electra, d. Oceanus
and Tethys)

see ch. 5
for other
offspring

Amphitrite
(Poseidon)

Psamathe
(Aeacus)

Thetis
(Peleus)

Iris:
Rainbow

Three-four
Harpies:
Aello
Celaeno and/or
Podarge
(Zephyrus)

Phocus

Achilles
(see ch. 18)

Galatea
(loved by Acis)

Eurybia   (Crius)[5]

Astraeus
(Eos: Dawn)
(see ch. 43)

Pallas (Styx)

Perses
(Asteria)

Xanthus
and
Balius
Ocypete

Victory: Nike
Strength: Cratus
Violence: Bia
Emulation: Zelus

Hecate

NOTES FOR CHART 4

[1]Pontus-Gaea   Hesiod says, "Sea produced Nereus, who never lies and is always true ... and is called the Old Man of the Sea." Then with Gaea, Sea produced "great Thaumas and heroic Phorcys, and one daughter with a beautiful face, Ceto, and one daughter with a heart of steel, Eurybia."

[2]Thalassa and the Telchines   Thalassa, the feminine personification of the sea, is generally called the mother of the Telchines, who may be called daughters or sons of the Sea, but are usually referred to as "semi-divine beings." One source says they "have been called fish children because they had flippers for hands and the heads of dogs." Ovid and Pausanias identify the Telchines as a race of beings living on Rhodes, skilled in metalwork, other useful arts, and magic. Ovid further says their "eyes defiled everything they looked upon, till Jupiter in his loathing drowned them in the waters of his brother Neptune." Yet another story is that the Telchines had foreknowledge of the weather and knew in advance of the coming of Deucalion's Flood, and fled to Asia Minor. Rhode is sometimes identified as the daughter of Poseidon and Halia, a sister of the Telchines.

[3]Charybdis   a whirlpool, the daughter of Poseidon and Gaea, who was thrown into the sea for stealing Heracles' cattle. Charybdis is associated with Scylla, and together they posed serious navigational problems for at least three famous mythological voyages: Jason and the Argo; Odysseus and his ships trying to get home to Ithaca from Troy; and Aeneas and his ships, who were forewarned and avoided the problem by detouring around the straits between Sicily and the "toe" of Italy.

[4]Nereus-Doris   Nereus is the son of Pontus, called by Homer, Hesiod, and others "the Old Man of the Sea"; Doris is the daughter of Oceanus and Tethys. It is generally said that Nereus and Doris were parents of fifty daughters, the Nereids, most of whom have no real identities or stories. Three lists of names, however, are cited by Homer, Hesiod, and Apollodorus. The most famous of the Nereids are Galatea, Amphitrite, Psamathe, and Thetis. Ovid tells the story of Galatea, loved by the cyclops Polyphemus, and her love for Acis, the son of Pan or Faunus (Roman). In anger at being rejected by Galatea, Polyphemus killed Acis, whereupon the latter was transformed into a river bearing his name. Amphitrite, identified as the daughter of Oceanus and Tethys by Apollodorus, is consistently called the wife of Poseidon, although this god, like his brother Zeus, had many mistresses and loves. Thetis, the most famous of the Nereids, married the mortal Peleus and became the mother of Achilles. Psamathe, by Aeacus, the son of Zeus and Aegina, bore a son Phocus,

who gave his name to the inhabitants of Phocis. Phocus was a half-brother of Telamon and Peleus, and according to Apollonius of Rhodes and others, was murdered out of jealousy by them.

[5]Eurybia-Crius   Eurybia, daughter of Pontus and Gaea, and Crius, Titan son of Uranus and Gaea, are the parents of Astraeus, Pallas, and Perses. Astraeus, which means "starry sky," married Eos, the dawn, and they became parents of the winds and stars. Pallas married Styx, the daughter of Oceanus and Tethys, by whom men and gods swore oaths that were not retractable.   These two had a "brood of abstractions," named by Apollodorus as Victory, Dominion, Emulation, and Violence; and named by Hesiod as Glory, Victory, Power, and Strength.   Hesiod continues:

> All these exalted children have their home and station always close to Zeus; they make no journey unless he leads the way; they always sit at the side of Zeus....   Zeus honored Styx and gave her special gifts: he made Styx the name by which gods swear, and he made her children partners of his home for all time.

Of the offspring of Pallas and Styx, one of the most notable references is to Bia (Violence) and Cratus (Strength) in Aeschylus' Prometheus Bound: these two are sent by Zeus, together with Hephaestus, to nail the Titan Prometheus to the side of a mountain.   As a river, Styx was the principal river of the Underworld, described by Virgil as the "awful river," the "black unlovely river," which flows nine times around the regions of Hades. The third son of Eurybia and Crius, Perses, married Asteria, daughter of Coeus and Phoebe, and had one child, the powerful daughter Hecate.

[6]Thaumas-Electra   Thaumas, the son of Pontus and Gara, and Electra, the daughter of Oceanus and Tethys, are the parents of Iris and the Harpies.   In Homer, Iris is the Rainbow messenger of the gods, principally of Zeus and Hera; and in Virgil she also acts to cut the threads of life and speed delivery of those who are dying.   Hesiod and Apollodorus name only two Harpies, Aello and Ocypete.   Homer names one and calls her Podarge; Virgil also names one and calls her Celeano.   In the Iliad, Homer refers to the Harpy Podarge as the mother by Zephyrus, the West-wind, of the two horses Xanthus and Balius.   These two horses went with Achilles to Troy, and when Patroclus died, they wept and would not obey.   Zeus sees the situation and says, "Ah unhappy pair, wherefore gave we you to King Peleus, to a mortal, while ye are ageless and immortal."   Later Xanthus speaks to Achilles and warns of his approaching death: "The day of doom is nigh thee, nor shall we be the cause thereof, but a mighty god and overpowering Fate."   After the death of Achilles, the horses are said to have passed into the ownership of Neoptolemus, the son of Achilles.

In the Argonautica, Apollonius of Rhodes relates an episode involving Phineus, the blind King of Thrace, who suffered persecution and near starvation because the Harpies continually fouled his food, and he could not eat.   Finally, this horrible Fate came to an end when his brothers-in-law, Zetes and Calais, came with Jason and the Argonauts and put the Harpies to flight.   They were forbidden to kill or in any wise harm them.   In this story the Harpies are described as bird-like women, notable for their "fetid stench."   In the Aeneid, Virgil relates a similar episode involving the Harpies and the men of Aeneas.   Again, the Harpies spoil the food, and the crew cannot eat it.   They are described as

> ... girls with the look of birds,

Chart 4   21

    Their bellies fouled, incontinent, their hands
    Like talons, and their faces pale with hunger...
    ... winged obscenities of Ocean.

In Homer, the image of the Harpies is merely that of
storm clouds of the Ocean and has none of the vile con-
notation associated with the Harpies of Apollonius of
Rhodes and Virgil.

[7]<u>Phorcys-Ceto</u>   brother and sister offspring of Pontus
                  and Gaea, became the parents of a
prodigious number of creatures, most of them monsters
of some order. There are many variants in the genealogy of this group.

Daughters of Nereus and Doris:[1]

Nereids
from the Iliad, sisters of Thetis:

Chart 5

Phorcys and Ceto[2]

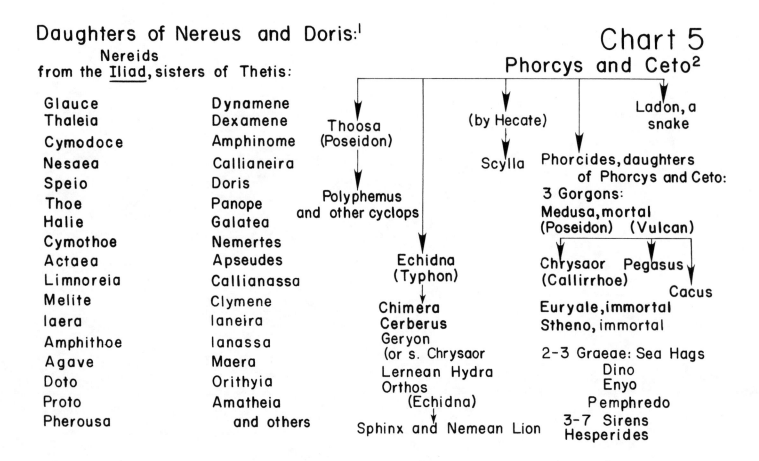

Glauce	Dynamene
Thaleia	Dexamene
Cymodoce	Amphinome
Nesaea	Callianeira
Speio	Doris
Thoe	Panope
Halie	Galatea
Cymothoe	Nemertes
Actaea	Apseudes
Limnoreia	Callianassa
Melite	Clymene
Iaera	Ianeira
Amphithoe	Ianassa
Agave	Maera
Doto	Orithyia
Proto	Amatheia
Pherousa	and others

Thoosa
(Poseidon)

Polyphemus
and other cyclops

(by Hecate)

Scylla

Ladon, a
snake

Phorcides, daughters
of Phorcys and Ceto:

3 Gorgons:
Medusa, mortal
(Poseidon) (Vulcan)

Echidna
(Typhon)

Chimera
Cerberus
Geryon
(or s. Chrysaor
Lernean Hydra
Orthos
    (Echidna)

Sphinx and Nemean Lion

Chrysaor Pegasus
(Callirrhoe)
                Cacus

Euryale, immortal
Stheno, immortal

2-3 Graeae: Sea Hags
        Dino
        Enyo
     Pemphredo
3-7 Sirens
Hesperides

NOTES FOR CHART 5

[1]The Nereids   daughters of Nereus and Doris. Al-
                though most of them do not figure in
mythological story, three complete lists of names are
assigned to these daughters.

From Homer, Iliad:

Then terribly did Achilles groan aloud, and his
queenly mother heard him as she sat in the
depths of the sea beside the old man her father.
Thereat she uttered a shrill cry, and the goddesses thronged about her, even all the daughters
of Nereus that were in the deep of the sea.
There were Glauce and Thaleia and Cymodoce,
Nesaea and Speio and Thoe and ox-eyed Halie,
and Cymothoe and Actaea and Limnoreia, and
Melite and Laera and Amphithoe and Agave, Doto
and Proto and Pherousa and Dynamene, and Dexamene and Amphinone and Callianeira, Doris and
Panope and glorious Galatea, Nemertes and Ap-
seudes and Callianassa, and there were Clymene
and Ianeira and Ianassa, Maera and Orithyia and
fair-tressed Amatheia, and other Nereids that
were in the deep of the sea....

From Apollodorus, The Library:

To Nereus and Doris were born the Nereids,
whose names are Cymothoe, Spio, Glauconome,
Nausithoe, Halie, Erato, Sao, Amphitrite, Eu-
nice, Thetis, Eulimene, Agave, Eudore, Doto,
Pherousa, Galatea, Actaea, Pontomedusa, Hip-
pothoe, Lysianassa, Cymo, Eione, Halimede,
Plexaure, Eucrante, Proto, Calypso, Panope,
Cranto, Neomeris, Hipponoe, Ianira, Polynome,
Autonoe, Melite, Dione, Nesaea, Dero, Evagore,
Psamathe, Eumolpe, Ione, Dynamene, Ceto, and
Limnoria....

From Hesiod, Theogony:

Nereus and fair-haired Doris, daughter of the
pure Ocean-stream, produced in the barren sea
children who were goddesses and who inspired
many hearts with love--Ploto and Eucrante and
Sao and Amphitrite; Eudora and Thetis and Ga-
lene and Glauce; Cymothoe and Speo and Thoe
and lovely Halia; Pasithea and Erato and Eunice
with her rosy arms; graceful Melite and Eulimene
and Agave; Doto and Proto and Pherusa and Dynamene; Nesaea and Actaea and Protomedea; Doris
and Panopea and beautiful Galatea; and lovely Hippothoe and Hipponoe with her rosy arms; Cymodoce, who along with Cymatolege and shapely
Amphitrite, is able to calm the waves of the
dark sea and the blasts of stormy winds; Cymo

CORBAN UNIVERSITY
LIBRARY
5000 Deer Park Drive SE
Salem, OR 97317-9392

and Eione and Halimede crowned with beauty; also
smiling Glauconome and Pontoporea; Leagora and
Euagora and Laomedea; Polynoe and Autonoe and
Lysianassa; Euarne with her lovely shape and per-
fect form; graceful Psamathe and divine Menippe;
Neso and Eupompe and Themisto and Pronoe; also Nemertes, who has the same unerring mind
as her immortal father.   These are the fifty
daughters of Nereus, and there is no stain on
them or on their father....

[2]<u>Phorcys-Ceto</u>   son and daughter of Pontus and Gaea.
                    Although many variations in this line
exist, the following relationships are generally recognized:
       (a) According to Homer in the <u>Odyssey</u>, Thoosa,
daughter of Phorcys and Ceto, is the mother, by Poseidon, of Polyphemus and other cyclops encountered by
Odysseus and his men.
       (b) Echidna is described by Hesiod as "half a
nymph with glancing eyes and fair cheeks, and half a
huge snake, great and awful with speckled skin ... a
nymph who dies not nor grows old all her days." Hesiod
also gives the following genealogy:

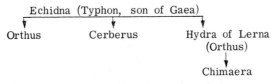

Echidna (Typhon, son of Gaea)

Orthus   Cerberus   Hydra of Lerna
                                      (Orthus)

                                      Chimaera

                                      Sphinx

                                      Nemean Lion

Apollodorus gives the following:

Tartarus-Gaea

    Echidna (Typhon, son of Gaea)

         Chimaera
         Orthus
         Ladon
         Caucasian Eagle
         Sphinx
         Crommyon Sow

Cerberus is referred to by Homer, Virgil, Apollodorus,
Ovid, and all other writers as the dog, with anything
from three to fifty heads, who guards the gates of the
Underworld, but no one seems much concerned with his
parentage. Ovid calls him "the Echidnean dog," following Hesiod.
       (c) Homer calls Scylla the daughter of Cratais;
Apollonius of Rhodes says that Scylla is "that wicked
monster borne to Phorcys by night-wandering Hecate,
whom men call Cratais." Located on a cliff opposite
Charybdis, Scylla was given to gobbling up sailors as
they passed by. Ovid tells the story of Scylla in some
detail: loved by the sea-deity Glaucus, Scylla rejected
his love. He consulted Circe, hoping for her magic
help in winning Scylla. Instead, Circe, who fell in love
with Glaucus herself, changed Scylla into a monster.
Ovid depicts the metamorphosis in grotesque detail:

       ... she saw her loins disfigured by barking mon-
       sters. At first, not believing that they were
       part of her own person, she tried to shrink away
       and drive them off, for she was afraid of the
       dogs' cruel jaws. But she dragged along with
       her the beasts she sought to escape, and when
       she looked for her thighs, her legs, her feet,
       she found gaping mouths like those of Cerberus.

GORDAN UNIVERSITY
(Library)
9000 Deer Park Drive SE
Salem, OR 91317-9392

Chart 5   25

She was standing upon a pack of wild dogs and, with truncated thighs and womb emerging from the mass, rested heavily on the backs of the wild beasts.

(d) The Phorcides are the daughters of Phorcys and Ceto, and are more specifically designated as the Gorgons, the Graeae (or Sea Hags), and possibly the Sirens and Hesperides. Of the three Gorgons--Medusa, Euryale, and Stheno--only Medusa was mortal, and she died when Perseus cut off her head. Hesiod says that from her, by Poseidon, came two offspring: Pegasus, the winged horse "who flew away and joined the gods," and Chrysaor, who married Callirrhoe, daughter of Oceanus and Tethys, and became the father of the "three-headed monster Geryon." Nothing else is known of Chrysaor, although Pegasus became famous in connection with Bellerophon and his daring adventures. Virgil incorporates in the _Aeneid_ the story of Cacus, a three-headed monster robber who belched flames and was finally killed by Heracles, and says that "Vulcan fathered this monster." Another mythology says that Medusa was the mother of Cacus by Hephaestus or Vulcan. There are no stories of the two immortal Gorgons, Euryale and Stheno.

Hesiod names two of the Graeae, the Gray Ones or Sea Hags, "Pemphredo well-clad, and saffron robed Enyo, sisters grey from their birth." Aeschylus in _Prometheus Bound_ refers to "the grey-haired three ... old, mumbling maids, swan-shaped, having one eye betwixt the three, and but a single tooth," among them. Apollodorus names them "Enyo, Pemphredo, and Dino, sisters of the Gorgons, and old women from their birth." The Sirens and the Hesperides are generally not treated as offspring of Phorcys and Ceto.

(e) Ladon, "the youngest, the awful snake who guards the apples of gold in the secret places of the dark earth at its great bounds," is thus described by Hesiod. In the _Argonautica_, Heracles is said to have killed Ladon when he stole the apples from the Hesperides while performing one of his Twelve Labors.

Chart 6

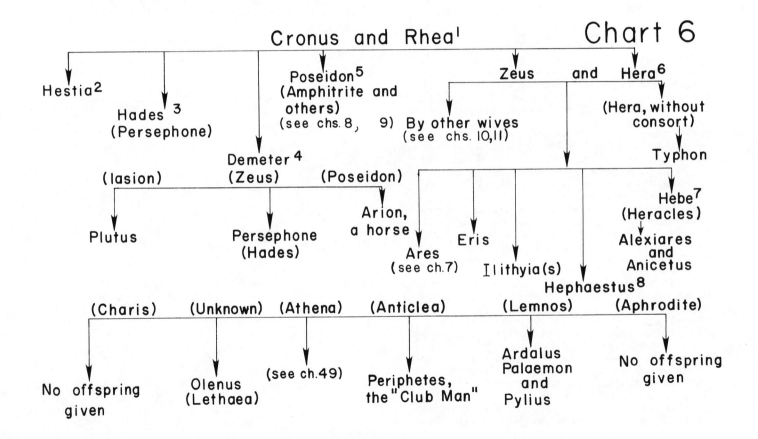

Cronus and Rhea[1]

Hestia[2]

Hades[3]
(Persephone)

Poseidon[5]
(Amphitrite and
others)
(see chs. 8, 9)

Zeus and Hera[6]

By other wives
(see chs. 10,11)

(Hera, without
consort)

Typhon

Demeter[4]

(Iasion) (Zeus) (Poseidon)

Plutus

Persephone
(Hades)

Arion,
a horse

Ares
(see ch.7)

Eris

Ilithyia(s)

Hebe[7]
(Heracles)

Alexiares
and
Anicetus

Hephaestus[8]

(Charis) (Unknown) (Athena) (Anticlea) (Lemnos) (Aphrodite)

No offspring
given

Olenus
(Lethaea)

(see ch.49)

Periphetes,
the "Club Man"

Ardalus
Palaemon
and
Pylius

No offspring
given

NOTES FOR CHART 6

[1]Cronus-Rhea Titan son and daughter of Uranus and Gaea, are the parents of six of the Olympian gods. In Roman mythology they are called Saturn and Ops.

[2]Hestia oldest daughter of Cronus and Rhea. No stories were told of her. As goddess of the household fire, the hearthside, she was most revered. As a maiden goddess, she had no descendants, and her name was never taken lightly. In Roman mythology, she became Vesta, and also related to the Roman household gods, the Lares and Penates. In his account of the fall of Troy, Virgil's Aeneas is outraged as he sees Helen, "hiding, of all places, at Vesta's shrine, clinging there in silence." In one of the two Homeric Hymns to Hestia, she is said to "tend the holy house of the lord Apollo at Pytho," and in the other Hymn she is said to "have gained an everlasting abode and highest honor." In the Homeric Hymn to Aphrodite, Hymn V, Hestia is described as "the pure maiden" who does not "love Aphrodite's works." Both Poseidon and Apollo had sought to wed Hestia, but she was "wholly unwilling and stubbornly refused." The Hymn goes on to say that "in all the temples of the gods she has a share of honor, and among all mortal men she is chief of the goddesses."

[3]Hades (or Ades) son of Cronus and Rhea, is called Pluto or Dis by the Romans. After Zeus had deposed Cronus in the war of the gods and Titans, the creation was divided among the three brothers: to Zeus, the Heavens and Earth; to Poseidon, the Ocean Waters; and to Hades, the Underworld, as god of the dead and god of the invisible. Understandably enough, there are few stories of Hades because of the grim and unpleasant nature of his domain. The only familiar story is the one in which he abducted Persephone, the daughter of Demeter and Zeus, and bore her away to be his Queen of the Underworld. Apollodorus calls Persephone the daughter of Zeus and Styx, but the usual account makes Persephone the daughter of Demeter. Even Apollodorus contradicts himself and later tells the story of Demeter's search for his daughter, and her anger when she learned that Hades had abducted the maid. Zeus ordered Hades to return the girl to her sorrowing mother, but Persephone had already eaten the fatal seed of the pomegranate, and the return could not be total. It was agreed that Persephone would spend six months of the year, or some writers say nine, with her mother on Earth, and the remaining months of the year in the Underworld with her husband. Ovid's version of the story differs but slightly with that of Apollodorus and other writers.

The name Hades should not be equated with the Underworld, nor should Hades and his kingdom be equated with the Christian concept of Satan and Hell.

Hades was not evil, and the only area of his domain in which punishment was meted out was Tartarus, a primordial creation of Gaea. For the most part the Underworld was simply the abode of the "piteous dead." The most hideous criminals of mythology, usually those who had in some way made an assault on the sanctity of the gods, were condemned to appropriate punishment in Tartarus. Although these punishments vary with the crimes of the individuals, mostly they are exercises in infinite futility: Tantalus reaching for water which he can never attain; Sisyphus rolling a stone to the top of a hill only to see it roll down again; the Danaids dipping water only to see it spill; Ixion whirling endlessly on the wheel. The names of these criminals vary according to the hero who had made a visit to the Underworld, but in general they all agree, and the punishments do not vary from story to story. On his Twelfth, or possibly the Eleventh, Labor, Heracles goes to the Underworld to get Cerberus the dog. While there he takes time to rescue Theseus, and to attempt to rescue Pirithous, both of whom have come to abduct Persephone from the Halls of Hades, but Heracles does not stay beyond bare necessity. Consequently, he does not report on anyone he has seen. In his visit to the Underworld, Odysseus reports that he saw Tityus, the Giant son of Gaea, stretched out with two vultures eating his liver. His crime had been to offer violence to Leto, the mother of Apollo and Artemis. Odysseus also saw Tantalus, standing in a pool of water that constantly receded when he tried to drink, and reaching for fruit that disappeared when he tried to eat; he saw Sisyphus, in violent torment, heaving a huge stone up a mountain only to see it eternally fall back again. Aeneas does not visit Tartarus in the Underworld, but the Sibyl gives him a lengthy account of those who are there: the Titans, crawling at the bottom; Aloeus' sons--Otus and Ephialtes --who had tried to climb onto Olympus; Salmoneus, who

presumed to be as powerful as Zeus; Tityus, his liver being eaten; Sisyphus, rolling his stone; Tantalus at his disappearing banquet; Pirithous and the Lapiths; Ixion on his wheel; Theseus, sitting in dejection; and Phlegyas wailing and crying forever. Ovid tells the story of Juno (Hera), who, in her hatred of Ino and Athamas, goes down to the "grim palace of dusky Dis" (Hades) to solicit the aid of the Furies in driving Ino and Athamas into a criminal madness. While there, Juno sees "Tityus, lying stretched out over nine acres, his entrails exposed for the vultures to tear; ... Tantalus, reaching for the water he can never grasp; Sisyphus, pursuing and pushing the stone that always comes rolling back; Ixion, whirling on his wheel; the fifty granddaughters of Belus, the Danaids, who killed their husbands, always dipping water which they just as quickly spill."

The Judges of Hades were Minos, Rhadamanthus, and Aeacus--all sons of Zeus by mortal women--and punishment was administered primarily by the Fury Tisiphone. The rivers referred to in the Underworld were the Acheron, Cocytus, Lethe, Phlegethon, and Styx. The boatman Charon ferried souls across, and Cerberus, the monster dog, stood guard.

[4]Demeter   goddess of agriculture, grain, and fertile soil. In Roman mythology, she became Ceres and assumed much the same functions. By Zeus, Demeter was the mother of Persephone, called Proserpine in Roman mythology, and also referred to as Kore, the maid. The story is told that Demeter also lay with Iasion, whom Apollodorus calls the brother of Dardanus, and bore the son Plutus, the god of wealth and riches. Hesiod describes Plutus as "a good spirit who goes everywhere on land and on the sea's broad back, enriching and giving great prosperity to whomever he meets and joins hands with." In the Odyssey, Homer says that Zeus killed Iasion when he found out about the

Chart 6   29

love affair, "hurling a dazzling thunderbolt." Apollodorus agrees with Homer, saying "Iasion loved Demeter, and in an attempt to defile the goddess he was killed by a thunderbolt." In the Iliad, Homer also says that Demeter had a son by Poseidon, Arion, "the swift horse of Adrastus, that was of heavenly stock." Adrastus, King of Argos, led the Argive invaders in the War of the Seven Against Thebes, and was the only leader who did not perish. According to Apollodorus, it was Arion who saved his life.

[5]Poseidon   god of the Ocean, called "Earth Shaker" and "god of the wavy locks" by Homer. His wife was Amphitrite, daughter of Nereus and Doris or of Oceanus and Tethys, who was the mother of Proteus, Triton, and others. Poseidon's amors were as numerous as those of his brother Zeus, but not so celebrated, primarily because Amphitrite was not always angrily chasing her rivals and working harm against them. Most of Poseidon's famous offspring were from mortal mothers, instead of goddesses. In Roman mythology, Poseidon is called Neptune.

[6]Zeus-Hera   son and daughter of Cronus and Rhea and supreme god and goddess of Olympus. Although Zeus took many consorts and had many offspring by mortals and immortals, he had only one wife and Queen, described by Homer as "white-armed, ox-eyed Hera." She is consistently represented as being very jealous of her husband's affairs, and her quarrels with her rivals form the basis for one of the largest and most dramatic groups of stories in mythology. By Zeus, Hera is usually called the mother of Area, the Ilithyias, Hephaestus, and Hebe. Apollodorus says that Hephaestus is the son of Hera without consort, produced when Zeus gave birth to Athena, but in Homer this god is clearly the son of Zeus and Hera, although he is portrayed as partial to his mother. The Ilithyias, or sometimes Ilithyia, are the two goddesses of Childbirth and are sent by Hera to deliver women in labor. On two notable occasions, Hera, in jealousy, held them back and thus prolonged the agony of her adversaries: when Leto was about to give birth to Apollo and Artemis, and when Alcmena was due to be delivered of Heracles and Iphicles. In both instances the father involved was Zeus.

There is some confusion as to the parentage of Eris, Enyo, and Ate, who are more identifiable as personifications than as mythological personages. (a) Hesiod calls Eris the daughter of Nyx, and Ate the daughter of Eris; (b) in Homer, Eris is called the "sister and companion of murderous Ares," and Ate is called the "eldest daughter of Zeus," the goddess of Delusion. The story is told that Ate created so much confusion among the gods that Zeus threw her off Olympus, where she now walks the Earth among mortals; (c) Enyo is referred to in the Iliad as "the sacker of cities," and as "carrying with her the turmoil of shameless hatred." In each instance she is in company with Ares, the god of War, and is sometimes called his sister. She most certainly is a goddess of War, identified by the Romans as Bellona.

[7]Hebe   goddess of Youth, named by Hesiod as a daughter of Zeus and Hera, and represented by Homer as cupbearer of the gods, although Hephaestus also pours for the Olympians. In Ovid, however, Hebe is said to have been replaced by the beautiful Trojan boy Ganymede, who has been transported to Olympus by Zeus in the form of a golden eagle. In the Aeneid, this replacement, "Ganymede's honors," is given as one of the reasons Juno (Hera) hates the Trojans and is determined to destroy them. At the death of his mortal parts, Heracles was received on Olympus as a deity. Apollodorus says, "Thereafter he obtained immortality, and being

reconciled to Hera he married her daughter Hebe, by whom he had sons, Alexiares and Anicetus." Homer and Hesiod also refer to this marriage with Hebe. When Odysseus visits the Underworld he sees Heracles "a phantom. For he himself is with the immortal gods," and is married to "Hebe of the fair ankles."

[8]Hephaestus   god of Fire, the builder, and the black- smith.   In the Iliad, he is represented in a variety of roles: club-footed cupbearer to the gods, at whose clumsiness the gods laugh; builder of the sep- arate houses in which the gods live; defender and pro- tector of his mother Hera against the angers of Zeus; the god who dried up the Xanthus River in one of the great battles near Troy; and finally as the great artist who fashioned the Shield of Achilles.   In the Iliad, Hephaestus is shown married to Charis, one of the Graces; in the Odyssey, however, Demodocus, the blind minstrel at Alcinous' court, tells a rowdy tale in which Hephaestus is married to Aphrodite.   True to her na- ture, Aphrodite was notoriously unfaithful, and in this tale she and Ares were tricked by Hephaestus and caught naked in bed in a net from which they could not escape or let go of each other.   Hephaestus called all the other gods in to see the sight--Poseidon, Hermes, and Apollo --and they laughed to see that the slow, lame Hephaes- tus had outwitted the bold and swift Ares.

The offspring of Hephaestus are not notable and hardly emerge with any distinction.   Ovid tells the story of Olenus and his wife Lethaea, who were turned to stones because of their pride and arrogance toward the gods.   Apollodorus tells the story of Hephaestus' abor- tive attempt to violate the goddess Athena.   When she would not accept him, he lost his seed, which fell to earth and became Erichthonias, fourth King of Athens. Periphetes is the son of Hephaestus and a nymph Anti- clea (not the same as Odysseus' mother), and his story

is told by Apollodorus and others.   Periphetes, called the "Clubman" from the club that he carried, was lame like his father and apparently used the club to aid him in walking.   His nature was evil, however, and he killed any passerby with his iron club.   He was finally killed by Theseus, King of Athens.   Ovid refers to Periphetes as "Vulcan's son brought down in spite of the club he carried." Apollodorus calls Palaemon, one of the Argo- nauts, a son of Hephaestus or of Aetolus; and Pau- sanias refers briefly to Ardalus, a son of Hephaestus, and says "they believe this Ardalus discovered the flute and call the Muses after him daughters of Ardalus." Two other brief references are made by Pausanias and by Aeschylus in The Euminides, to "children of Hephaes- tus," who built a road for Apollo when the god first went to Delphi.   Hephaestus is frequently associated with the Island of Lemnos, where he fell when Zeus threw him off Olympus, and one source says that Philoctetes, the Greek warrior who was abandoned by his companions on the Island of Lemnos, was cared for by sons of Hephaestus, Ardalus, Palaemon, and Pylius.

Vulcan, in Roman mythology, is basically the same as Hephaestus, except that no great skills were attributed to the Roman god.

Chart 7

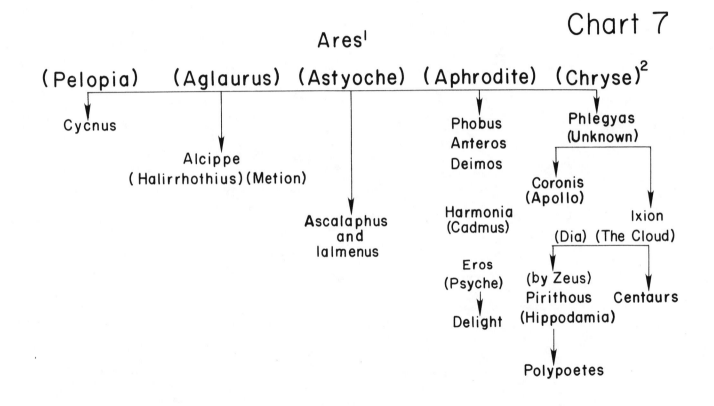

Ares[1]

(Pelopia)   (Aglaurus)   (Astyoche)   (Aphrodite)   (Chryse)[2]

Cycnus

Alcippe
(Halirrhothius)(Metion)

Ascalaphus
and
Ialmenus

Phobus
Anteros
Deimos

Harmonia
(Cadmus)

Eros
(Psyche)

Delight

Phlegyas
(Unknown)

Coronis
(Apollo)

Ixion

(Dia) (The Cloud)

(by Zeus)
Pirithous   Centaurs
(Hippodamia)

Polypoetes

NOTES FOR CHART 7

[1]Ares   god of War, who in the Iliad is called "bane of
         mortals, blood-stained stormer of walls," and
is himself wounded in battle by Diomedes.   When he
was hurt, Homer says, "brazen Ares bellowed loud as
nine thousand warriors," and went speedily up to Olympus, complaining to Zeus of the violent deeds that immortals must suffer from mortals.   Ares gets no sympathy from his father, who says, "Sit thou not in any
wise by me and whine, thou renegade.   Most hateful to
me art thou of all gods that hold Olympus, for ever is
strife dear to thee and wars and fightings.   Thou hast
the unbearable, unyielding spirit of thy mother, even of
Hera."
         Several offspring of Ares are important in myth-
ology.   Cycnus, son of Ares and Pyrene, challenged
Heracles to combat and would have killed him, but Zeus
hurled a thunderbolt between the two and parted them on
a draw.   Another Cycnus, or a variation on the first
story, the son of Ares and Pelopia, was slain by Heracles, according to Apollodorus, and Ares would have
then slain Heracles, but Zeus prevented it.   Ares had
a daughter Alcippe, by Aglaurus, daughter of Cecrops of
Athens.   In attempting to rape Alcippe, Halirrhothius,
son of Poseidon and a nymph Euryte, was caught and
killed by Ares.   Apollodorus and other writers say that
for this Ares was tried in the Aeropagus before a jury
of twelve gods and was acquitted.   This episode is also
referred to by Euripides in his Iphigenia in Taurus:

"there is a tribunal, erst ordained of Zeus, to cleanse
the War-God's blood-stained hands," and again in this
author's Electra:

> There is a Hill of Ares, where first sat
> Gods to give judgment touching blood-shedding,
> When fierce-souled Ares, Halirrhothius slew,
> The Sea-king's son, in wrath for outrage done
> His daughter.

Two sons of Ares took ships to Troy, as Homer
says in the famous Catalog of Ships:

> And they that dwelt in Aspledon and Orchomenus
> of the Minyae were led by Ascalaphus and Ial-
> menus, sons of Ares, whom, in the palace of
> Actor, son of Azeus, Astyoche conceived of
> mighty Ares.... And with these were ranged
> thirty hollow ships.

These two are also named by Apollodorus as members
of the Argo crew, but their names do not appear in the
list of Argonauts by Apollonius of Rhodes.   Ascalaphus
is killed at Troy by Deiphobus, a son of Priam, "and
he fell in the dust and clutched the ground with his
palm."   When Ares hears of his son's death, he angrily
declares that he will go to the aid of the Greeks, against
the orders of Zeus, and avenge the slaying.   He is re-

strained from doing so only by Athena, who says this is not the first great man to die, nor will it be the last.

By Aphrodite, Ares is also said to be the father of several abstractions: Deimos (Fear), Phobus (Alarm), and Anteros (Terror), but these are also referred to as attendants of Ares, not his offspring. Harmonia, who married Cadmus of Thebes, claimed Aphrodite and Ares as her parents, and was given a necklace made by Hephaestus on her wedding day. This necklace proved to carry a fatal charm, since all who wore it perished tragically. Eros is said by Hesiod to have existed from the beginning, and to have presided over the creating and ordering of all things, mortals, and gods; the most familiar Eros, however, is the young son of Ares and Aphrodite, best known as the Roman god of love Cupid. This is the well-known youngster with bow and arrows, ready to let go one of his fatal darts at any moment. This god himself fell in love with Psyche and their daughter was Delight.

Ares, who is also called Enyalius by Homer, is related to Mars of Roman mythology; however, Mars was also an early vegetation and agricultural deity, and this function was never applied to Ares.

[2]Chryse   daughter of Halmus, King of Orchomenus, whom Pausanias calls a son of Sisyphus. By Ares, Chryse was the mother of the notorious Phlegyas. The story is told that when Apollo violated Coronis, the daughter of Phlegyas, and then either killed her or had Artemis kill her, Phlegyas marched against Apollo's temple and reduced it to ashes. The god in turn slew Phlegyas and sent him to Tartarus, where, Virgil says, he screams "through the halls forever: 'Being warned, learn justice; reverence the gods.'" Phlegyas was also the father of a son, Ixion, another criminal who was sent to Tartarus.

By Dia, daughter of Deioneus of Phocis, Ixion (or Zeus) was the father of Pirithous, who became King of the Lapithae and a friend of Theseus of Athens. In order to obtain his daughter in marriage, Ixion promised Deioneus a valuable gift; however, when the father-in-law came to collect, Ixion threw him into a pit of burning coals, and the old man perished miserably. Unable to find any human forgiveness for this treacherous crime, which has been referred to as the first mythological murder, Ixion was pitied by the gods who invited him to dine with them. Instead of humility and gratitude, Ixion showed contempt for the gods by trying to seduce Hera. Zeus created a cloud in the shape of Hera, and Ixion assaulted it. From this union came the race of Centaurs, half-man and half-horse, who lived in and around the area of Mount Pelion. Ixion was sent to Tartarus, where he was bound to a wheel, spinning in eternal motion. At the celebrated wedding of Pirithous and Hippodamia, daughter of Adrastus of Argos, war broke out between the Centaurs and Lapiths, and many on both sides were slaughtered. At Troy, Nestor, son of Neleus, refers to this war, in which he also had taken part, and names some of the great warriors who were there: Pirithous, Dryas, Caeneus, Exadius, Polyphemus, and Theseus. "Mightiest were these of all men reared upon the earth," Nestor calls them in the Iliad. The same story, with far greater detail, is retold by Ovid.

Pirithous is generally associated with the adventures of his great friend Theseus, and from one adventure Pirithous did not escape: when he and Theseus went to the Kingdom of Hades to abduct Persephone. One of the sons of Pirithous, Polypoetes, took forty ships and went to Troy as leader of the Lapiths. It is in this passage that Homer calls Pirithous the son of Zeus. It is not recorded whether Polypoetes died at Troy, but Apollodorus says that he and others "journeyed by land to Colophon and buried Calchas."

Chart 7   35

Some of the Centaurs have individualized stories, and many of them are named in Ovid's account of the War between the Lapiths and the Centaurs. Sophocles makes use of the story of Nessus in his tragedy <u>The Trachinian Women.</u> The centaur Nessus tried to rape Deianira, the wife of Heracles, and was shot for his deed. Before he died, Nessus gave Deianira a robe that had been soaked in his own blood and told her that the robe would regain Heracles' love should he ever forsake her. In Sophocles' play, Deianira sends this robe to Heracles upon his return with a new bride, and it proves to be his death. After putting the robe about his shoulders, he is consumed with unbearable pain, and so orders his funeral pyre and accepts death as his only release from suffering. Thus, Nessus brings about his revenge.

The most familiar and the most benevolent of Centaurs is Chiron, wise and gentle. Apollodorus says he is the offspring of Cronus and Philyra and accounts for several events involving Chiron: saving Peleus when he would have been killed by other Centaurs; receiving the infant Ascelpius and teaching him the art of healing; training Actaeon to be a hunter and later carving an image of Actaeon to soothe the dogs that had unwittingly torn their master to pieces; giving Peleus an ashen spear that Achilles would later take with him to Troy. Chiron is frequently referred to as the teacher of other heroes: Achilles, Aeneas, Heracles, Jason, etc. As told by Apollodorus, it was Heracles who finally brought about the death of the noble centaur; accidentally Heracles dropped one of the Hydra-poisoned arrows on Chiron's foot and mortally wounded him. Since Chiron was immortal and could not die, he was condemned to unending pain until someone should assume his immortality and thus allow him to die. Prometheus agreed to relieve the centaur of his burden, and so Chiron passed into the Kingdom of Hades.

36

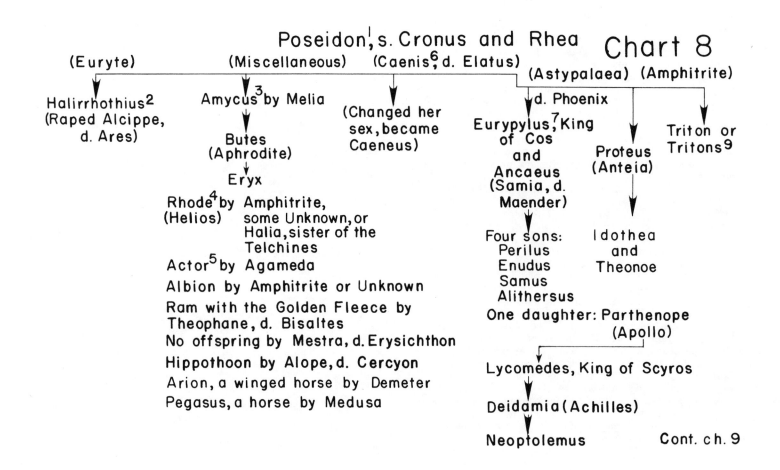

Poseidon, s. Cronus and Rhea Chart 8

(Euryte)   (Miscellaneous)   (Caenis[6], d. Elatus)

(Astypalaea) (Amphitrite)

Halirrhothius[2]
(Raped Alcippe,
d. Ares)

Amycus[3] by Melia

Butes
(Aphrodite)

Eryx

(Changed her
sex, became
Caeneus)

d. Phoenix

Eurypylus[7], King
of Cos
and
Ancaeus
(Samia, d.
Maender)

Proteus
(Anteia)

Triton or
Tritons[9]

Rhode[4] by Amphitrite,
(Helios)   some Unknown, or
Halia, sister of the
Telchines
Actor[5] by Agameda
Albion by Amphitrite or Unknown
Ram with the Golden Fleece by
Theophane, d. Bisaltes
No offspring by Mestra, d. Erysichthon
Hippothoon by Alope, d. Cercyon
Arion, a winged horse by Demeter
Pegasus, a horse by Medusa

Four sons:
Perilus
Enudus
Samus
Alithersus
One daughter: Parthenope
(Apollo)

Idothea
and
Theonoe

Lycomedes, King of Scyros

Deidamia (Achilles)

Neoptolemus

Cont. ch. 9

NOTES FOR CHART 8

[1]Poseidon   son of Cronus and Rhea, became the god of the sea and water when Zeus overthrew Cronus and became ruler of the gods. According to Homer, Poseidon is the younger brother of Zeus, but in other writers he is older than Zeus. In Roman mythology, Poseidon is called Neptune; he is the god of earthquakes, "Earth Shaker," the god of "wavy locks," and is frequently associated with horses. Two of his notable offspring are horses: Arion by Demeter, and Pegasus by Medusa. He is also the sire, by Theophane, of the Ram with the Golden Fleece.

Poseidon has an important role in the Iliad and an even greater role in the Odyssey. For instance, in the former he takes sides against the Trojans, but is not totally without sympathy for them, as is clearly demonstrated when he saves Aeneas from the sword of Achilles. Poseidon says that it is ordained for Aeneas to escape, "that the race of Dardanus perish not without seed and be seen no more." In the Aeneid, Poseidon maintains the same concerned attitude toward the Trojans when he puts down a mighty storm that his sister Hera has persuaded the Winds to create. At the end of the Trojan War, Poseidon and all the other gods turn against the Greeks for their outrageous behavior at the sack of Troy--defiling the temples, desecrating the holy images, raping Cassandra, the priestess of Apollo--and determine to give the Greeks a rough passage home. Poseidon, none too happy at seeing Troy destroyed, and especially the Wall that he and Apollo had built, needs no urging to turn "the wide Aegean sea into a turmoil." It is Poseidon who speaks the grim warning in The Trojan Women, that he who conquers today may be the conquered tomorrow.

[2]Halirrhothias   the son of Poseidon by Euryte. The story of this son who was killed by Ares for ravishing his daughter Alcippe is generally told in connection with Ares, who was tried by a jury of twelve gods and acquitted of the crime.

[3]Amycus   King of the Bebryces, a son of Poseidon by Melia, a Bithynian nymph. Apollonius of Rhodes calls him "the haughtiest of men," who would never let his guests go until he had challenged them in boxing. In the Argonautica, he boasts and brags until he is challenged by Polydeuces (Pollux), one of the Dioscuri, who kills him in the boxing match.

[4]Rhode   also called Rhodos, is the eponym for the Island of Rhodes. Apollodorus calls her the daughter of Poseidon and Amphitrite, although she is called a sister of the Telchines by Pausanias. She is uniformly called the wife of Helios, and mother of one set of Heliades. Apollodorus also names Benthesicyme of Ethiopia a daughter of Poseidon and Amphitrite and sister to Rhode.

5Actor, Albion, Theophane, Mestra, Alope, etc.   Of these only slight mythology exists. Actor (the name of many other figures) as a son of Poseidon has no story; Albion, a son of Amphitrite and Poseidon, is of very late origin and is said to have reigned over what is now Great Britain; Theophane or Bisaltis, daughter of Bisaltus, was changed into a sheep, and Poseidon, assuming the shape of a ram, became the father of the Ram with the Golden Fleece.   This and the story of Mestra, or Metra, are told by Ovid.   Mestra, loved by Poseidon, had received from the god the power to change herself into whatever shape she chose.   Her father, Erysichthon of Thessaly, defied Demeter by chopping down a tree beloved by the goddess.   For punishment, Demeter called upon Hunger, whom she detested, to inhabit the house of Erysichthon and render him eternally hungry.   Mestra helped her father by assuming different shapes of animals which he sold, trying to provide enough food for her gluttonous parent.   The story of Alope, daughter of Cercyon, is referred to by Pausanias.   By Poseidon, she became the mother of an infant whom she exposed to avoid being detected, but when she was later discovered, her father put her to death, and Poseidon changed her into a fountain.   The infant was cared for by shepherds, and later was identified as Hippothoon, King of Eleusis.

Arion and Pegasus, both horses, have been discussed elsewhere.

6Caenis   after being assaulted by Poseidon, obtained the god's permission to change her sex.   She became Caeneus, and was the great warrior who fought in the War of the Lapiths and the Centaurs.   In this altercation, he was killed and transformed into a "bird with tawny wings."   Nestor, who tells the story in some detail in Ovid, says it was a bird he had "never seen before or since."

7Eurypylus   This name is a common one, there being some six or seven other figures who are so called.   This Eurypylus was a son of Poseidon by Astypalaea, an obscure daughter of Phoenix.   Eurypylus became King of Cos, and was killed by Heracles when he laid waste the city.   Ancaeus, by the same mother is a son of Poseidon who sailed with the Argonauts, and, according to Apollonius of Rhodes, after the death of Tiphys was voted by the shipmates to steer the Argo.   According to Apollodorus, Ancaeus had four sons and one daughter, Parthenope, who became the mother of Lycomedes by Apollo.   It was to the court of Lycomedes, King of Scyros, that Achilles' mother sent her son to avoid going to the Trojan War.   While here, Achilles married Deidamia, the daughter of the king, and became father of his son Neoptolemus.

8Proteus   son of Poseidon and Amphitrite, was a prophet, but getting an answer from him depended upon holding him still while he answered.   He, like his father and many other sea deities, had the ability to assume any shape he liked.   In Homer's Odyssey, Menelaus relates an experience with Proteus.   Stranded in Egypt on their way home from Troy, Menelaus wants to know if he and Helen will ever get home.   The daughter of Proteus, Eidothea or Idothea, advised Menelaus that the "old man of the sea" will give up the answer if he is caught and held fast, no matter what fearsome shape he assumes.

9Triton   a name that sometimes, as in Virgil's Aeneid, is used as a plural, but generally is a reference to a single deity.   Triton is represented as blowing on an echoing conch shell, and according to Ovid it was Triton whom Poseidon called forth to blow the signal for retreat to all the waters covering the earth and sea after the Great Flood that Zeus had sent to destroy the

Chart 8   39

impious human race.   Like all the gods, Triton was
jealous of mortals who presumed to have greater skills
or talents than the gods.   Virgil tells the story of
Misenus, a son of Aeolus, who was foolish enough to
challenge Triton in a trumpet contest.   Naturally Misenus lost, and Triton "held him down between the rocks,
and drowned him under the foaming waves."   Aeneas
conducts a magnificent funeral for Misenus and buries
him in a place that has since then been called Cape
Misenum, located at the northern end of the Bay of
Naples.

Poseidon, cont.

Chart 9

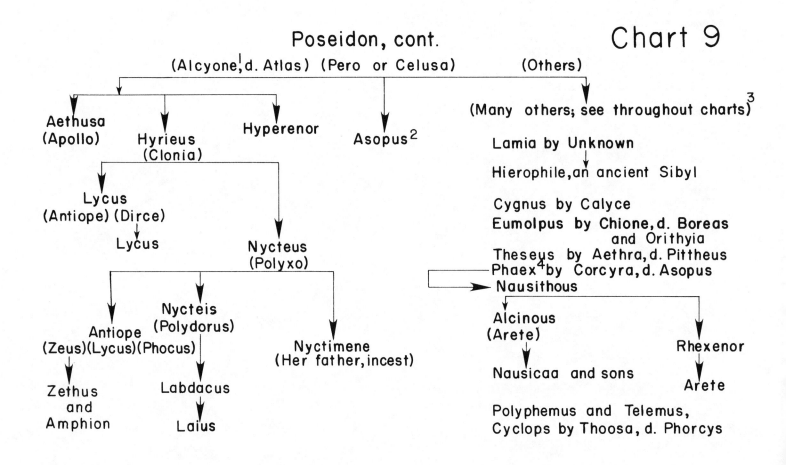

(Alcyone, d. Atlas) (Pero or Celusa)   (Others)

(Many others; see throughout charts)[3]

Aethusa
(Apollo)

Hyrieus
(Clonia)

Hyperenor

Asopus[2]

Lamia by Unknown

Hierophile, an ancient Sibyl

Lycus
(Antiope) (Dirce)

Lycus

Nycteus
(Polyxo)

Cygnus by Calyce
Eumolpus by Chione, d. Boreas
          and Orithyia
Theseus by Aethra, d. Pittheus
Phaex[4] by Corcyra, d. Asopus
Nausithous

Antiope
(Zeus)(Lycus)(Phocus)

Nycteis
(Polydorus)

Nyctimene
(Her father, incest)

Alcinous
(Arete)

Rhexenor

Zethus
and
Amphion

Labdacus

Nausicaa and sons

Arete

Laius

Polyphemus and Telemus,
Cyclops by Thoosa, d. Phorcys

NOTES FOR CHART 9

[1]Alcyone   daughter of Atlas and Pleione, was the moth-
          er by Poseidon of three notable offspring:
Aethusa, who by Apollo was the mother of Eleuther;
Hyrieus, the father of Lycus and Nycteus; and Hyperenor.
The story of Lycus and Antiope, the daughter of Nycteus,
is a familiar one.   She was either carried away by, or
willingly went with, Zeus by whom she had twins, Amphion and Zethus.   Later she married her uncle, Lycus.
His first wife, Dirce, mistreated and imprisoned Antiope, until such time that the latter's sons were grown
to manhood.   They took Thebes, killed Lycus, and tied
Dirce to the tail of a wild bull, which dragged her to
death.   In becoming rulers of Thebes, Amphion and
Zethus had also deposed Laius, the infant son of Labdacus, for whom Lycus was acting as regent, and sent
him into exile.   It is said that Amphion was a great
musician, and received a lyre from Hermes.   With
Zethus, he built the great seven-gated wall of Thebes.
Zethus married Thebe, the twin sister of Aegina, daughters of Asopus and Metope, but there is no record of
any children they may have had.   Apollodorus says that
Amphion married Niobe, daughter of Tantalus, and had
seven daughters and seven sons who were killed by
Apollo and Artemis; in the Odyssey, however, Homer
indicates that there were two Amphions: the son of
Antiope and the son of Iasus, who married Niobe.   At
any rate, no descendant of Amphion or Zethus ever occupied the throne of Thebes, and the kingdom reverted

to Laius, who was followed by the ill-fated Oedipus and
the sons of Oedipus.

[2]Asopus   the river god, is generally called a son of
          Oceanus and Tethys.   One mythology calls
Asopus the son of Poseidon.   Since there are two rivers
of this name, one that flows through Sicyonia and another that flows through southern Boeotia, the different
parentage may be the result of local tradition.

[3]Others   Many others are shown throughout the charts,
          women who were pleased to claim Poseidon
as the father of an illustrious son: Aethra, for instance,
said Poseidon was the father of Theseus.   Tyro, married to Cretheus, nevertheless called her twins, Neleus
and Pelias, sons of the Sea-god.   Calyce, a daughter of
Aeolus, was the mother by Poseidon of the Cygnus who
was strangled by Achilles early in the Trojan War.

[4]Phaex   son of Poseidon and Corcyra, daughter of the
          Asopus, is the eponym for the Phaeacians, a
people who lived on the island of Scherie.   The most
notable of Phaex' descendants was Nausithous, who had
led the people to their home from Hypereia, driven out
by their notorious neighbors the Cyclops.   Homer makes
considerable use of the court of Alcinous, son of Nausithous, in the Odyssey, since it is here that Odysseus
is washed ashore, and is later given hospitality and wel-

come. It is to Alcinous' court that Odysseus tells of
his ten-year adventure from the time he left Troy when
the war was over. After his brief stay with the Phaeacians, Odysseus is carried home to Ithaca in one of
their ships. In connection with this event, there is the
curious myth that Poseidon, angry with the Phaeasians
for having given so much aid to sea-stranded sailors,
turned the Phaeacian ship and its crew to stone as it
came into port from Ithaca. The Phaeacians also figure
in a long episode in the Argonautica. It is here that
the angry Colchians demand the return of Medea, which
is promised by Alcinous if the marriage of Jason and
Medea has not been consummated. The marriage, therefore, took place rather hurriedly, and Jason and Medea
became man and wife in what was then called Macris'
cave, later renamed Medea's cave. The Colchinians
dared neither challenge Alcinous' decision or return to
King Aeetes without Medea, and so they asked and were
given permission to settle among the Phaeacians.

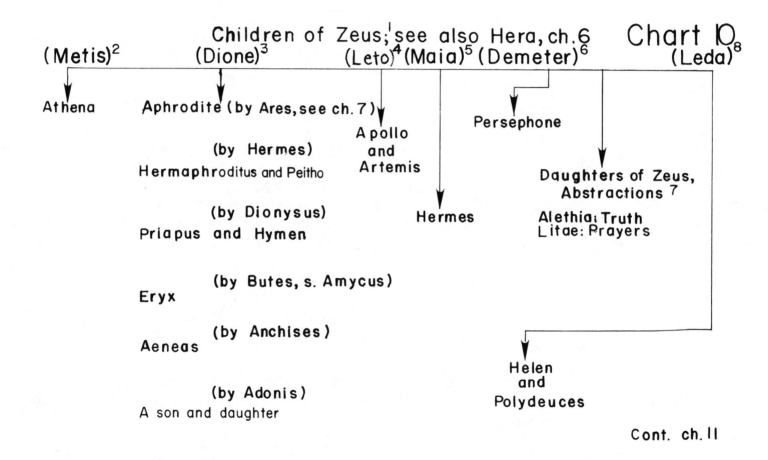

Children of Zeus; see also Hera, ch.6   Chart IO[8]

(Metis)[2]   (Dione)[3]   (Leto)[4] (Maia)[5] (Demeter)[6]   (Leda)[8]

Athena   Aphrodite (by Ares, see ch.7)

Apollo
and
Artemis

Persephone

(by Hermes)
Hermaphroditus and Peitho

(by Dionysus)
Priapus and Hymen

Hermes

Daughters of Zeus,
Abstractions [7]

Alethia: Truth
Litae: Prayers

(by Butes, s. Amycus)
Eryx

(by Anchises)
Aeneas

(by Adonis)
A son and daughter

Helen
and
Polydeuces

Cont. ch. 11

Zeus, cont. Chart II

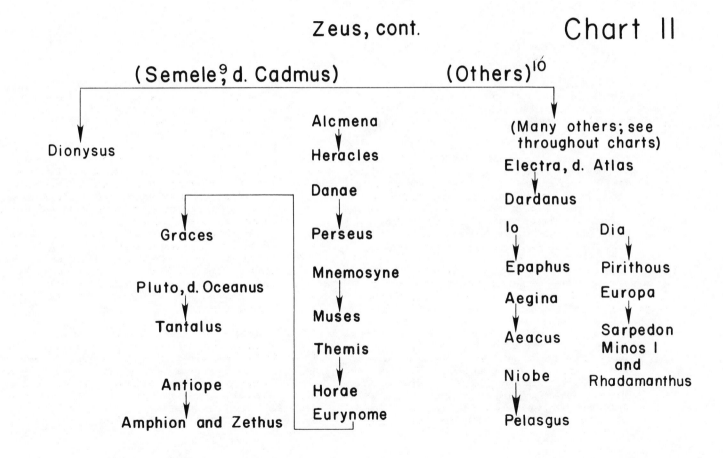

(Semele,[9] d. Cadmus) (Others)[10]

Dionysus

Alcmena
↓
Heracles

Danae
↓
Perseus

Graces

Pluto, d. Oceanus
↓
Tantalus

Mnemosyne
↓
Muses

Themis
↓
Horae

Antiope
↓
Amphion and Zethus

Eurynome

(Many others; see
throughout charts)

Electra, d. Atlas
↓
Dardanus

Io
↓
Epaphus

Aegina
↓
Aeacus

Niobe
↓
Pelasgus

Dia
↓
Pirithous

Europa
↓
Sarpedon
Minos I
and
Rhadamanthus

NOTES FOR CHARTS 10 AND 11

[1]Zeus   son of Cronus and Rhea, is called "father of gods and men" by Homer.   In the Iliad, Zeus himself gives some indication of how widespread his paternity is by reciting to Hera an extensive catalog of his amors:

> ... not when I was seized with love of the wife of Ixion, who bore Pirithous; nor of Danae, daughter of Acrisius, who bore Perseus; nor the daughter of far-famed Phoenix that bare me Minos and the god-like Rhadamanthus; nor of Semele, nor of Alcmena in Thebes, and she brought forth Heracles, and Semele bore Dionysus, the joy of mortals; nor of Demeter; nor of glorious Leto....

Extensive though this list may be, it is rather modest in comparison to the number of progeny that mythological tradition attributes to him.   As one study of mythology says:

> ... one could prolong the list which was enriched by the regional pride of the various provinces of Greece or even small towns, eager to give themselves a divine ancestor.   We have seen, in fact, how a number of Zeus' offspring became the ancestors of a tribe or the founder of cities. But some of these unions of the god can be explained in other ways: Some are solar myths;

for instance, the union of Zeus, god of the luminous ether, with Leto and Leda, who seem to have been deities of the night.   Others are merely allegorical accounts of historical facts; the Phoenician Europa brought to Crete by a bull could represent the contribution of Asiatic civilization to that of Crete, symbolized by the bull-god.   Finally, others are romanticized expression of great natural phenomena; in the shower of gold which penetrates to the subterranean Danae it is easy to recognize the rays of the sun which germinate the seed buried in the ground.

In attributing to Zeus all these adventures, the Greeks then were not guilty of irreverence toward their god.   They were all translating the emotions they felt in the face of nature's great mysteries into gracious poetic form.   Or else, more naively, they were creating for themselves a noble ancestry.

[2]Metis   daughter of Oceanus and Tethys, was the first wife of Zeus and personifies Wisdom.   According to Hesiod, she was destined to give birth to Athena and "an unruly son, future king of god and men." Zeus prevented this possibility by swallowing Metis. Later, Athena is said to have issued from the top of her father's head, full grown and armed from head to foot.   Athena, or the Roman Minerva, is one of the most familiar fig-

ures in all mythology.   She is called the goddess of
wisdom, and goddess of defensive warfare.   As a goddess of war, she should not be confused with Ares or
the Roman Mars, who is god of the brutality and killing
of war.   Athena is the patron goddess of brave and
heroic warriors, and she is also associated with various
arts and culture, as was her city Athens in ancient
times.   In power and authority she is almost equal to
Zeus, having access to the thunderbolt and wearing the
Aegis, the great shield of Zeus, which renders her invulnerable.   Athena never married, although she was
the champion of a number of great men: Jason, Odysseus, Achilles, and others.   It was Athena who presided at the trial of Orestes and voted for acquittal of
his mother's murder when the jury of citizens voted six
to six.   Athena is referred to by many names: Pallas,
either from the giant Pallas whom Athena killed in the
War of the Giants and in whose skin she clothed herself,
or from Pallas, a daughter of Triton, whom Athena
loved and accidentally killed; Parthenos, because she
was a virgin goddess; Tritogeneia, related to her patron-
age of navigation interests; and Minerva, the name by
which she is regularly identified in Roman myth.

[3]Dione   is called a Titan by Apollodorus, and by Hesi-
           od is referred to as a daughter of Oceanus
and Tethys.   Homer does not specify her lineage, but
calls her simply "the fair goddess," who is the mother
of Zeus' daughter Aphrodite.   Except for her role in the
Iliad, she has no mythology.   Here she acts primarily
as a comforter for Aphrodite when the goddess of love
is wounded by the warrior Diomedes, and speaks a dire
warning against mortals who are so foolish as to wound
gods.

     Aphrodite is said by Homer in the Odyssey to be
the wife of Hephaestus, but she is better known for some
of her other liaisons.   By several of the gods--Ares,

Hermes, Dionysus--she is the mother of a dozen offspring.   Aeneas, son of Anchises, is the most famous
of her sons by mortals, but she was also charmed by
the ill-fated Adonis.   The story is familiarly told by
Ovid and many others.   In Euripides' Hippolytus, the
death of Adonis by a wild boar, Artemis says, will be
her revenge on Aphrodite, who has just been responsible
for the death of Hippolytus, a dedicated follower of
Artemis.   The following genealogy of Adonis is recon-
structed from Ovid and Apollodorus:

Pygmalion, King of Cyprus
(Galatea, the statue that Pygmalion
         created and to which Aphrodite
         gave life)

Paphos, eponym for the island sacred
        to Aphrodite

Cinyras

Myrrha: Smyrna
(by her father)

Adonis
(Aphrodite)

a son and a daughter

Aphrodite, called Venus in Roman mythology, is also
referred to as Cypris or Cytherea; the myth that says
Aphrodite was created from the foam of the ocean places
her origin near the island of Cyprus or perhaps the
island of Cythera.

[4]Leto   daughter of the Titans Coeus and Phoebe, by
          Zeus was the mother of Apollo and Artemis.

[5]Maia   one of the Pleiades, daughters of Atlas and
          Pleione, by Zeus was the mother of Hermes.

[6]Demeter   daughter of Cronus and Rhea, and therefore
            sister of Zeus, by whom she had Persphone.

[7]Abstractions   Alethia, better known as the Roman Veri-
                 tas, was Truth personified, the daughter
of Zeus, or Jupiter, and the mother of Virtue. Litae,
meaning Prayers, are daughters of Zeus, described in
the Iliad as "halting and wrinkled and of eyes askance,"
following behind Eris to repair the damage she does.

[8]Leda   daughter of Thestius, married Tyndareus and
         by him was the mother of Castor, Clytemnestra,
and possibly other lesser-known daughters; by Zeus, who
assumed the shape of a swan when he visited her, she
was the mother of Helen and Polydeuces or Pollux.

[9]Semele   daughter of Cadmus, one of four ill-fated sis-
           ters--Semele, Autonoe, Ino, and Agave--all
of whom met violent ends. Semele was consumed by
flames when she insisted that Zeus reveal himself to her
in his divine splendor. As the mother of Dionysus, however, she was rescued from Hades and became the goddess Thyone on Olympus.

[10]Others   The list here is representative, and many
            others are shown throughout the charts.

Chart 12

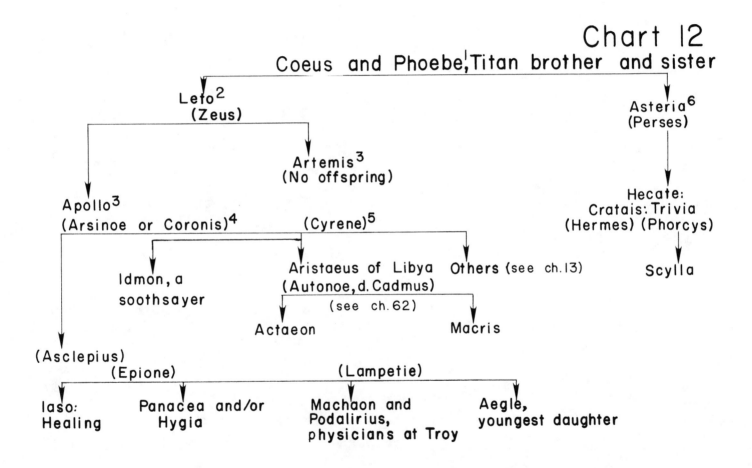

Coeus and Phoebe, Titan brother and sister

Leto[2]
(Zeus)

Asteria[6]
(Perses)

Artemis[3]
(No offspring)

Hecate:
Cratais: Trivia
(Hermes) (Phorcys)

Apollo[3]
(Arsinoe or Coronis)[4]   (Cyrene)[5]

Scylla

Idmon, a
soothsayer

Aristaeus of Libya
(Autonoe, d. Cadmus)   Others (see ch. 13)

(see ch. 62)

Actaeon   Macris

(Asclepius)
          (Epione)   (Lampetie)

Iaso:
Healing

Panacea and/or
Hygia

Machaon and
Podalirius,
physicians at Troy

Aegle,
youngest daughter

Chart 13

Apollo, cont.

(Psamathe)[7]   (Others)[8]

Linus of Argos
(see ch. 3)

(Others; see throughout charts)

Corybantes by Thalia

Dorus, Laodocus, and Polypoetes by Phthia

Eleuther by Aethusa

Miletus by Aria

Mopsus by Manto

Delphus and Cycnus by Thyra or Celaeno (see ch. 15)

Ismenus by Melia

Philammon by Chione (see ch. 43)
(Argiope)

Thamyris

Ion by Creusa

NOTES FOR CHARTS 12 AND 13

[1]Coeus-Phoebe   Titan brother and sister, are consistently said to have had two daughters,
Leto and Asteria.

[2]Leto   called Latona in Roman mythology, is generally
represented as the fond mother of two glorious
offspring.   Stories involving Leto are fairly numerous,
and usually have a theme of persecution or lack of respect for divinity.   Hera persecuted her "over the whole
earth," Apollodorus says, until she came to Delos,
where Artemis and Apollo were born.   The giant Tityus
is said to have attempted an assault on her, was killed
by Apollo and Artemis, and was thrown into Tartarus,
where an eagle perpetually eats at his liver.   Ovid relates the story in which Leto turns the Lycians into
frogs because they haughtily and cruelly refused to give
her water.   The most frequently told story is the one in
which Apollo and Artemis, at their mother's request,
kill all the children of Niobe.   This is also an instance
of persecution, since Niobe boasted that she had many
children--the number varies--whereas Leto had borne
but two.   In the Iliad, Leto flies to the aid of her daughter when Artemis and Hera get into an ear-boxing match.
Artemis and her arrows might slay the daughters of
Niobe without difficulty, but the young goddess is no
match for Hera, who soundly slaps her and scatters the
arrows all over Olympus.   Leto is never represented
as consort of anyone except Zeus, and no other offspring
are attributed to her.

[3]Apollo and Artemis   two of the most prominent figures
in Greek mythology, are referred
to by a variety of names: Delius and Delia after Delos,
where they were born; Cynthius and Cynthia after Mount
Cynthus, their birthplace on Delos; and Phoebus and
Phoebe after Leto's mother Phoebe.   Artemis is also
related to Diana of Roman mythology, and the attributes
of the Greek Apollo and the Roman Apollo are nearly
identical.

Artemis is the goddess of hunting, protector of
animals, and, curiously enough, since she was a virgin
goddess, friend and helper of women in childbirth.
Sometimes it was said that Artemis was the slayer of
women who died of women's diseases, as Odysseus on
his trip to the Underworld asks his mother's shade,
"Was it long disease, or did the archer, Artemis, as-
sail thee with her gentle shafts, and slay thee?" Most
of the stories of Artemis involve violence of an ex-
treme nature, and on at least two occasions she is connected with human sacrifice.

Her role in killing the giant Tityus for his actions toward Leto has already been referred to, and she
is also said by Odysseus in the Odyssey to have slain
the giant Orion out of jealousy toward Eos, who loved
Orion.   Other versions of this story say that Orion was
killed for challenging Artemis to a match of quoits; or
that Orion was shot by Artemis for attempting to violate
one of her maidens.   One further variation of the tale is
that Orion died of the bite of a deadly scorpion sent by

Artemis because he had dared to violate her chastity. Artemis and Apollo are also said to have killed the Aloads, Otus and Ephialtes, who presumed to ascend into the heavens. Apollodorus says Artemis "changed herself into a deer and leaped between them, and in their eagerness to hit the quarry they threw their darts at each other."

Artemis is generally said to have caused the Calydonian Boar Hunt, which resulted in much disaster and the loss of nearly an entire family. Oeneus, the King of Calydon, forgot to sacrifice to Artemis, and in great wrath she sent a boar of extraordinary size and strength that ravaged the land and cattle and killed the people. To hunt this boar, Oeneus called together all the great heroes of the day and offered as prize the skin of the beast to whomever who should kill it. The boar was killed by the huntress Atalanta, but the aftermath of the hunt was disastrous, and many of the family of Oeneus, including his son Meleager, perished as a result. On another occasion, Artemis was also forgotten in the sacrifice. Admetus, who married Alcestis, forgot Artemis, and when he opened his marriage chamber he found it full of coiled snakes. Apollo, who had been bound to serve Admetus for a year, advised him to appease the goddess, which he hastily attended to.

Artemis and Heracles came to a near-clash as Heracles was performing his Third Labor, bringing the golden hind of Cerynitia alive to Mycenae. This animal was sacred to Artemis, and Heracles did not want to in any wise harm it. After hunting it unsuccessfully for a whole year, Heracles finally gave up and wounded it. Artemis with Apollo met Heracles, and would have snatched the hind away and rebuked him, except he pleaded necessity and placed all the blame on Eurystheus, who had imposed the labor. With this plea Heracles appeased the anger of the goddess who then cured the hind of its wound and allowed him to take the animal alive to Mycenae. The story of Actaeon and his encounter with Artemis did not end on quite so happy a note. Actaeon, son of Autonoe, a daughter of Cadmus, and Aristaeus, a son of Apollo, was a great hunter. One day he chanced to see Artemis bathing, whereupon she changed him into a deer, and his fifty dogs tore him to pieces.

There are several instances in which Artemis destroys those who challenge her honor. The story of Niobe's children and their destruction by Artemis and Apollo has been referred to in connection with Leto. Another familiar story is that of Callisto, daughter of Lycaon of Arcadia, who was a companion of Artemis in the hunt, wore the same dress, and swore an oath of chastity. Zeus loved Callisto against her will, and wishing to deceive Hera, turned her into a bear. One account says Hera persuaded Artemis to shoot her down as a wild beast, but another version says Artemis shot her because Callisto violated her oath of chastity. The role of Artemis in the destruction of Adonis has been referred to earlier in connection with Aphrodite, who loved Adonis. Broteas, another hunter, a son of Tantalus, did not honor Artemis and boasted that he feared nothing, not even fire. Artemis subsequently drove him mad, and he threw himself into the fire.

And finally it was Artemis who was responsible for the sacrifice of Iphigenia, the daughter of Agamemnon. The story is a familiar one and is referred to by nearly all classic writers except Homer, who says nothing about the matter. Artemis began her hostility with Atreus, father of Agamemnon, who had cheated her of a sacrifice of a golden lamb; with Agamemnon her anger came full circle when he boasted that "not even Artemis could shoot better," and killed a deer sacred to her. The fleet on its way to Troy was calmed at Aulis, and the prophet Calchas gave out that only the sacrifice of the fairest of Agamemnon's daughters could appease the goddess and cause the winds to blow. Hence, Iphigenia

was brought to Aulis and, according to one version of
the myth, was sacrificed on the altar of Artemis; another version says that at the moment of slaughter Artemis snatched her away and substituted a deer. According to the latter story, Iphigenia became a priestess
in the temple of Taurian Artemis, and her duty was to
consecrate human beings for death on the altar. These
events are treated in two plays by Euripides, Iphigenia
at Aulis and Iphigenia in Tauris, and are referred to
directly in Aeschylus' trilogy the Oresteia.

Apollo shares many stories with Artemis, but a
great many others have no connection with the sister.
Apollo is perhaps the most complex of the Greek gods,
and as such his mythology is the most extensive. He
is called the god of truth, is associated with light, music, archery, prophecy, health, and medicine. His functions also relate to the care of flocks and herds, and
the founding of cities.

As archer god, Apollo is usually associated with
Artemis; on other occasions, however, he acts indepen-
dently. For instance, one of his earliest acts was to
come to Delphi, where Themis kept her oracles, and
kill the great Python that guarded the temple. He then
took over, and Delphi thereafter became the center of
Apollo's prophecy. On two occasions Apollo and Heracles are associated: Apollo is said to have given Heracles his marvelous bow and arrow and to have taught
him the craft of archery; later, Heracles, in great anger
at not receiving an answer to a question he asked of
Apollo's oracle, plundered the temple and would have
established one of his own. He and Apollo fought until
Zeus, who loved Heracles and did not want him harmed,
hurled a thunderbolt and parted them. As an archer,
Apollo was finally responsible for the death of Achilles.
When the Greeks left Aulis, they stopped at Tenedos,
where Apollo's son Tenes was king. Achilles killed
Tenes, and was at that time warned by his mother Thetis

that Apollo would kill him in turn. This the god did,
ten years later, when he guided the arrow shot by Paris
into the vulnerable spot on Achilles' heel.

As a god of music, Apollo plays the lyre for the
other gods in the Iliad. The story of how Apollo obtained the lyre from his brother, the god Hermes, is
the plot of the fragmentary play by Sophocles The Track-
ers. Apollo's cattle were stolen by Hermes, who had
fashioned the lyre from the tortoise shell. In tracking
his cattle, Apollo came across the lyre and was so en-
chanted with it that he offered to give Hermes the cattle
in exchange for the instrument. Hermes readily accepted the bargain, and Apollo also gave the younger
god the office of divine keeper of herds. The story of
Marsyas and his encounter with Apollo the musician is
a grim one. Marsyas, foolish as all mortals who challenge gods, engaged Apollo in a musical contest. It
was agreed that the winner should do as he liked to the
loser. Marsyas lost, and Apollo hung him to a pine
tree where he was flayed alive. This story is told by
Ovid and other writers.

Apollo as the god of prophecy is illustrated by
the story of Cassandra, a daughter of Priam. Apollo
loved Cassandra and gave her the gift of prophecy. Following this, Cassandra refused the god her favors, and
he, unable to take back his gift, deprived her of the
power to induce belief in her prophecies. Cassandra's
story is referred to by numerous writers, but is told
in some detail in Aeschylus' Agamemnon. Apollo is
also said to have given the gift of prophecy to Melampus,
son of Amythaon and Idomene. Idmon, the son of Apollo
and Cyrene, received his gift from his father, and was
the prophet who sailed with Jason and the Argonauts.
Many other stories of Apollo are related to his offspring,
and are discussed under their names.

[4]Arsinoe or Coronis   mother of Asclepius, called Aes-

culapius by the Romans. Arsinoe, daughter of Leucippus, is rarely given as the mother, and the story is usually told of Coronis, daughter of Phlegyas. Loved by Apollo, Coronis was nonetheless unfaithful, and the god was told of this by the raven, which at that time was a snow-white bird. Apollo killed Coronis, but he thanked the informer by cursing it and turning it black. The child Asclepius was saved, and was given to the centaur Chiron for educating. Chiron taught him the art of healing, and he began to save men from death; on some occasions he is even said to have raised men from the dead. Zeus, afraid that men might learn to live forever, killed Asclepius with the Thunderbolt. Apollo in turn slew the Cyclops, or the sons of the Cyclops, who had made the Thunderbolt. Zeus would have cast him into Tartarus, but Leto, Apollo's mother, begged for a lesser sentence. Instead, Zeus ordered Apollo to serve as bonded slave to a mortal for one year. This task the god performed willingly, serving Admetus, the son of Pheres.

Asclepius is said to be the father of a variety of offspring, all having some relation to health and medicine. Machaon and Podalirius are named by Homer in the Iliad as warriors and healers who go to Troy to help cure the wounded Greeks. Quintus of Smyrna says that Machaon was killed by Eurypylus, a grandson of Heracles who came to aid the Trojans; and that Podalirius cured Philoctetes' great wound and was with the Greeks in the Wooden Horse.

[5]Cyrene   a daughter of the river god Peneus, or a daughter of Hypseus, a king of the Lapiths and a son of the Peneus. Apollo carried her to Libya in Africa, where she became the mother of Aristaeus and Idmon, a soothsayer. Aristaeus, after he had traveled over most of the world, came to Thebes, where he married Autonoe, a daughter of Cadmus. They had a son, Actaeon, who perished at the hands of Artemis, and a daughter, Macris, who is said to have nursed the infant Dionysus on Mount Nysa, a mythological location related to the god's name. Macris later took refuge from Hera on the Island of Scherie among the Phaeacians, and lived there in a cave. It was in this cave, Apollonius of Rhodes says, that Jason and Medea spent their wedding night, and after that the cave was called the cave of Medea. Aristaeus is best known as "the bee-man" who introduced the care and use of honey-bees into Greece; and in a much less favorable situation, he is reputed to have chased Eurydice, the wife of Orpheus, and to have caused her to step on the snake that caused her death.

Idmon, sometimes called the son of Abas, "was not really Abas' son, but one whom Apollo had fathered"; he was the soothsayer of the Argonauts. Apollonius of Rhodes says that he knew he would die before the journey ended, but he went anyway. He was killed by a wild boar in the land of Bithynia before the ship reached Colchis. He was given a magnificent funeral by Jason and the Argonauts, and his father Apollo strictly commanded the people of that country to honor him.

[6]Asteria   daughter of Coeus and Phoebe, married Perses, son of Crius and Eurybia. Hecate is called "the only daughter of her mother" by Hesiod, and it is not generally recognized that Hecate was the mother of any offspring. She is associated with Hermes in his function as conductor of dead souls to Hades, and one mythology calls her the mother of Scylla. She is identified with magic, sorcery, and witchcraft, and was said to inhabit crossroads, graveyards, or places of execution. The most familiar devotee of Hecate is perhaps Medea, daughter of Aeetes of Colchis, and wife to Jason. In the Argonautica, Medea performs lengthy rites to honor Hecate and prays for the help of the goddess to win

Jason's love.   In Euripides' <u>Medea</u>, Medea calls her
"Queen of Night, whom I revere above all, and for fel-
low-worker chose. " Medea, herself a sorceress, then
calls on Hecate to aid her in a terrible revenge she is
plotting against Jason because he is taking another wife.
Although Hecate is usually identified with witchcraft or
sorcery, she has a much broader scope than this, according to Hesiod.   He says Zeus "exalted her above
all with gifts and honors. " Her rights extended over
the earth, sea, and heavens, and prayers to her could
obtain all manner of benefits: victory in battle, a plentiful catch of fish, greater fertility in animals, or success
in winning games.   This all-inclusive power is unique,
and no one else "is endowed with every privilege which
the gods possess. " Hecate is not mentioned in Homer,
and is referred to only briefly by Virgil.

[7]<u>Psamathe</u>   daughter of Crotopus, a king of Argos, was
               the mother of Linus by Apollo.   See Chart
3 for all Linus stories.

[8]<u>Others</u>   Some of the more prominent figures are
               treated throughout the charts in the genealogies
of their mothers.   A list of Apollo's other offspring
could become almost indefinite, but since most of these
figures have little or no mythology only a few are suggested here:

>   Dorus, Laodocus, and Polypoetes by Phthia were
>   killed by Aetolus, who called the country Ae-
>   tolia after himself.
>
>   Eleuther by Aethusa, the daughter of Alcyone and
>   Poseidon, is the eponym for a town in Boeotia
>   and another one in Crete.
>
>   Miletus by Aria, daughter of Cleochus, is the
>   eponym for the city in Caria.

Mopsus by Manto, daughter of the prophet Tiresias, was himself a prophet who proved himself
wiser than Calchas and thereby caused the
death of Calchas.

Thamyris, the son of Philammon and Argiope,
was related to Apollo through his father, and
was a great poet-musician who dared to challenge the Muses to a contest; he lost, and the
Muses deprived him of his sight and poetic
gift.

Oceanus and Tethys, Titan brother and sister[1]   Chart 14

Nymphs[2]

Daughters: Oceanids[3]

Sons: River gods[11]

Peitho	Pasithea	Europa[6]	Nile	Peneus
Admeta	Plexaura	Metis (Zeus)	Alpheus (Arethusa)	(see ch. 16)
Ianthe	Galaxaura	(see ch. 10)	(see ch. 15)	Hermus
Electra (Thaumas)	Dione (Zeus)[5]	Eurynome (Zeus)	Eridanus	Caicus
(see ch. 4)	(see ch. 10)	(see ch. 15)	Strymon (Euterpe)	Sangarius
Doris (Nereus)	Melabosis	Telesto	(see ch. 3)	(see ch. 16)
(see ch. 4)	Thoe	Chryseis	Maender	Ladon of
Prymo	Polydora	Asia (Iapetus)[7]	Ister	Arcadia
Urania	Cerceis	(see ch. 19)	Phasis	(see ch. 16)
Hippo	Pluto (Zeus)	Calypso[8]	Achelous	Parthenius
Clymene (Iapetus)	(see ch. 44)	Eudora	(see ch. 16)	Evenus
(see ch. 2)	Perseis (Helios)	Tyche[9]	Nessus	Ardescus
Rhodea	Ianira	Amphiro	Rhodius	Scamander:
Callirrhoe (Chrysaor)	Acaste	Ocyrrhoe	Haliacmon	Xanthus of Troy
(see ch. 5)	Xanthe	Styx (Pallas)[10]	Heptaphorus	(see ch. 16)
Zeuxo	Petraea	(see ch. 4)	Granicus	
Clytie[4]	Menesto		Asopus (Metope)	
(loved Helios)	Idyia (Aeetes)		(see ch. 17)	
(see ch. 42)	(see ch. 42)		Simois of Troy	

NOTES FOR CHART 14

[1]Oceanus-Tethys   Titan brother and sister, were succeeded by Poseidon as principal god of the sea and other waters. Oceanus, oldest of the Titans, did not take part in the War of the Gods and Titans, hence no enmity existed between him and Zeus. Homer calls him "Oceanus, from whom the gods are sprung. "

[2]Nymphs   The word has become generalized to mean "maiden"; originally it referred to a class of female deities, lesser than the gods, to whom they were frequently daughters or wives. They are classified as to nymphs of the land and nymphs of the water in the following categories:

(a) Dryades and Hamadryades -- presided over the woods.

(b) Oreades -- presided over the mountains.

(c) Napaeae -- presided over hills and dales.

(d) Oceanids -- daughters of Oceanus, presided over the sea.

(e) Nereids -- daughters of Nereus, presided over the sea.

(f) Naiades -- presided over rivers, fountains, streams, and lakes.

Hesiod calls all nymphs daughters of Oceanus and Tethys, "three thousand slender-ankled daughters ... scattered far and wide, watching over the land and the depths of the sea. "

[3]Oceanids   sea nymphs, daughters of Oceanus and Tethys. This list of forty-one by Hesiod is called "the eldest, " but there are others that "are known to the peoples living near them. " Apollodorus names only seven: Asia, Styx, Electra, Doris, Eurynome, Amphitrite, and Metis. In Hesiod, Amphitrite is called a Nereid. Most of the Oceanids have no mythological stories; hence only a few are discussed here. Others are discussed throughout the charts in the genealogies of their husbands.

[4]Clytie   was loved and then deserted by Helios, the sun god, who by then was in love with Leucothoe, the daughter of King Orchamus of Persia. Clytie in rage and jealousy told the father, who ordered Leucothoe buried alive. Clytie did not regain the sun god's love, but grieved herself to death and was changed into a sunflower or marigold. The stories of Clytie and Leucothoe are told by Ovid.

[5]Dione   is called one of the Titans by Apollodorus. By Zeus she is the mother of Aphrodite, according to Homer.

[6]Europa   not to be confused with the more famous Europa, sister of Cadmus. There is no mythology of the Oceanid Europa, her name being merely an eponym for the continent.

[7]Asia   eponym for the continent, is called the wife of the Titan Iapetus by Apollodorus; however, his wife is usually called Clymene, another Oceanid.

[8]Calypso   more commonly called the daughter of Atlas, as in Homer's Odyssey. If there are two figures by this name, the Oceanid has no mythology.

[9]Tyche   named by Hesiod simply as one of the Oceanids; the word itself means fortune or luck, not necessarily good or bad. She was worshipped as a local deity in charge of the fortunes of the city, and beyond this she has no mythology. She was called Fortuna by the Romans.

[10]Styx   referred to by Hesiod as the "most exalted" of the daughters of Oceanus, she married Pallas. The waters of the Styx River were so cold and poisonous that it was said to have its origin in the Underworld. The gods held the Styx in great awe, and swore their sacred oaths by its waters.

[11]River Gods   called the sons of Oceanus and Tethys, "the swirling rivers." This list is given by Hesiod, who says there are many others, three thousand, "roaring as they flow." Like their sisters, the Oceanids, most of the river gods have little or no mythology. Some of them are discussed under Charts 15 and 16, and still others are shown throughout the charts, as founders of notable families.

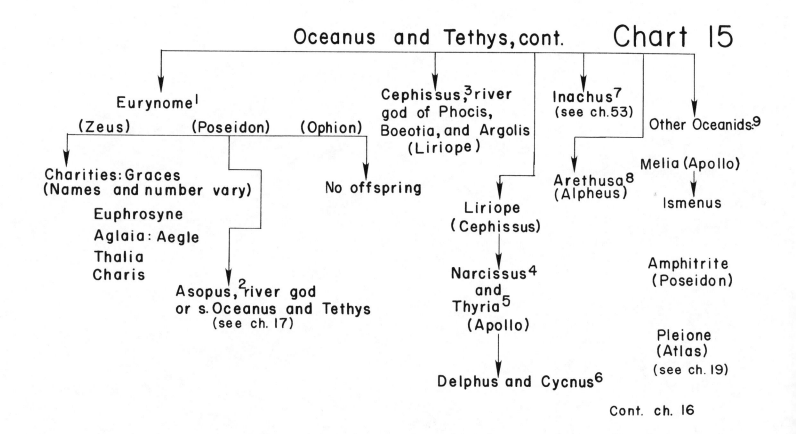

Oceanus and Tethys, cont. Chart 15

Eurynome[1]

(Zeus) (Poseidon) (Ophion)

Cephissus,[3] river god of Phocis, Boeotia, and Argolis (Liriope)

Inachus[7] (see ch. 53)

Other Oceanids:[9]

Charities: Graces (Names and number vary)

Euphrosyne
Aglaia: Aegle
Thalia
Charis

No offspring

Asopus,[2] river god or s. Oceanus and Tethys (see ch. 17)

Liriope (Cephissus)

Narcissus[4] and Thyria[5] (Apollo)

Delphus and Cycnus[6]

Arethusa[8] (Alpheus)

Melia (Apollo)

Ismenus

Amphitrite (Poseidon)

Pleione (Atlas) (see ch. 19)

Cont. ch. 16

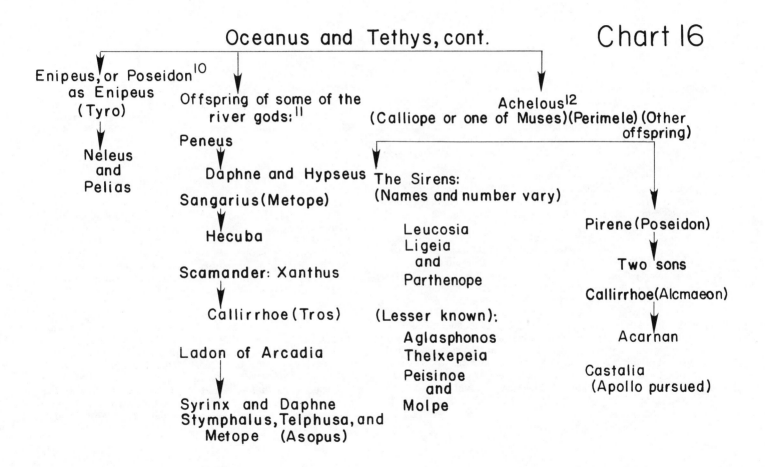

Oceanus and Tethys, cont.   Chart 16

NOTES FOR CHARTS 15 AND 16

[1]Eurynome   daughter of Oceanus and Tethys, is referred to by Apollonius of Rhodes as the
wife of Ophion, by whom there were no offspring.
Hesiod calls her the mother by Zeus of the Charities,
"three daughters with beautiful faces," Euphrosyne (Joy),
Aglaia (Pageantry), and Thalia (Festivity). Their names
and number vary, and they are more commonly called
the Graces from Roman mythology. In the Iliad,
Hephaestus is married to Charis, referred to as one of
the Graces. Other than personifying such qualities as
beauty and charm, the Graces have no mythology.

[2]Asopus   a river god, son of Oceanus and Tethys, according to Hesiod and Apollodorus. A more
obscure myth says he was the son of Eurynome and
Poseidon or Zeus. All accounts agree, however, that
he married Metope, daughter of the river Ladon, and
had two sons and from twelve to twenty daughters.
There are at least five rivers by this name: one each
in Thessaly, Boeotia, Peloponnesus, Macedonia, and
Phoenicia. Which offspring belonged to which river is
confused and uncertain, the genealogy changing according to the local origin of the poet telling the myth.
Apollodorus, the source for most of these remarks, is
referring to the Asopus of Sicyonia, located on the
coast of the Peloponnesus at the eastern end of the Gulf
of Corinth.

[3]Cephissus   a river in Phocis, Boeotia, Attica, and
Argolis, is not named by Hesiod as one
of the river gods. In his story of Narcissus and Echo,
Ovid calls Cephissus and Liriope the parents of Narcissus.

[4]Narcissus   son of Cephissus and Liriope, has been
referred to earlier in connection with Echo,
a daughter of Gaea, who loved Narcissus in vain until
she became thin and withered away to nothing but a voice.
Not long after, a young man who loved Narcissus in
vain, prayed to Nemesis that he would fall in love and
be unable to gain his loved one. The prayer was heard,
and Narcissus soon after fell in love with his own re-
flection in a pool of water. Unable to attain the object
he loved, Ovid says, "he was worn and wasted away
with love, and slowly consumed by its hidden fire."

[5]Thyria (or Thyra) a daughter of the Cephissus, her
name is the eponym for the city near
Delphi. Her son Delphus by Apollo built Delphi and
dedicated it to his father. Sometimes the mother of
Delphus is said to be Celaeno, the Pleiade.

[6]Cycnus   the name means swan, and there are at least
four well-known sons by this name: a son of
Ares, a son of Poseidon, a kinsman of Phaeton, and a

son of Apollo.   In each example, the story is much the same; the youth dies or is killed and is changed into a swan.   The son of Apollo by Thyria is said to have drowned himself in a lake which ever after was inhabited by swans.

[7]Inachus   a son of Oceanus and Tethys, who gave his name to the river in Argos.   He is called the father of Io by Aeschylus in Prometheus Bound, although Apollodorus constructs another genealogy for her. See Chart 53.

[8]Arethusa   a daughter of Oceanus, a wood nymph who hunted with Artemis or Diana.   Ovid tells the story of her pursuit by the river god Alpheus.   To escape the god, she was changed into a fountain near Syracuse.

[9]Other Oceanids   (a) Melia, wife of the river god Inachus, according to Apollodorus; or one of the Nereids, mother of Ismenus by Apollo, according to Pausanias.   (b) Amphitrite, wife of Poseidon, is called a Nereid by Hesiod, and Oceanid by Homer, Virgil, and Apollodorus.   (c) Pleione, daughter of Oceanus, was the mother of the seven sisters, the Pleiades, by Atlas.

[10]Enipeus   a river in Peloponnesus with which Tyro, daughter of Salmoneus, fell in love.   Poseidon assumed the shape of the river, and by the god Tyro had twins, Neleus and Pelias.

[11]Progeny of Other River Gods   (a) Peneus, the father of Daphne, whose familiar story is told by Ovid.   Loved and then pursued by Apollo, Daphne called on the gods to help her escape, and she was changed into the laurel.   Apollo crowned

himself with the laurel and decreed that the laurel should thereafter be sacred to him.   (b) Sangarius by the nymph Metope was the father of Hecuba, according to one myth; however, Homer says Hecuba was a daughter of Dymas, "who dwelt in Phrygia by the streams of Sangarius. "   Euripides and Virgil call Hecuba the daughter of Cisseus.   (c) Scamander, called Xanthus by the gods, was the father of Callirrhoe, who married Tros, by whom she was the mother of Ilus, Ganymede, and Assaracus.   There are at least five other women in mythology with this name who should not be confused with the wife of Tros.   (d) Ladon, who is sometimes called the father of Daphne, was the father of Syrinx, a nymph loved by Pan.   Like Daphne, she tried to escape her lover, and was changed into a reed.   Ovid tells the story of her transformation and how the god then made himself a pipe from the reeds.   The only other well-known offspring of Ladon was Metope, who married Asopus, the river god, and was mother of a notable line of sons and daughters.

[12]Achelous   largest river in Greece, is said to be the oldest of the three thousand sons of Oceanus and Tethys.   Other accounts say the Achelous was the son of Helios and Gaea and sprang into existence after the Great Flood.   By one of the Muses, Achelous is usually called the father of the Sirens.   Their names and number vary, but usually three are given: Parthenope, Ligeia, and Leucosia.   Apollodorus names Pisinoe, Agalaope, and Thelxiepia, and says, "One of them played the lyre, another sang, and another played the flute, and by these means they were fain to persuade passing mariners to linger; and from the thighs they had the forms of birds. "   Apollonius of Rhodes says that "at one time they had been handmaids of Demeter's daughter ... but now, half-human, half-bird in form, they spent their time watching for ships. "   Except for Orpheus, who out-

played them on his lyre, they would have added many Argonauts to the men who had perished under the spell of their song. The best-known story of the Sirens is the one told by Homer in the Odyssey. Warned in advance by Circe, Odysseus put wax in his sailors' ears and had himself bound to the mast of his ship. In this manner, the crafty Odysseus was able to hear their song, but was in no danger of being overwhelmed himself or of losing any of his men. Apollodorus refers to the prophecy that the Sirens would die when they were thus defeated, but Homer says nothing about this aspect of the story.

As to other wives and offspring of Achelous, Ovid tells the story of Perimele, a daughter of Hippodamus, who was thrown from a cliff by her father because Achelous had courted and seduced her. The river god caught her and prayed to his father Oceanus to save her. This not being possible, however, Perimele was changed into an island in the Ionian Sea. Pirene, a daughter of Achelous, had two sons by Poseidon, one of whom was killed by Artemis. Pirene grieved herself to death and was changed into a fountain, which Pausanias reports as having seen in Corinth. Callirrhoe was the second or third wife of Alcmaeon, whose brutal murder was avenged when their two sons, Acarnan and Amphoterus, grew miraculously to manhood in a night's time. Castalia, eponym for the town near Phocis, was loved by Apollo.

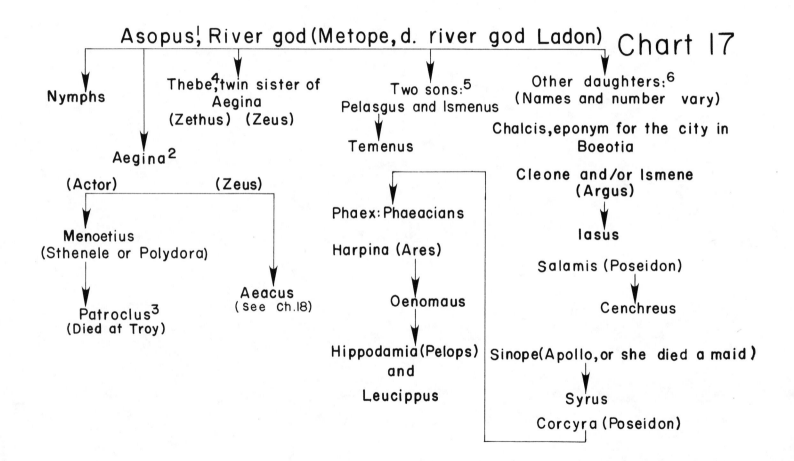

Asopus,[1] River god (Metope, d. river god Ladon)   Chart 17

Nymphs

Thebe,[4] twin sister of
Aegina
(Zethus) (Zeus)

Aegina[2]

(Actor)   (Zeus)

Menoetius
(Sthenele or Polydora)

Patroclus[3]
(Died at Troy)

Aeacus
(See ch.18)

Two sons:[5]
Pelasgus and Ismenus

Temenus

Phaex: Phaeacians

Harpina (Ares)

Oenomaus

Hippodamia (Pelops)
and
Leucippus

Other daughters:[6]
(Names and number vary)

Chalcis, eponym for the city in
Boeotia

Cleone and/or Ismene
(Argus)

Iasus

Salamis (Poseidon)

Cenchreus

Sinope (Apollo, or she died a maid)

Syrus

Corcyra (Poseidon)

NOTES FOR CHART 17

[1]Asopus   a river god, usually called the son of Oceanus and Tethys; by Metope, a daughter of the river god Ladon, Asopus was the father of a notable line of progeny. Apollodorus says Asopus and Metope were parents of two sons and twenty daughters. A more conservative estimate is two sons and twelve daughters.

[2]Aegina   the most famous daughter of Asopus, was carried off by Zeus and became the mother of Aeacus. In honor of her, Zeus named the island, then called Oenone, after her. Later she married Actor, son of Myrmidon, by whom she had other sons, including Menoetius, the father of Patroclus. Menoetius went with the Argonauts to Colchis, but did not especially distinguish himself, since he is not mentioned by Apollonius of Rhodes after the introduction of the crew.

[3]Patroclus   son of Menoetius, called Actorides by Homer, after his grandfather Actor; Homer, however, does not give the mother of Patroclus. Apollodorus says she was Sthenele, daughter of Acastus; or Periopis, daughter of Pheres; or Polydora (also called Polymele), a daughter of Peleus by Antigone, the daughter of Eurytion, a son of Actor. The story is told that in a game of dice, Patroclus killed a son of Amphidamas, and with his father fled to the court of his kinsman Peleus, where he became a close friend of Achilles. Patroclus accompanied Achilles to Troy, where he was killed in the tenth year of the war by Hector, who in turn was killed by Achilles. These events are narrated in the later books of Homer's Iliad.

[4]Thebe   daughter of Asopus, married Zethus, a son of Zeus and Antiope. With the help of his brother Amphion, Zethus built and fortified with the great wall the city of Thebes, which one source says he then named for his wife. However, another tradition says the city was called Thebes from the time of Cadmus. Zethus succeeded Lycus as King of Thebes and was himself succeeded by Laius, son of Labdacus, who was a kinsman. There is no evidence that Zethus and Thebe bore children.

[5]Two Sons   Pelasgus or Pelagon and Ismenus are eponyms for the Pelasgians and the Ismenus River of Boeotia near Thebes. Pelasgus is also said to be the son of Zeus and Niobe, a daughter of Phoroneus.

[6]Other Daughters   the names and number vary, and there is little or no mythology connected with these figures, who are primarily eponyms for the cities or islands where they lived. Some of them are discussed elsewhere in the charts.

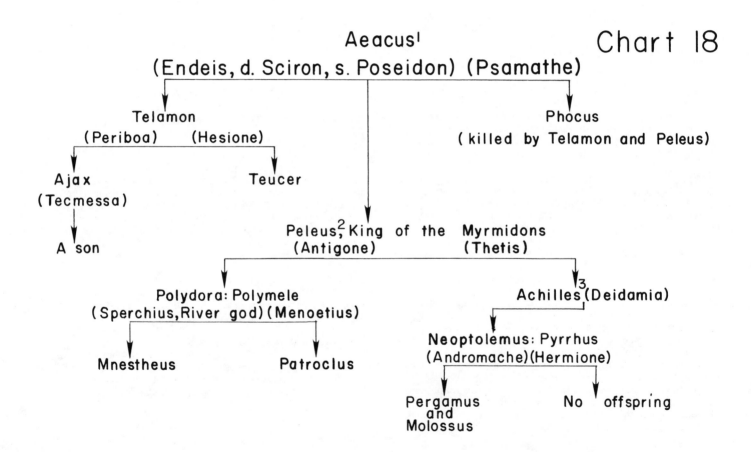

Chart 18

Aeacus[1]
(Endeis, d. Sciron, s. Poseidon) (Psamathe)

Telamon
(Periboa)   (Hesione)

Phocus
(killed by Telamon and Peleus)

Ajax
(Tecmessa)

Teucer

A son

Peleus[2] King of the Myrmidons
(Antigone)   (Thetis)

Polydora: Polymele
(Sperchius, River god) (Menoetius)

Achilles[3] (Deidamia)

Mnestheus

Patroclus

Neoptolemus: Pyrrhus
(Andromache) (Hermione)

Pergamus
and
Molossus

No offspring

NOTES FOR CHART 18

[1]Aeacus son of Aegina and Zeus, married Endeis, a daughter of Sciron, by whom he had two famous sons, Telamon and Peleus. Later, he married the Nereid Psamathe, by whom he had the son Phocus. After his death, Aeacus became one of the judges in the Underworld, sharing the honor with Minos and Rhadamanthus, two sons of Zeus by the Phoenician Europa. In life, Aeacus is represented as "the most pious of men," who honored the gods.

Telamon and Peleus, both members of the Argo crew, were said by Apollonius of Rhodes to have "killed their brother Phocus in a mad moment, and to have put a long way between Aegina and themselves." Apollodorus also tells the story:

> ... his brothers Peleus and Telamon plotted against him and the lot falling on Telamon, he killed his brother in a match by throwing a quoit at his head, and with the help of Peleus carried the body and hid in in a wood. But the murder being detected, the two were driven fugitives from Aegina by Aeacus.

Telamon went to the court of Cychreus, a son of Poseidon and Salamis, daughter of Asopus. Cychreus dying childless, left his kingdom of Salamis, named for his mother, to Telamon. By Periboa, daughter of Alcathous, a son of Pelops, Telamon was the father of Ajax. Telamon went with Heracles on his expedition to Troy, where they laid waste the city and killed Laomedon and all his sons except Priam. Hesione, the daughter of Laomedon, was given as a war prize to Telamon, and became the mother of Teucer, a natural son. Both Ajax and Teucer later fought in the Trojan War. Ajax killed himself in the tenth year of the war, when he was not awarded the great shield of Achilles for which he and Odysseus had competed. Teucer survived the war, but was later exiled by his father, who did not forgive him for failing to avenge the death of Ajax. According to Virgil, Teucer went to Cyprus, where he built a town that he called Salamis after his native country. The story of the death of Ajax is best told by Sophocles in his tragedy Ajax, but Quintus of Smyrna also gives an interesting account of the event.

[2]Peleus a king of the Myrmidons in Thessaly, is best known as the father of Achilles by the Nereid Thetis. After the murder of his brother Phocus, he fled to the court of Eurytion (or Eurytus), where he was purified of the crime and married Antigone, daughter of Eurytion, by whom he had a daughter, Polydora, also called Polymele. It was apparently after this that Peleus married Thetis and became the father of Achilles. Peleus went with Jason on the Argo, and by reason of being married to Thetis, he was able to enlist the aid of the Nereids in getting the ship safely through the

Wandering Rocks.   Later Peleus also went to the Caly-donian Boar Hunt, where he accidentally killed Eurytion, his father-in-law and former host.   He fled again, this time to the court of Acastus, the son of Pelias in Iol-chus, where he nearly lost his life because of a treacher-ous woman.   Astydamia, the wife of Acastus, fell in love with Peleus, and when he would not return her af-fection, she lied to her husband that Peleus had attempted to violate her virtue.   Acastus, reluctant to break the law of hospitality, did not kill him at once, but ordered him left defenseless in a mountain wood where he would be killed by wild animals.   Zeus saw the injustice about to be done to his grandson, and made possible his res-cue by Chiron, the centaur.   Peleus then marched against Acastus, seized the throne and killed both the king and Astydamia.   Later the sons of Acastus, Archan-der and Architeles, expelled Peleus and reclaimed their kingdom.   Peleus escaped to the island of Cos, where, according to one story, he died in exile.   A reference is made to Peleus' difficulties with the sons of Acastus in Euripides' The Trojan Women.   In this play, Neop-tolemus departed hastily from Troy because he had "heard tidings of wrong to Peleus ... how the seed of Pelias exiles him."

The marriage of Thetis and Peleus was one of the most celebrated events in mythology.   Both Zeus and Poseidon had sought Thetis in marriage, but the Titan goddess Themis, or her son Prometheus, prophe-sied that the son of Thetis would be greater than his father.   After this, the two gods withdrew their suit, and Zeus determined to marry her to a mortal, Peleus being the only one so honored.   Their marriage was celebrated on Mount Pelion by gods and mortals alike, with feasting and gifts, and singing by the Muses.   It was to this famous wedding that Eris, goddess of Dis-cord, was not invited.   The marriage of Thetis and Peleus, however, was apparently of short duration.

Homer depicts the goddess living with her aged father Nereus and her sisters in the depths of the sea while her husband, now old, lives out a miserable and soli-tary life in his halls.   After the birth of Achilles, Thetis tried to make her son immortal by hiding him in the fire at night and anointing him with ambrosia by day. Caught by Peleus and thus frustrated in her purpose, Apollonius of Rhodes says, she threw the screaming in-fant on the floor and rushed out of the house never to return.   Another version of the story says that Thetis dipped Achilles in the river Styx to make him immortal, but overlooked the heel by which she held him.   In the play Andromache, Euripides shows Thetis appearing to Peleus and, because of her love for her son Achilles, bestowing immortality on the aged father.

[3]Achilles   celebrated son of Thetis and Peleus, is the epic hero of Homer's Iliad, and in spite of his tragic pride and stubborn arrogance, is called the greatest warrior of them all.   His death occurs after the conclusion of the Iliad, in the tenth year of the Tro-jan War, at the hands of Paris and the god Apollo.   In the Odyssey, Achilles is in the Underworld and speaks to Odysseus of the value he places on life:

> Noble Odysseus, do not commend death to me.
> I would rather serve on the land of another man
> Who had no portion and not a great livelihood
> Than to rule over all the shades of those who are
>   dead.

Another, perhaps later, tradition says that Achilles be-came immortal and went to the Blessed Isles at his death.

Apollodorus tells the story that Thetis tried to prevent Achilles from going to the war by sending him to the court of Lycomedes dressed as a girl.   Appar-

Chart 18   73

ently, however, his costume did not fool everyone, for
while there he became the father of Neoptolemus by the
king's daughter, Deidamia. After Achilles' death, Neoptolemus is brought to Troy, and is among the survivors
when the city falls. It was he who killed old King Priam
and Priam's young son Polites. In Euripides' The Trojan Women, Hector's widow, Andromache, becomes his
war prize, but later, according to Virgil and Euripides,
she was abandoned by Neoptolemus when he married
Hermione, the daughter of Helen and Menelaus. In
Euripides' Andromache, Neoptolemus is slain by Orestes, the son of Agamemnon and Clytemnestra, who
claims Hermione as his betrothed. In Virgil's Aeneid,
Andromache is portrayed as married to Helenus, prophet
son of Priam, whom Neoptolemus also took captive and
did not kill.

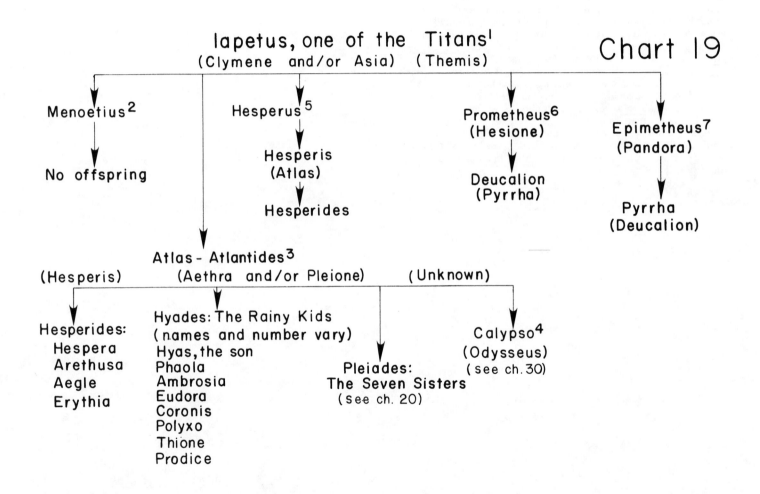

Iapetus, one of the Titans[1]
(Clymene and/or Asia)   (Themis)

Chart 19

Menoetius[2]

No offspring

Hesperus[5]

Hesperis
(Atlas)

Hesperides

Prometheus[6]
(Hesione)

Deucalion
(Pyrrha)

Epimetheus[7]
(Pandora)

Pyrrha
(Deucalion)

Atlas - Atlantides[3]
(Hesperis)   (Aethra and/or Pleione)   (Unknown)

Hesperides:
Hespera
Arethusa
Aegle
Erythia

Hyades: The Rainy Kids
(names and number vary)
Hyas, the son
Phaola
Ambrosia
Eudora
Coronis
Polyxo
Thione
Prodice

Pleiades:
The Seven Sisters
(see ch. 20)

Calypso[4]
(Odysseus)
(see ch. 30)

Chart 20
The Pleiades: Daughters of Atlas and Pleione

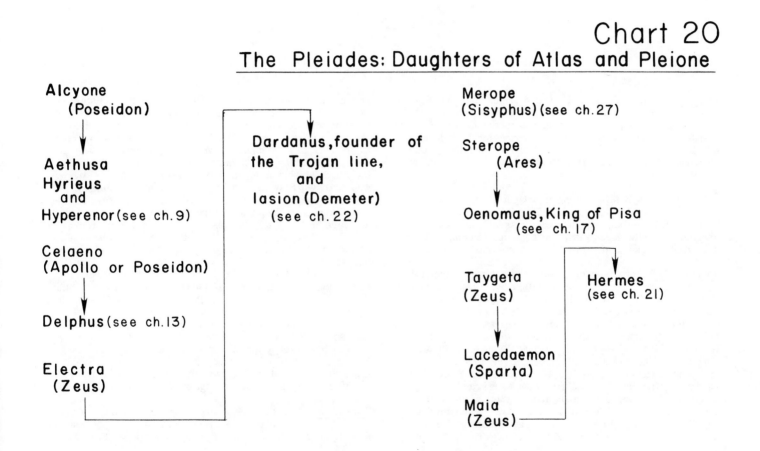

Alcyone
(Poseidon)

↓

Aethusa
Hyrieus
and
Hyperenor(see ch.9)

Celaeno
(Apollo or Poseidon)

↓

Delphus(see ch.13)

Electra
(Zeus)

Dardanus,founder of
the Trojan line,
and
Iasion(Demeter)
(see ch.22)

Merope
(Sisyphus)(see ch.27)

Sterope
(Ares)

↓

Oenomaus,King of Pisa
(see ch.17)

Taygeta
(Zeus)

Hermes
(see ch.21)

↓

Lacedaemon
(Sparta)

Maia
(Zeus)

NOTES FOR CHARTS 19 AND 20

[1]Iapetus   Titan son of Uranus and Gaea, married Clymene or Asia, daughters of Oceanus and
Tethys, and was generally regarded as the father of humankind.   There is no mythology connected with Iapetus
or his wives.   Clymene means "famous" and is a name
attached to at least a dozen women; Asia is the eponym
for the continent.

[2]Menoetius   son of Clymene and Iapetus, has no mythology except this description by Hesiod:
"Lawless Menoetius, because of his savage insolence and
overbearing boldness, was struck by the smoking thunderbolt of Zeus and sent down to the lower darkness. "

[3]Atlas-Atlantides   son of Iapetus, was himself the father of many offspring, the Atlantides,
a collective name for the Hesperides, Hyades, and Pleiades.   The Hesperides are also called daughter of Nyx
or of Phorcys and Ceto.   Whatever variation in their
family, their function is consistent: to guard and care
for the golden apples that Hera gave Zeus on their wedding day.   The names and number of the Hesperides
vary; Apollodorus names Hespera, Arethusa, Aegle, and
Erythia.   The Hyades, the Rainy Kids, were daughters
of Atlas who pined away and died of grief when their
brother Hyas was killed by a wild boar.   Some myths
say that Hyas was killed by an enraged lioness, or that
he died of a serpent bite.   When the sisters died, they
became a cluster of stars in the head of the constellation Taurus.   The names and number of the Hyades vary
from two to seven.   The list given here is from Hyginus,
Poetica Astronomica.   The Pleiades, seven sisters (see
Chart 20), are the best known of the Atlantides, and at
their deaths they too became a constellation.   One of
the stars is very dim, and it is said that this is Merope,
who married Sisyphus, a notorious criminal, and that
she hides her face in shame.   Another myth says that
the dim star is Electra, mother of Dardanus, who hides
her face in grief for the destruction of her city Troy.
Merope, Electra, and the other Pleiades are discussed
elsewhere in the charts in the genealogies of their husbands.

[4]Calypso   is called one of the Oceanids by Hesiod, and
the daughter of Atlas by Homer.   The moth-
er of Calypso is not named by either writer.   At the
beginning of the Odyssey, Calypso has held Odysseus on
her island of Ogygia for seven years and would continue
to hold him except that Zeus sent Hermes and ordered
her to allow him to continue on his way home.   Some
mythologies say that Calypso bore children by Odysseus,
but this is not generally recognized.

[5]Hesperus   son of Iapetus and brother of Atlas.   As
the evening star, appearing after the sun-
set, Hesperus is sometimes called the son of Eos, the

Dawn.   His daughter Hesperis married Atlas and became the mother of the Hesperides.

[6]Prometheus   son of Iapetus and Themis, according to
                     Aeschylus.   Hesiod says he was the son
of Iapetus and Clymene.   In Hesiod, Prometheus is
called "a cunning trickster" because he stole "the radi-
ant light of all-consuming fire" and gave this blessing
to humanity.   To punish him, Zeus ordered Hephaestus
to chain Prometheus to a high crag of the Caucasus
Mountains, where an eagle would eternally eat out his
immortal liver.   This segment of the story is treated
in Aeschylus' tragedy Prometheus Bound.   Also on the
voyage of the Argo, the ship passes this locality, and
the Argonauts hear the screams of the god as the bird
eats.   During the centuries between Hesiod and Aeschylus, the image of Prometheus changed from "cunning
trickster" to benefactor of humankind.   In the great
tragedy by Aeschylus, Prometheus says Zeus gave nothing to "miserable men."   Not only did Prometheus be-
stow the gift of fire, but also that of blind hope--mortals
would no longer know the date of their own death.   There
are at least two versions of the god's release: Heracles, by the will of Zeus, killed the eagle and set him
free; or Zeus set him free out of gratitude for the secret that the son of Thetis, with whom Zeus was in love,
would be stronger than his father.   By Hesione, an
Oceanid, Prometheus was father of Deucalion, the only
male survivor of the Great Flood that Zeus sent to destroy mankind.

[7]Epimetheus   called a "half-wit" by Hesiod, fell victim
                     to and married the artificial woman Pan-
dora, whom Zeus had sent to plague man.   By Pandora,
Epimetheus was father of Pyrrha, who married Deucalion and with whom she survived the Great Flood.

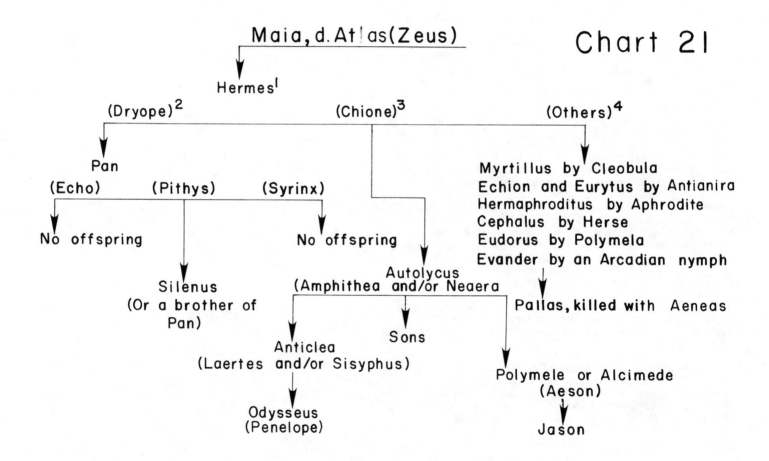

Maia, d. Atlas(Zeus)

Chart 21

Hermes[1]

(Dryope)[2] (Chione)[3] (Others)[4]

Pan

(Echo) (Pithys) (Syrinx)

No offspring No offspring

Silenus
(Or a brother of
Pan)

Myrtillus by Cleobula
Echion and Eurytus by Antianira
Hermaphroditus by Aphrodite
Cephalus by Herse
Eudorus by Polymela
Evander by an Arcadian nymph

Autolycus
(Amphithea and/or Neaera

Anticlea
(Laertes and/or Sisyphus)

Sons

Pallas, killed with Aeneas

Polymele or Alcimede
(Aeson)

Odysseus
(Penelope)

Jason

NOTES FOR CHART 21

[1]<u>Hermes</u>   son of Maia, one of the Pleiades, and Zeus, is generally referred to as a messenger god, but his functions are far more extensive.   He was the god of travelers, contests, games of chance, and particularly of runners; he was also the god of thieves, pickpockets, and highwaymen.   As god of the twilight, his function was to conduct the souls of the dead to the Underworld.   He is called Mercury in Roman mythology, and his functions are much the same as in Greek. Hermes is a prominent figure in Homer, although he takes no side in the war.   In the <u>Iliad,</u> perhaps his most interesting role is to conduct Priam to the tent of Achilles to claim the dead body of Hector; in the <u>Odyssey,</u> he appears first to inform Calypso that the gods want Odysseus to set sail for home, and again at the end to conduct the souls of the dead suitors to the halls of Hades.   One of the most familiar stories of Hermes is that in which he steals Apollo's cattle.   He was also the slayer of the hundred-eyed Argus, who tormented Io. By several wives, Hermes was the father of a number of well-known offspring.

[2]<u>Dryope</u>   an Arcadian nymph, mother of Pan by Hermes. Other genealogies of Pan are rarely given.   As the son of Hermes, Pan assumed the functions of a god of shepherds and pastoral life.   He usually inhabited the woods and the rugged mountains.   Represented as a man-goat, Pan had a monstrous appearance, two small horns on his head, hairy legs and thighs, and a tail.   In his pursuit of certain nymphs, he was generally unsuccessful.   For instance, his pursuit of Syrinx, daughter of the Ladon River god, resulted in her being changed into a reed rather than accept his embraces.   His adventure with Echo, daughter of Gaea, was equally unsuccessful.   The nymph Pithys was loved by Pan and the North Wind Boreas.   She scorned the latter, upon which he dashed her against a rock and she became a pine tree.   One myth says that Pithys was the mother of Silenus, son of Pan, but according to others Silenus was a brother of Pan.

[3]<u>Chione</u>   also called Philonis, daughter of Daedalion, claimed that she was loved by two gods on the same night, Apollo and Hermes.   She was the mother of twins, Philammon, son of Apollo, who became a great musician; and Autolycus, son of Hermes, who became a notorious robber.   Chione became so proud of her affairs with the gods that she preferred her own beauty to that of Artemis, for which the goddess promptly shot her.

Autolycus is represented by Homer as the grandfather of Odysseus, in fact the one who named him-- Odysseus, child of wrath.   His grandmother is called Amphithea, and "sons" of Autolycus are referred to several times by Homer, but are not named.   Anticles, the daughter of Autolycus, in Homer, is the mother of

Odysseus by Laertes.   Another story is that Autolycus was so impressed with the craftiness of Sisyphus that he allowed him to enjoy the favors of his daughter Anticlea, by whom she conceived Odysseus a few days before she married Laertes.   This story has no sanction in Homer; however, it is referred to in Euripides' Iphigenia at Aulis, where Odysseus is called "the seed of Sisyphus. "   To be related to Sisyphus was considered a disgrace; hence, making Odysseus his son according to an obscure myth was a discrediting device used by the playwright.   In the Odyssey, Homer says that Autolycus "excelled all men in thievery and in oaths, " because the god Hermes had given him this skill, but Hermes is not called his father.   Apollodorus calls Autolycus "a son of Hermes" and includes him as one of the Argonauts; however, in his catalog of crew members, Apollonius of Rhodes says "Deileon, Autolycus, and Phlogius, sons of Deimachus of Thessaly, " joined the Argonauts when the Argo stopped at Sinope.

From Apollodorus comes the story that Polymele, or Alcimede, daughter of Autolycus, married Aeson, the father of Jason.   Apollonius of Rhodes, however, constructs a different genealogy for Jason.

[4]Other Offspring   (a) By Cleobula, Hermes was father of Myrtillus, the famous charioteer of Oenomaus, King of Pisa.   Pelops bribed Myrtillus to help win the hand of Hippodamia by causing the death of her father, Oenomaus, in a chariot race.   Later Pelops killed Myrtillus and threw his body into the sea.   (b) By Antianira, Hermes was the father of Echion and Eurytus, two of the Argonauts named by Apollonius of Rhodes. (c) Aphrodite and Hermes were parents of Hermaphroditus, who became both male and female in one body. (d) By Herse, daughter of Cecrops of Athens, Hermes is said to have been the father of Cephalus; however, there are many other genealogies of Cephalus given.

(e) Eudorus, a son of Hermes and Polymela, daughter of Phylas, went to Troy with Achilles, according to Homer in the Iliad.   (f) Evander, a son of Hermes by an Arcadian nymph, founded a town on the Tiber River in Italy and named it Pallantium, after his home in Arcadia.   Pallas, a son of Evander, was killed while fighting with Aeneas against Turnus in the Aeneid.

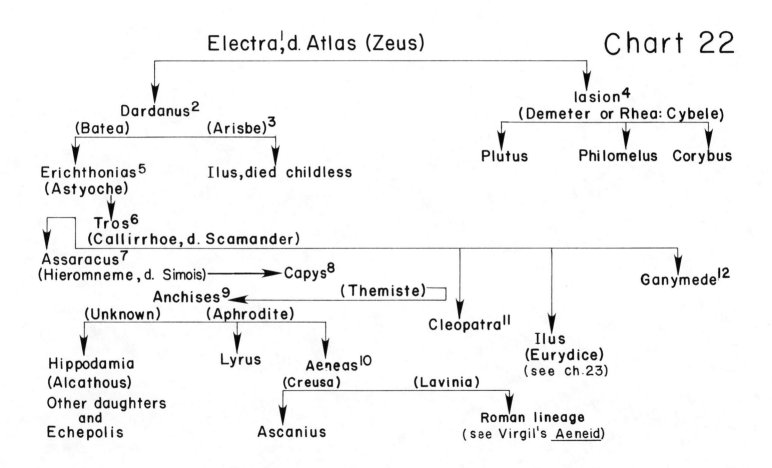

Electra, d. Atlas (Zeus)   Chart 22

Dardanus[2]

(Batea)   (Arisbe)[3]

Erichthonias[5]   Ilus, died childless
(Astyoche)

Tros[6]
(Callirrhoe, d. Scamander)

Assaracus[7]
(Hieromneme, d. Simois) ──────→ Capys[8]

Anchises[9] ←── (Themiste)

(Unknown)   (Aphrodite)

Hippodamia   Lyrus   Aeneas[10]
(Alcathous)   (Creusa)   (Lavinia)

Other daughters
and
Echepolis   Ascanius   Roman lineage
(see Virgil's Aeneid)

Iasion[4]
(Demeter or Rhea: Cybele)

Plutus   Philomelus   Corybus

Ganymede[12]

Cleopatra[11]

Ilus
(Eurydice)
(see ch. 23)

NOTES FOR CHART 22

[1]Electra   daughter of Atlas and Pleione, by Zeus was
          the mother of Dardanus, founder of the Tro-
jan line, and Iasion.   At her death, she became one of
the Pleiades.   In the Argonautica, Samothrace is referred to as Electra's island, where she gave birth to
her sons.

[2]Dardanus   son of Electra and Zeus, is generally re-
            ferred to as the founder of the Trojan line.
In the Iliad, Dardanus is said to have been loved by
Zeus above all the children born to him of mortal wom-
en.   One story says Dardanus killed his brother Iasion
to obtain the kingdom, but then fled to Asia Minor,
where he married Batea and Arisbe, daughters of Cretan
Teucer, the first king of Troy.   Virgil calls the Trojans
"Teucer's line."   The death of Iasion is more frequently
said to have been caused by the wrath of Zeus (see below, Note 4).

[3]Arisbe   daughter of Teucer of Crete and wife of Dar-
          danus, is the eponym for the city in the Troad
from which Asius, the son of Hyrtacus, brought troops
to fight with the Trojans of Troy.   Apollodorus names
another Arisbe, a daughter of Merops, as the first wife
of Priam, by whom he had a son, Aesacus.   Later this
Arisbe was given in marriage to Hyrtacus.

[4]Iasion   son of Electra and Zeus, who loved Demeter

and in an attempt to defile the goddess was
killed by Zeus with a thunderbolt.   This account of
Iasion's death by Apollodorus says that Dardanus then
left Samothrace because of grief for his brother.   Homer
and Hesiod are almost identical in their references to
Iasion as the lover of Demeter in a "thrice-ploughed"
field, but Hesiod says nothing about the death of Iasion.
Homer says Zeus "smote him with his bright thunderbolt
and slew him."   Plutus, the son of Demeter and Iasion,
is the god of wealth, described by Hesiod as "a kindly
god who goes everywhere over land and the sea's wide
back and into whose hands he comes he makes rich, bestowing great wealth upon him."
        Less familiar are other sons by Demeter and
Iasion, Philomelus and Corybus.   Of these only Corybus
has a slight mythology.   One story says he accompanied
his uncle Dardanus to Asia Minor, where he introduced
the worship of his mother, the earth goddess Demeter
or Cybele, the Phrygian Rhea.

[5]Erichtonias   son of Dardanus by Bates.   According to
              Apollodorus, Ilus was his half-brother.
This Ilus died childless, and Erichthonias succeeded to
the kingdom.   Most of Dardanus' descendants are enu-
merated by Aeneas in the Iliad, although Homer does
not name the mother of Tros.   Apollodorus says Erichthonias married Astyoche, daughter of the Simois, and
became the father of Tros.

[6]Tros   succeeded his father as ruler of the kingdom
            and named the city Troy after himself.   By
Callirrhoe, a daughter of the Scamander, he was father
of a daughter, Cleopatra, and three sons, Ilus, Assaracus, and Ganymede.   The only story told of Tros is that
he made war against Tantalus, believing him to have
abducted Ganymede (see below, Note 12).

[7]Assaracus   son of Tros, married Hieromneme, a
                  daughter of the Simois, according to Apol-
lodorus, and became the father of Capys.   Homer does
not name the wife of Assaracus.

[8]Capys   married Themiste, daughter of Ilus, and there-
             fore his cousin, by whom he was the father of
Anchises.

[9]Anchises   father of Aeneas by the goddess Aphrodite;
                also, according to Apollodorus, the father
of Lyrus, who died young.   According to Homer,
Anchises was also the father of a daughter, Hippodamia,
who was married to Alcathous, killed by Idomeneus in
the Iliad.   Hippodamia is called the "eldest of Anchises'
daughters," but no others are named, nor is the mother's
name given.   Echepolis, also, is referred to in the Iliad
as "son of Anchises" who lived in Sicyon, then under
the rule of Mycenae.   He is said by Homer to have given
Agamemnon a valuable mare "without price, to the end
that he might not follow him to windy Ilios, but might
abide at home and take his joy," since he lived in great
wealth.
         According to Virgil in the Aeneid, Anchises is
saved from destruction at the fall of Troy by his son
Aeneas, who carries the old man on his shoulders
through the burning city to the coast.   He travels with
Aeneas as far as Sicily, where he dies and is buried on
Mount Eryx by his son and Acestes, King of Sicily.

Later, when Aeneas visits the Underworld, Anchises is
represented in the Elysian Fields, able to foretell all
that the Fates have in store for Aeneas and the Trojans,
destined to become the Romans.

[10]Aeneas   son of Anchises and Aphrodite, married
               Creusa, a daughter of Priam, by whom he
was the father of Ascanius.   At the fall of Troy, Aeneas
led his son and carried his father to safety, but Creusa
was lost.   When Aeneas returned to find her, he could
only hear her voice, urging him to leave at once; it was
not her destiny to leave.   He must continue, Creusa
tells him, and marry another wife and establish a new
race.   This wife will be Lavinia, the daughter of Latinus
and Amata, and the marriage leads to the Roman lineage.
These events either take place or are foretold in Virgil's
Aeneid.
         In the Iliad, Aeneas is represented as a heroic
warrior fighting for the Trojans, but some of his advantages derive from being god-protected.   His mother
Aphrodite saves him on one occasion, only to drop him
when she herself is wounded by Diomedes; he is then
saved by Apollo.   When Aeneas recklessly confronts
Achilles, Poseidon saves him from certain death because
it is "not destined that the race of Dardanus should perish."   The Aeneid ends with Aeneas fighting and slaying
Turnus, the Latin contender for leadership and Lavinia's
hand; however, Ovid tells of Aeneas becoming a god,
largely through the intercession of his mother Venus
(Aphrodite), after she had "cleansed away all that was
mortal in him."   According to Ovid, Aeneas was made
a "god whom the Roman people welcomed with a temple
and altars, giving him the name Indiges."

[11]Cleopatra   a daughter of Tros and Callirrhoe, accord-
                  ing to Apollodorus.   The name is a fairly
common one in mythology, and the different figures should

Chart 22   85

not be confused.   There are no stories about this Cleopatra.

12<u>Ganymede</u>   son of Tros and Callirrhoe, was abducted
                    by Zeus because of his great beauty and
carried to Olympus, where he became cupbearer to the
gods.   He is generally represented as being carried
away on the back of an enormous golden eagle.

Ilus[1], s. Tros and Callirrhoe
(Eurydice)

Chart 23

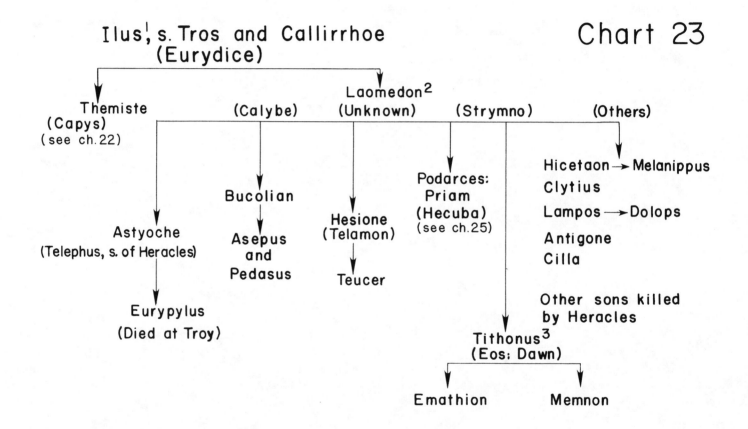

Themiste
(Capys)
(see ch.22)

(Calybe)

Laomedon[2]
(Unknown)

(Strymno)

(Others)

Astyoche
(Telephus, s. of Heracles)

Bucolian

Hesione
(Telamon)

Podarces:
Priam
(Hecuba)
(see ch.25)

Hicetaon → Melanippus

Clytius

Lampos → Dolops

Antigone

Cilla

Eurypylus
(Died at Troy)

Asepus
and
Pedasus

Teucer

Other sons killed
by Heracles

Tithonus[3]
(Eos: Dawn)

Emathion

Memnon

NOTES FOR CHART 23

[1]Ilus   son of Tros and Callirrhoe, who, according to
Apollodorus, migrated to Phrygia, and there,
competing in games held by the king, was victorious in
the wrestling matches.   As a prize he received fifty
youths and fifty maidens and a dappled cow.   An oracle
then commanded him to follow the cow and wherever she
should lie down, there he should found a city.   Ilus followed until the cow came to what was called the hill of
Até, and there he built a city and called it Ilium.   This
story is also told of Cadmus, who founded Thebes under
similar oracular commands.   Ilus married Eurydice, a
daughter of Adrastus of Argos, by whom he was the
father of Laomedon.   Apollodorus also names Themiste
as a daughter of Ilus who married Capys, her cousin.

[2]Laomedon and His Sons   According to Apollodorus,
Laomedon was the father of
five sons by Strymo, daughter of the Scamander: Tithonus, Lampos, Clytius, Hicetaon, and Podarces; and
three daughters: Hesione, Cilla, and Astyoche.   Homer
names the sons of Laomedon who are sitting with Priam
in the famous wall scene of the Iliad: Lampos and Clytius and Hicetaon.   Elsewhere in the Iliad, Tithonus is
referred to as the consort of Dawn, the goddess Eos.
Bucolian is named by Homer and Apollodorus as a natural son of Laomedon by the nymph Calybe.   Bucolian is
the father of twin sons, Aesepus and Pedasus, who are
both killed, in the Iliad, by Euryalus, the son of Mecis-

teus.   Melanippus, the son of Hicetaon, is killed in the
war by Antilochus, son of Nestor; and Dolops, the son
of Lampos, is killed by Menelaus.
As to the sons of Laomedon, a contradictory
story is told that Heracles killed them and their father
in his raid on Troy some time prior to the Trojan War.
Laomedon had angered Poseidon and Apollo after the two
gods had built the great wall of Troy, and in retaliation
they were devastating the land with a plague and a sea
monster.   The oracle said nothing would appease the
monster except an annual offering of one of the virgin
maidens of the kingdom.   In due time, Laomedon's
daughter Hesione was chosen, and subsequently exposed
on a cliff near the sea.   About this time, Heracles, in
company with Telamon and other heroes, was in this
area and offered to rid the land of the monster in exchange for a number of fine Trojan horses.   Heracles
killed the monster, but Laomedon failed to keep his part
of the bargain; Heracles then laid seige to the city and
destroyed it, killing Laomedon and his sons, except
Podarces, later called Priam, whom he set on the throne.
Hesione was given to Telamon, and by him became the
mother of Teucer, who fought in the Trojan War beside
his half-brother Ajax.   Except for Antigone, whom Ovid
calls a daughter of Laomedon, nothing is known of the
other daughters.   Antigone dared to compete with Hera
in beauty and was changed into a bird, "a shining white
stork, who still applauds herself with clattering beak. "

[3]<u>Tithonus</u> son of Laomedon, who was loved and carried away by Dawn, the goddess Eos, by whom he had two sons, Memnon of Ethiopia and Emathion. See Chart 43, notes.

Other Trojans[1]

Chart 24

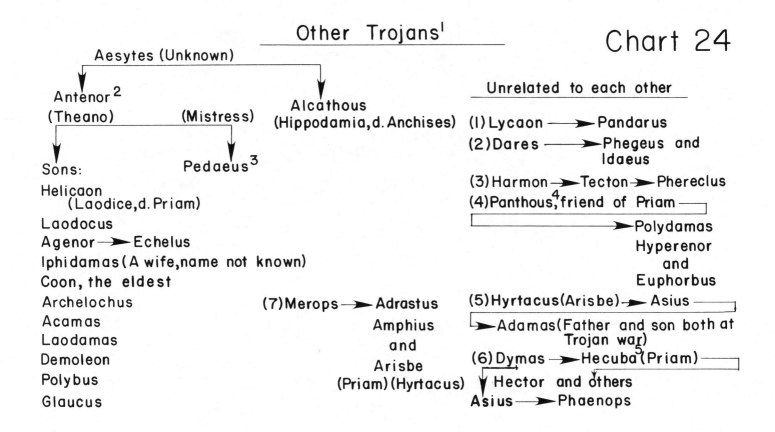

Aesytes (Unknown)

Antenor[2]
(Theano)   (Mistress)   Alcathous
                                  (Hippodamia, d. Anchises)

Sons: Pedaeus[3]
Helicaon
    (Laodice, d. Priam)
Laodocus
Agenor ➤ Echelus
Iphidamas (A wife, name not known)
Coon, the eldest
Archelochus   (7) Merops ➤ Adrastus
Acamas   Amphius
Laodamas   and
Demoleon   Arisbe
Polybus   (Priam) (Hyrtacus)
Glaucus

Unrelated to each other

(1) Lycaon ➤ Pandarus
(2) Dares ➤ Phegeus and
                  Idaeus
(3) Harmon ➤ Tecton ➤ Phereclus
(4) Panthous,[4] friend of Priam ─
    ➤ Polydamas
                  Hyperenor
                    and
                  Euphorbus
(5) Hyrtacus (Arisbe) ➤ Asius ─
    ➤ Adamas (Father and son both at
                  Trojan war)
(6) Dymas ➤ Hecuba (Priam) ─[5]
  ↓ Hector and others
Asius ➤ Phaenops

NOTES FOR CHART 24

[1]Other Trojans and Their Allies   After the famous cata-
                                     log of Achaean ships
in the Iliad, Homer gives a briefer, but nonetheless
valuable, catalog of Trojan allies and their leaders:

(a) The Trojans were led by great Hector, the
     son of Priam.

(b) Of the Dardanians, the valiant son of Anchises
     was Captain, Aeneas, whom fair Aphrodite
     conceived to Anchises amid the spurs of Ida.

(c) With him were Antenor's two sons, Archelous
     and Acamas.

(d) They that dwelt in Zeleia, beneath the neth-
     ermost foot of Ida, the Troes, were led by
     the son of Lycaon, Pandarus, to whom Apol-
     lo himself gave the bow.

(e) From Adrasteia in the land of Apaesus, and
     Pityeia and the steep mountain of Tereia,
     these were led by Adrastus and Amphius,
     sons of Merops of Percote, above all men
     skilled in prophecy.

(f) They that dwelt about Percote and Practius
     and that held Sestus and Abydus and goodly
     Arisbe, were led by Asius, son of Hyrta-
     cus.

(g) Hippothous led the tribes of the Pelasgi, and
     Pylaeus, sons of Pelasgian Lethus, son of
     Teutamus.

(h) Of the Thracians Acamas led and Peirous,
     all of them that the strong stream of the
     Hellespont encloseth.

(i) Euphemus was captain of the Ciconian spear-
     men, the son of Ceas' son Troezenus.

(j) Pyraechmes led the Poeonians, out of Amydon
     from the wide-flowing Axius.

(k) The Paphlagonians were led by Pylaemenes,
     from the land of the Eneti.

(l) Of the Halizones Odius and Epistrophus were
     captains from Alybe, where is the birthplace
     of silver.

(m) Of the Mysians the captains were Chromis
     and Ennomus.

(n) From Ascavia, Phorcys and godlike Ascanius
     led the Phrygians.

(o) Maeonians had captains <u>Mesthles</u> and <u>Antiphus</u>, sons of Telaemenes, whose mother was the nymph of the Gygaean lake.

(p) <u>Nastes</u> led the Carians who held Miletus and the mountain of Phthires, and <u>Amphimachus</u>, sons of Nomion.

(q) <u>Sarpedon</u> and peerless <u>Glaucus</u> were captains of the Lycians from afar out of Lycia, from the eddying Xanthus.

In addition to the names given in this catalog, many other Trojans and Trojan allies are named throughout the <u>Iliad</u>. Most of these individuals are specified as being killed by Achaeans or as killing Achaeans. The Catalog of Achaean leaders and their number of ships, as well as many others who fought and died or survived at Troy, are given in the notes to Chart 48.

[2]<u>Antenor</u>   son of Aesytes, is said by Virgil in the <u>Aeneid</u> to have escaped the destruction of <u>Troy</u> and founded the city of Padua, Italy. Theano, his wife, is said by Homer to be the daughter of Cisseus and a priestess of Athens. As to the escape of Antenor, Apollodorus says that "when Glaucus, son of Antenor, fled to his house, Odysseus and Menelaus recognized and rescued him by their armed intervention." In the <u>Iliad</u>, Antenor entertained Odysseus and Menelaus when they went into Troy to seek the release of Helen, and it was Antenor who advocated that the Trojans send Helen and her property back to the Greeks. Other sources also indicate that Antenor and his family were spared in the sack of Troy, and that the Greeks hung a leopard's skin in front of Antenor's house as a sign that they were to be unmolested.

[3]<u>Pedaeus</u>   son of Antenor, but, according to Homer, "was in truth a bastard, howbeit goodly Theano had reared him carefully even as her own children, to do pleasure to her husband." Pedaeus was killed by Meges during the Trojan War.

[4]<u>Panthous</u>   friend of Priam. In the wall scene of the <u>Iliad</u>, certain Trojan elders sit with Priam and observe the fighting warriors. These are described as beyond the age of battle, their voices grown thin like cicadas: Panthous, Thymoetes, Lampos, Clytius, Hicetaon, Ucalegon, and Antenor. Of these, Antenor and members of his family are most often referred to throughout the <u>Iliad</u>.

[5]<u>Hecuba</u>   Apollodorus says Priam first married Arisbe, the daughter of Merops, then gave her to Hyrtacus and married Hecuba. Euripides in his play <u>Hecuba</u> says she was the daughter of Cisseus; however, in the <u>Iliad</u>, Asius, the son of Dymas, is Hecuba's brother, and is referred to as Hector's uncle (see Chart 25, Note 2).

94

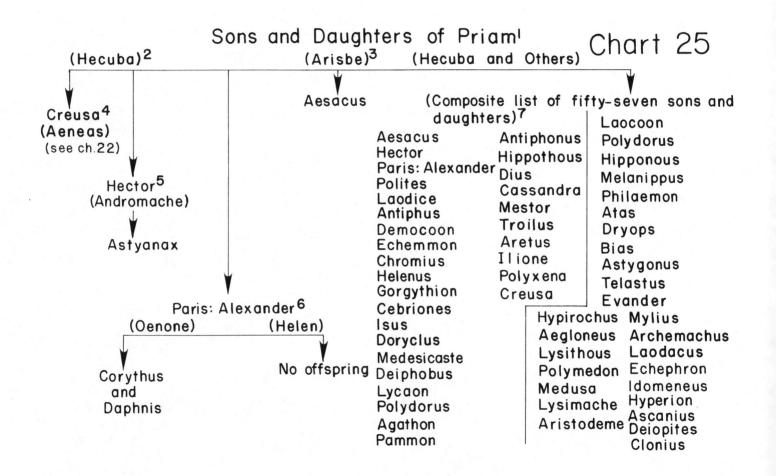

Sons and Daughters of Priam[1]   Chart 25

(Hecuba)[2]   (Arisbe)[3]   (Hecuba and Others)

Aesacus   (Composite list of fifty-seven sons and
                                daughters)[7]
Creusa[4]   Laocoon
(Aeneas)   Aesacus   Antiphonus   Polydorus
(see ch.22)   Hector   Hippothous   Hipponous
                              Paris: Alexander Dius   Melanippus
                              Polites   Cassandra   Philaemon
Hector[5]   Laodice   Mestor   Atas
(Andromache)   Antiphus   Troilus   Dryops
                              Democoon   Aretus   Bias
                              Echemmon   Ilione   Astygonus
Astyanax   Chromius   Polyxena   Telastus
                              Helenus   Creusa   Evander
                              Gorgythion
                              Cebriones   Hypirochus Mylius
                              Isus   Aegloneus   Archemachus
                              Doryclus   Lysithous   Laodacus
Paris: Alexander[6]   Medesicaste   Polymedon   Echephron
(Oenone)   (Helen)   Deiphobus   Medusa   Idomeneus
                              Lycaon   Lysimache   Hyperion
                              Polydorus   Aristodeme Ascanius
Corythus   No offspring   Agathon   Deiopites
and   Pammon   Clonius
Daphnis

NOTES FOR CHART 25

[1]Sons and Daughters of Priam   are traditionally referred to as fifty in
number, although "fifty" is sometimes used to designate
only sons.   Near the end of the Iliad, Priam, speaking
to Achilles, says: "I begat sons the best in the broad
land of Troy, yet of them I avow that not one is left.
Fifty I had; nineteen were born to me of the same womb,
and the others women of the palace bare." Homer, however, does not refer to the names of the fifty sons.   Virgil makes still another reference to the traditional fifty:
"The fifty marriage chambers, the proud hope of an
everlasting line, are violated," Aeneas says when he is
relating the fall of Troy.   After the death of Hector,
there are at least nine sons still alive, as shown when
Priam calls them together and speaks to them of his
plan to ransom Hector's body: Helenus, Paris, Agathon, Pammon, Antiphonus, Polites, Deiphobus, Hippothous, and Dius.   Priam outlived all of his sons, except Helenus, who was taken captive by Neoptolemus,
the son of Achilles, and allowed to live.   Priam was
killed on the altar by the murderous son of Achilles at
the final sack of Troy.

[2]Hecuba   second wife of Priam, mother of nineteen
children by Priam.   Her role in the Iliad is
slight, although she is the principal character in Euripides' The Trojan Women, and in this play the fall of
Troy is seen through her suffering and loss.   In casting
lots for the captive Trojan women, Odysseus drew Hecuba as his slave.   It was not her fate, however, to continue with Odysseus, and Homer in the Odyssey makes
no reference to Hecuba's final disposition.   The story
of Hecuba's destiny is told by Euripides in his play
Hecuba, and also by Ovid.   Many years earlier, when
the Trojan War was just beginning, Priam and Hecuba
had sent their youngest son Polydorus, together with a
great treasury of money and jewels to their son-in-law
Polymestor, King of Thrace.   The king betrayed their
trust, killed the boy, and took the wealth.   When Hecuba
learned of this, she plotted against Polymestor, and was
successful in gouging out his eyes.   The people of Thrace
attacked Hecuba with stones and weapons; but then, as
Ovid tells the story, "with harsh growls she snapped at
the rocks they threw and, when she tried to speak, uttered barks instead of words." Thus she was transformed into a red bitch, and long after this Hecuba
continued to howl mournfully as she roamed the hills of
Thrace, remembering her great sufferings.

[3]Arisbe   a daughter of Merops, who first married
Priam and was the mother of Aesacus, Pri-
am's oldest son.   Having learned dream interpretation
from his grandfather Merops, Aesacus was asked by
Priam to interpret Hecuba's dream just before the birth
of Paris.   In this dream she gave birth to a firebrand,
and the fire spread over the whole city and burned it.

Aesacus declared that the child about to be born was to be the ruin of his country. Apollodorus and Ovid both refer to the transformation of Aesacus into a bird. Having caused the death of a nymph of the Cebren whom he loved, or who was his wife, Aesacus tried to die also by leaping into the sea; but the goddess took pity, "clothed him in feathers, and would not let him die." Still he longed to die, and repeatedly dashed his body into the sea, but to no avail; he had been changed into a sea diver.

[4]Creusa   daughter of Priam and Hecuba, according to Apollodorus and Virgil. She is represented as the wife of Aeneas, and is lost in the destruction of Troy.

[5]Hector   oldest son of Priam and Hecuba. In the Iliad, Hector is married to Andromache, daughter of Eetion, King of Thebe in Cilicia. Achilles is said to have killed Eetion and Andromache's seven brothers and taken her mother into captivity. Later, the mother's father ransomed her, but she had since died. Homer tells the story, but does not name Andromache's mother or the mother's father. Hector is referred to many times by Virgil and Euripides, but he is best studied in Homer's Iliad, where he meets his death at the hands of Achilles. At the fall of Troy, Andromache passed into slavery to Achilles' son Neoptolemus, by whom she had children. It is Andromache who concludes the Iliad, lamenting that now, with the death of Hector, Troy will fall and the women be carried into slavery. Hector's young son Astyanax, also called Scamandrius, will become a slave or be "hurled from the wall." In Euripides' play The Trojan Women, the death of the young boy Astyanax, thrown from the wall by Neoptolemus, is used to point up the ultimate atrocity of war.

[6]Paris   second son of Priam and Hecuba, was destined even before birth to be the ruin of his country. To avert this disaster Priam gave the infant to a shepherd with orders to destroy it. The shepherd, however, did not kill Paris, but merely exposed him on Mount Ida, where other shepherds found him and brought him up as their own son. He married Oenone, a nymph of Ida, by whom he had sons and lived a prudent and happy life as Alexander or Alexandrus. In the meantime, at the marriage of Thetis and Peleus, Eris had thrown her golden apple of discord into the assembly of the goddesses, Hera, Athena, and Aphrodite. Inscribed "For the Fairest," the apple was claimed by all three goddesses, and the other gods, not wishing to arbitrate such a tricky business, chose Alexandrus because he was known to be a wise and fair man. Each goddess promised the shepherd the gift she was best equipped to deliver: Hera, authority and power; Athena, glory in battle; Aphrodite, the world's most beautiful woman. His judgment was in favor of Aphrodite. Subsequently, Alexandrus became identified as Priam's son Paris, recognized by his sister Cassandra, a prophetess.

There are several versions of the reason Paris went to Sparta. One story says he set forth with firm purpose to go to Sparta and get Helen. Another myth is that he set forth with a fleet to the island of Salamis to ransom his father's sister Hesione, held there by Telamon, the son of Aeacus. Remembering that Aphrodite had promised him the most beautiful of women, he then turned his course toward Sparta, intending to abduct Helen. Other details of the story are consistent among the authors who refer to the abduction: Menelaus was in Crete at the time, attending the funeral of Catreus, his mother's father; Helen and Menelaus had a young daughter, Hermione, who was deserted by her mother; and not only Helen, but also a great deal of Spartan wealth went with Paris back to Troy. As to Helen's

Chart 25   97

willingness to go with Paris, there are varying degrees of opinion, from her total consent to her total reluctance. Homer says she was willing to go at first, but later regretted her decision and guilt in the matter.

Paris did not distinguish himself in the Trojan War, although he did wound several notable Greeks in battle, and usually he is said to have slain, with Apollo's help, great Achilles. In the Iliad, the dying Hector tells Achilles that Paris and Apollo will kill him at the Gates of Troy. The death of Paris by Philoctetes is related in detail by Quintus of Smyrna in the Posthomerica. After Paris was mortally wounded, he required his men to carry him to Mount Ida, where his wife Oenone had said she would cure him if he were ever wounded. When the time came, however, she could not forgive him for leaving her and allowed him to die. Later she repented of her action and either hanged herself or threw herself on Paris's funeral pyre.

[7]Offspring of Priam   traditionally numbered as fifty sons, this composite list of fifty-seven names is based on Homer, Virgil, and Apollodorus. Most of Priam's offspring have little or no identity; a great many of them are merely referred to as being killed by one of the Greeks.

(1) Aesacus -- son of Priam and Arisbe (see Note 3 above).

(2) Hector -- oldest son of Priam and Hecuba (see Note 5 above).

(3) Paris -- second oldest son of Priam and Hecuba (see Note 6 above).

(4) Polites -- son of Priam and Hecuba, was killed in the final destruction of Troy by Neoptolemus. Priam looked helplessly on while Polites was slaughtered, and was himself killed shortly thereafter. Virgil says Polites had a son, named Priam after his grandfather, who followed Aeneas on the voyage to Italy.

(5) Laodice -- called by Homer the loveliest of all the daughters of Priam and Hecuba, was married to Helicaon, a son of Antenor. Another myth says she fell in love with Acamas, son of Theseus, from Athens, when he first came with the Greeks to Troy. Later she married the son of Antenor. Apollodorus and Quintus of Smyrna say that at the Fall of Troy Laodice prayed to the gods that the earth might swallow her before she became a slave, and one of them granted her request.

(6) Antiphus -- son of Priam and Hecuba, was killed by Agamemnon in the Iliad.

(7) Democoon -- a natural son of Priam who lived at Abydos, but came to Troy and was killed by Odysseus.

(8) Echemmon -- a natural son of Priam, was killed by Diomedes.

(9) Chromius -- a natural son of Priam, was killed by Diomedes.

(10) Helenus -- a prophet, the only son of Priam and Hecuba who survived the Fall of Troy. There are several versions of the means by which he survived: that he was captured by Odysseus and forced by promises or threats

to reveal the secret of capturing Troy; that he willingly betrayed his country to the enemy in order to survive; or that he fell prisoner to Neoptolemus, who spared his life because Helenus warned him of a tempest that would be fatal to all who sailed on that day. Virgil represents Helenus in the Aeneid as married to Andromache, after the slaying of Neoptolemus by Orestes, and ruling over his own lands. Aeneas visits Helenus and Andromache in his wanderings after escaping from Troy.

(11) Gorgythion -- son of Priam by a Thracian mistress, Castianeira, was killed by Teucer.

(12) Cebriones -- natural son of Priam, was killed by Patroclus.

(13) Isus -- natural son of Priam, was killed by Agamemnon.

(14) Doryclus -- natural son of Priam, was killed by Ajax, son of Telamon.

(15) Medesicaste -- natural daughter of Priam, was married to Imbrius, son of Mentor. He was killed by Teucer.

(16) Deiphobus -- son of Priam and Hecuba, was still alive at the end of the Iliad. Virgil tells the story that after the death of Paris, Deiphobus became the husband of Helen. At the Sack of Troy, Helen betrayed him to Menelaus, who hacked him to death. Aeneas saw the mutilated shade of Deiphobus in the Underworld.

(17) Lycaon -- son of Priam and Laothoe, daughter of Altes. He had once before been captured by Achilles and sold to a son of Jason on Lemnos. In his second encounter with Achilles, Lycaon pleads for his life, but it is not spared. Achilles chides him for making so much of death: "Patroclus is dead, and he was better by far than you are."

(18) Polydorus -- in the Iliad is called the youngest son of Priam and "the favorite." His mother was Laothoe, the same as the mother of Lycaon. Polydorus was killed by Achilles (see also Polydorus, No. 32, below).

(19) Agathon -- son of Priam whose mother is not named. He is one of the nine sons still alive at the end of the Iliad. There is no specific reference to his death in other works.

(20) Pammon -- son of Priam and Hecuba, was still alive at the end of the Iliad. Quintus of Smyrna says Pammon was killed by Neoptolemus at the Sack of Troy.

(21) Antiphonus -- son of Priam whose mother is not named. He was killed with Pammon by Neoptolemus.

(22) Hippothous -- natural son of Priam, was still alive at the end of the Iliad. There is no specific reference to his death.

(23) Dius -- son of Priam whose mother is not named. He was still alive at the end of the Iliad, and there is no further reference to his death.

Chart 25   99

(24) Cassandra -- daughter of Priam and Hecuba, was loved by Apollo, who gave her the gift of prophecy in return for her favors. After receiving the gift, however, Cassandra refused the god; but he, unable to take back the gift, nonetheless caused that no one should ever believe her prophecies. She was generally regarded as a raving maniac. At the Fall of Troy, Ajax the son of Oileus, dragged Cassandra from Athena's temple and raped her. She was given to Agamemnon as a war prize and returned with him to Argos, where she and the king were murdered by Clytemnestra. Cassandra knew her fate and Agamemnon's, but had no power to prevent its coming.

(25) Mestor -- natural son of Priam, spoken of as "dead" but was not killed during the action of the Iliad.

(26) Troilus -- son of Priam and Hecuba, or according to Apollodorus, Hecuba's son by Apollo. He is referred to by Priam as "dead," along with Mester, near the end of the Iliad, although they are not killed during the action of the Iliad. Virgil refers to a scene engraved on Dido's temple to Hera in which Troilus is killed: "poor youngster, Achilles was much too good for him."

(27) Aretus -- natural son of Priam, killed by Automedon.

(28) Ilione -- eldest and most beautiful daughter of Priam, according to Virgil. Another mythology says she was married to Polymestor, King of Thrace (see Note 32, below).

(29) Polyxena -- daughter of Priam and Hecuba, was sacrificed on the tomb of Achilles by Neoptolemus when Troy fell. The story as told by Virgil, Apollodorus, Euripides, and Quintus of Smyrna is that Polyxena was dragged to the grave and slaughtered by the son of Achilles to appease his father's restless spirit.

(30) Creusa -- daughter of Priam and wife of Aeneas (see Note 5, above).

(31) Laocoon -- son of Priam who tried to persuade the Trojans against bringing the wooden horse inside the walls of the city. Virgil says that the Trojans believed that he and his two small sons were killed by two enormous serpents because Laocoon had hurled a spear against Athena's offering, the horse.

(32) Polydorus -- son of Priam and Hecuba, like the other Polydorus, is also called the "youngest of Priam's sons." This son was sent to Polymestor, King of Thrace, for safety throughout the war. When Polymestor heard that Troy had fallen and Priam was dead, he killed Polydorus and threw his body into the sea or buried it in a shallow grave very near the sea. Later Hecuba avenges this murder by blinding Polymestor and killing his two small sons. In this version of the story, Polymestor is called Priam's "friend," and there is no reference to Ilione, Priam's daughter, as Polymestor's wife. Virgil incorporates this story into the Aeneid, and Euripides' play Hecuba is based upon Hecuba's revenge for the murder of her son.

(33-57) Hipponous through Aristodeme -- these names
are all derived from Apollodorus.   Except
for Hipponous, who is called the son of Priam
and Hecuba, the others are natural sons of
Priam whose mothers are not given; the last
three are natural daughters by one mother
whose name is not given.   There are no
stories or events related to any of these offspring.

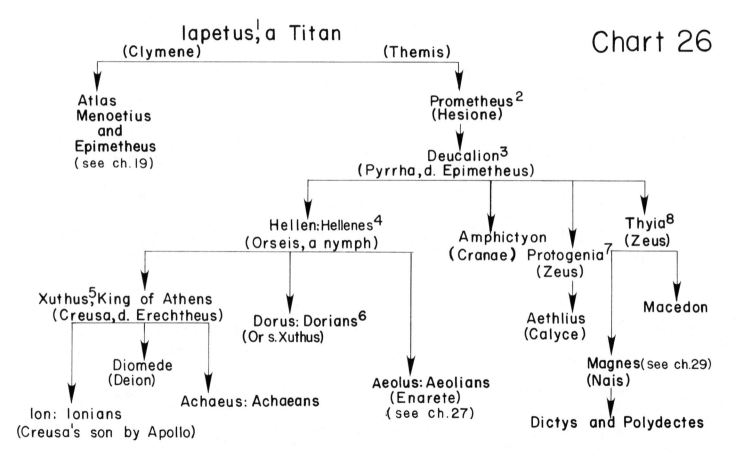

Chart 26

Iapetus, a Titan[1]

(Clymene)

(Themis)

Atlas
Menoetius
and
Epimetheus
(see ch.19)

Prometheus[2]
(Hesione)

Deucalion[3]
(Pyrrha, d. Epimetheus)

Hellen: Hellenes[4]
(Orseis, a nymph)

Amphictyon
(Cranae)

Protogenia[7]
(Zeus)

Thyia[8]
(Zeus)

Xuthus, King of Athens[5]
(Creusa, d. Erechtheus)

Dorus: Dorians[6]
(Or s. Xuthus)

Aethlius
(Calyce)

Macedon

Diomede
(Deion)

Achaeus: Achaeans

Aeolus: Aeolians
(Enarete)
(see ch.27)

Magnes(see ch.29)
(Nais)

Ion: Ionians
(Creusa's son by Apollo)

Dictys and Polydectes

NOTES FOR CHART 26

[1]Iapetus   Titan son of Uranus and Gaea; by Themis, also a Titan, is the father of Prometheus; by Clymene, one of the Oceanids, was the father of three other sons.

[2]Prometheus   son of Iapetus and Themis, according to Aeschylus in Prometheus Bound. Prometheus was the father of Deucalion, the sole male survivor of the Great Flood that Zeus sent to destroy humankind.

[3]Deucalion   son of Prometheus, married his cousin Pyrrha, daughter of Epimetheus. It is commonly said that the Great Flood occurred during the age of Deucalion's reign, or that the Flood occurred during the reign of Cranaus of Athens. Acting on the advice of his father, Deucalion built a ship that floated on the water and thus saved himself and his wife Pyrrha. After the flood waters had receded, Deucalion and Pyrrha consulted the oracle of Themis and were told to repopulate the earth by "throwing the bones of their mother over their shoulders." At first they were puzzled over the meaning of the oracle, but then decided that it meant the stones of the earth. The stones thrown by Deucalion became men, and those thrown by Pyrrha became women. Apollodorus says Deucalion and Pyrrha had two sons, Hellen and Amphictyon, and a daughter Protogenia. Hesiod, in The Catalogue of Women, names Thyia as another daughter.

[4]Hellen   son of Deucalion and Pyrrha who gave the name Hellenes to his subjects. Apollodorus names Orseis, a nymph, as his wife, by whom he had three sons: Xuthus, Dorus, and Aeolus.

[5]Xuthus   married Creusa, daughter of Erechtheus, King of Athens. Apollodorus says they had two sons, Achaeus, who gave his name to the Achaeans, and Ion, for whom the Ionians were named. Euripides, in his drama Ion, says Ion was the son of Creusa and Apollo, and was adopted by Xuthus. The daughter Diomede married Deioneus of Phocis.

[6]Dorus   became ruler of the country in the Peloponnese and called his subjects Dorians after himself.

[7]Amphictyon and Protogenia   named by Apollodorus as the second and third offspring of Deucalion and Pyrrha. Amphictyon, a soothsayer, married Cranae, a daughter of Cranaus, and ruled over Attica after Cranaus. Protogenia became the mother by Zeus of Aethlius. Calyce, a daughter of Aeolus, married Aethlius, and by him, or Zeus, became the mother of Endymion, who led a group of Aeolians from Thessaly and founded Elis.

[8]Thyia   another daughter of Deucalion and Pyrrha. In The Catalogue of Women, Hesiod says: "And

she conceived and bare to Zeus who delights in the thunderbolt two sons, Magnes and Macedon, rejoicing in horses, who dwell round about Pieria and Olympus. And Magnes again begot Dictys and Polydectes." Apollodorus, however, calls Magnes a son of Aeolus and Enarete and says: "Magnes married a Naiad nymph, and sons were born to him, Polydectes and Dictys; these colonized Seriphus." Polydectes became King of Seriphus and received with great kindness Danae and her son Perseus, who had been set afloat on the Ocean. Later, he fell in love with Danae, and when she refused him, he would have acted violently except for the intervention of his brother Dictys. Perseus, after growing into manhood, returned from his adventure of slaying Medusa and by showing the Gorgon's head turned Polydectes to stone. Dictys then became King of Seriphus.

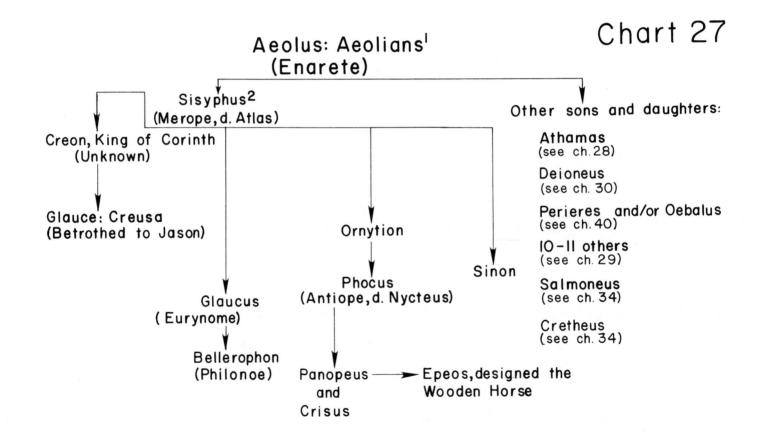

Chart 27

Aeolus: Aeolians[1]
(Enarete)

Sisyphus[2]
(Merope, d. Atlas)

Creon, King of Corinth
(Unknown)

Glauce: Creusa
(Betrothed to Jason)

Glaucus
(Eurynome)

Bellerophon
(Philonoe)

Ornytion

Phocus
(Antiope, d. Nycteus)

Panopeus
and
Crisus

Epeos, designed the
Wooden Horse

Sinon

Other sons and daughters:

Athamas
(see ch. 28)

Deioneus
(see ch. 30)

Perieres and/or Oebalus
(see ch. 40)

10-11 others
(see ch. 29)

Salmoneus
(see ch. 34)

Cretheus
(see ch. 34)

NOTES FOR CHART 27

[1]Aeolus son of Hellen, is the eponym for the Aeolians. He married Enarete, by whom he had seven sons and five daughters. Apollodorus gives the following: Cretheus, Sisyphus, Athamas, Salmoneus, Deion (Deioneus), Magnes, and Perieres; Canace, Alcyone, Pisidice, Calyce, and Perimede. In The Catalogue of Women, Hesiod says the sons of Aeolus were "Cretheus, and Athamas, and clever Sisyphus, and wicked Salmoneus and overbold Perieres." Aeolus, the son of Hellen, should not be confused with Aeolus, the guardian of the winds.

[2]Sisyphus married Merope, daughter of Atlas and Pleione, by whom he had a son, Glaucas, according to Homer and Apollodorus. Ovid, Virgil, Pausanias, and Euripides attribute other offspring to Sisyphus. For instance, in Iphigenia at Aulis, Euripides calls Odysseus a son of Sisyphus, but this relationship is not generally recognized. Many stories are told of the notorious Sisyphus, the most familiar being that of his punishment in Tartarus, eternally rolling a rock to the top of a hill, and the rock eternally rolling back down. Several reasons for this punishment are given: that Sisyphus told Asopus of Zeus' abducting his daughter Aegina; that Sisyphus captured Death and would not let him go until Ares freed him; or that Sisyphus died and was given permission by Hades to return to earth for a short time, but did not honor his word and would

not return to the Underworld until he was sent for. As for other forms of wrong-doing, Sisyphus is said to have violated his niece Tyro, daughter of Salmoneus, who killed her children by him. The story is also told that Sisyphus, "craftiest of men," outwitted Autolycus, the son of Hermes, and a crafty thief himself. Autolycus came to admire Sisyphus so much that he gave his daughter Anticlea to him. Later Anticlea married Laertes and became the mother of Odysseus.

Several offspring attributed to Sisyphus have stories of some interest. Creon of Corinth died a miserable death at the hands of Medea. His daughter Glauce, called Creusa, also died in the same incident, burned to death by a poisoned robe that Medes had sent Glauce on her wedding day. Euripides incorporates these events into his drama Medea; however, it is from Hyginus that the father of Creon is called Sisyphus. Pausanias names Ornytion as a son of Sisyphus and father of Phocus, who led a colony of Corinthians into Phocis. Here Phocus cured Antiope, daughter of Nycteus, of her madness and married her. Afterwards they became parents of Panopeus and Crisus. The story has been referred to earlier, as told by Apollodorus, that Antiope first married Lycus of Thebes, and by Zeus was the mother of Zethus and Amphion. After her sons killed Lycus and Dirce--his second wife, who was a follower of Dionysus--the god struck Antiope mad, and she wandered about Greece until she was cured by Phocus.

In the Iliad, Epeos, the son of Panopeus, wins the boxing match at the funeral games for Patroclus; later he
is referred to in the Odyssey as the one who built the
Wooden Horse.   In the Aeneid, Virgil calls him the one
"who designed the thing," and also says he was inside
the Wooden Horse when it was brought into Troy.

Sinon the Greek is referred to by numerous writ-
ers--Homer, Virgil, Apollodorus, Pausanias, and Quintus of Smyrna; but none of these writers calls him the
son of Sisyphus.   One little-known source specifies his
father; however, he may have been related to Sisyphus
on the basis of his sly and treacherous actions.   Homer
simply refers to him as a relative of Odysseus.   Virgil
tells the story in greatest detail: After the Wooden
Horse had been built and sent to the Trojans, Sinon deliberately allowed himself to be captured by the Trojans,
pretending that his fellow Greeks were about to sacrifice him, as they had sacrificed Iphigenia ten years
earlier, for a safe return home.   The Trojans took pity
on him and brought him into the city.   After the Wooden
Horse was finally pulled into Troy, it was Sinon who un-
bolted it in the middle of the night, and thus allowed the
Greeks to overrun the city.   Quintus of Smyrna says that
the Trojans first tortured Sinon, cutting off his ears and
nose, before they brought him into their midst, but Virgil says nothing about such unfavorable acts of the Trojans.

In the Iliad, Glaucus, one of the Trojan allies,
and Diomedes, the Greek warrior, face each other in
single combat.   Instead of fighting at once, they talk
about their families, and from this conversation the
following genealogy is constructed:

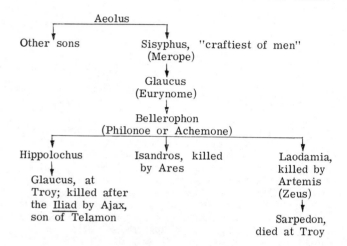

Sarpedon, or another Sarpedon, is also called the son
of Zeus by Europa.   In this episode, Glaucus also relates the story of Bellerophon, his grandfather.   Proetus,
King of Argos, drove Bellerophon out of the city because
his wife Anteia, also called Stheneboa, claimed that Bellerophon had tried to assault her, the truth being that
she loved Bellerophon, and he had refused her attentions.
Proetus, unwilling to murder his guest and thus violate
the law of Zeus, planned Bellerophon's death by sending him to his wife's father, Iobates of Lycia, with a
letter instructing the king to kill Bellerophon.   Instead,
Iobates set him many dangerous and impossible tasks
to do, thinking that he would thus perish.   Bellerophon,
however, performed all his tasks, one of which was to
slay the monster Chimera.   Because the gods took a
lively interest in the fate of Bellerophon, they provided
him with a winged horse, Pegasus, the semidivine offspring of Poseidon and Medusa.   After the Chimera was

Chart 27

109

slain, Iobates was so impressed that he gave Bellerophon one of his daughters to wife and made him successor to the kingdom, having no sons himself.

After listening to Glaucus, Diomedes remembers that his grandfather, Oeneus of Calydon, had once entertained Bellerophon for twenty days. Diomedes says he does not remember his own father, Tydeus, who died as one of the Seven Against Thebes. On the basis of their grandfathers' friendship, Glaucus and Diomedes pledge their respect to each other and refuse to fight even though they are enemies at war.

110

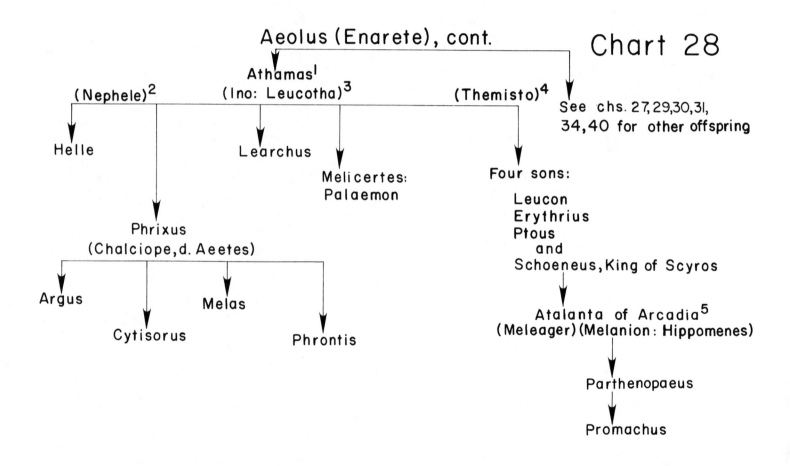

Aeolus (Enarete), cont.

Chart 28

Athamas[1]

(Nephele)[2]   (Ino: Leucotha)[3]   (Themisto)[4]

See chs. 27,29,30,31,
34,40 for other offspring

Helle

Learchus

Melicertes:
Palaemon

Four sons:

Leucon
Erythrius
Ptous
and
Schoeneus, King of Scyros

Phrixus
(Chalciope, d. Aeetes)

Argus

Cytisorus

Melas

Phrontis

Atalanta of Arcadia[5]
(Meleager)(Melanion: Hippomenes)

Parthenopaeus

Promachus

NOTES FOR CHART 28

[1]Athamas   son of Aeolus who ruled over Boeotia. By two or three wives he had a number of well-known and mostly ill-fortuned children. Apollodorus says that after the death of Ino and her sons, Athamas was banished from Boeotia. Having inquired of an oracle where he should dwell, he was told that he should live in the place where he should be entertained by wild beasts. After traveling a great distance, he fell in with wolves that were devouring a sheep, but when they saw him they fled. Athamas then settled in that country and called it Athamantia after himself. Here he married Themisto, daughter of Hypseus.

[2]Nephele   the first wife of Athamas, a cloud goddess, by whom he had a daughter, Helle, and a son, Phrixus. Because of her unstable nature, Nephele deserted Athamas, or he put her away, and married Ino, a daughter of Cadmus and Harmonia, by whom he had two sons, Learchus and Melicertes. Apollodorus tells the story of Ino's jealousy against Nephele's children:

> Ino plotted against the children of Nephele and persuaded the women to parch the wheat; and having got the wheat they did so without the knowledge of the men. But the earth, being sown with parched wheat, did not yield its annual crops; so Athamas sent to Delphi to inquire how he might be delivered from the dearth. Now Ino persuaded the messengers to say it was foretold that the infertility would cease if Phrixus were sacrificed to Zeus. When Athamas heard that, he was forced by the inhabitants of the land to bring Phrixus to the altar. But Nephele caught him and her daughter up in a cloud, and gave them a ram with a golden fleece which she had received from Hermes.

In their struggle to escape, Helle slipped into the sea and was drowned in what was later called the Hellespont after her. Phrixus continued to Colchis, where King Aeetes received him and gave him one of his daughters, Calciope in marriage. Phrixus sacrificed the ram to Zeus and gave Aeetes the golden fleece. In the Argonautica, Phrixus is represented as being dead by that time, but his wife and four sons are alive. Argus, Cytisorus, Melas, and Phrontis, the sons of Phrixus, are in fact picked up by Jason and the Argo after their small craft has run ashore near Colchis.

[3]Ino (or Leucotha)   daughter of Cadmus and Harmonia, and second wife to Athamas. After the escape of Helle and Phrixus, Hera caused further harm to befall the family. Angry because Ino had nursed the infant god Dionysus, who was the son of Zeus and Semele, Ino's sister, Hera sent the fury Tisiphone

to stir up madness in Athamas' household. Ovid tells the story in some detail, and other writers frequently make references to the disaster. Athamas, thinking his wife and sons were a lioness and her cubs, seized his son Learchus and dashed him to death against a rock; Ino fled with Melicertes in her arms and plunged over a cliff into the waters below. Aphrodite pitied Ino and Melicertes and begged her uncle, Poseidon, to take pity and "add them to the company of seagods." This Poseidon did, and the new deities became Palaemon and Leucotha, whose functions were to aid distressed mariners at sea. Leucotha came to the aid of Odysseus in the Odyssey when she gave him an immortal veil that enabled him to swim to the land of the Phaeacians.

[4]Themisto   third wife of Athamas, daughter of Hypseus, himself a son of the river god Peneus. After the deaths of Ino and her sons, Athamas was banished from Boeotia or else went voluntarily into exile. He married Themisto and had four sons, Leucon, Erythrius, Schoeneus, and Ptous. Pausanias relates a story which conflicts with the usual story of Ino and the fate of her two sons. Themisto tried to kill the children of Ino, who lived in the house as a serving maid, but, tricked by Ino, Themisto accidentally killed her own children. Upon discovery of the truth, she then killed herself.

[5]Atalanta   of Boeotia and/or Arcadia. Hesiod, in The Catalogue of Women, calls Atalanta the daughter of Schoeneus, son of Athamas of Boeotia. Apollodorus calls her the daughter of Iasus, son of Lycurgus of Arcadia. Whatever genealogy is assigned to Atalanta, the basic elements of her story are the same:

(a) She was a virgin huntress.

(b) She was a chief participant in the Calydonian Boar Hunt.

(c) She was loved by Meleager of Calydon.

(d) She was finally won in marriage by Melanion or Hippomenes, son of Megareus of Anchestus.

(e) She was the mother of a son, Parthenopaeus.

Opinion varies, however, as to the parentage of Parthenopaeus. Apollodorus lists him in the following genealogy as a brother of Adrastus:

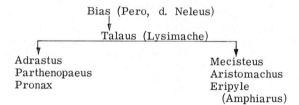

Bias (Pero, d. Neleus)

Talaus (Lysimache)

Adrastus	Mecisteus
Parthenopaeus	Aristomachus
Pronax	Eripyle
	(Amphiarus)

Apollodorus also says that Parthenopaeus had a son, Promachus, who marched "with the Epigoni against Thebes." Later, Apollodorus, contradicting himself, in listing the Seven Against Thebes says, "Parthenopaeus, son of Melanion, was an Arcadian." In Aeschylus' Seven Against Thebes, Parthenopaeus, who assaults the Gate of Boreas, is called a "waif of Arcady whose dam littered among the mountains."

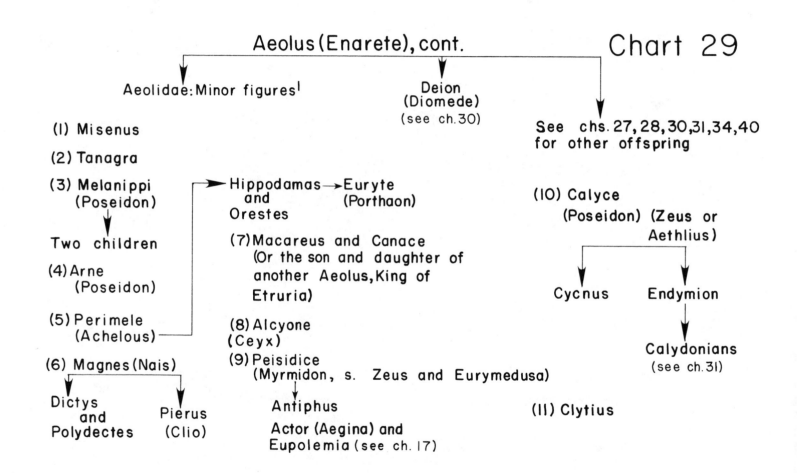

Aeolus (Enarete), cont.

Chart 29

Aeolidae: Minor figures[1]

Deion
(Diomede)
(see ch. 30)

See chs. 27, 28, 30, 31, 34, 40
for other offspring

(1) Misenus

(2) Tanagra

(3) Melanippi
(Poseidon)

Two children

(4) Arne
(Poseidon)

(5) Perimele
(Achelous)

(6) Magnes (Nais)

Dictys
and
Polydectes

Pierus
(Clio)

Hippodamas → Euryte
and   (Porthaon)
Orestes

(7) Macareus and Canace
(Or the son and daughter of
another Aeolus, King of
Etruria)

(8) Alcyone
(Ceyx)

(9) Peisidice
(Myrmidon, s. Zeus and Eurymedusa)

Antiphus

Actor (Aegina) and
Eupolemia (see ch. 17)

(10) Calyce
(Poseidon) (Zeus or
Aethlius)

Cycnus   Endymion

Calydonians
(see ch. 31)

(11) Clytius

NOTES FOR CHART 29

[1]Aeolidae: Minor Figures   (1) Misenus -- a son of Aeolus who escaped the Fall of Troy and followed Aeneas to Italy. He was killed by Poseidon's son Triton (see Chart 8, Note 9). Aeneas buried him on a promontory that bears his name.

(2) Tanagra -- a daughter of Aeolus, or the Asopus, who gave her name to a town in Boeotia, near the Euripus, between the Asopus and Thermodon.

(3) Melanippi -- a daughter of Aeolus or of some other king. The story as told by Hyginus is that she had two sons by Poseidon, and that her father put out both her eyes and confined her to prison. The two children were exposed, but survived and were subsequently given to Metapontus, a son of Sisyphus, as his own sons. His wife Theano later had two sons of her own and contrived to murder the sons of Melanippi. The scheme miscarried and Theano's sons were the victims. Metapontus exiled Theano, or she committed suicide, and married Melanippi, whom he had long known was the mother of the twins.   Poseidon restored Melanippi's eyesight, and her sons became Metapontus' successors.

(4) Arne -- daughter of Aeolus who was loved by Poseidon. She gave her name to a city in Thessaly and to another city in Boeotia. Ovid says she was changed into a bird, "the black-footed, black-winged jackdaw."

(5) Perimele -- daughter of Aeolus who bore two sons, Hippodamas and Orestes, by the river god Achelous. Hippodamas was the father of Euryte, who married Porthaon of Calydon and became the mother of numerous children, including Oeneus.

(6) Magnes -- son of Aeolus who married Nais, a nymph by whom he became the father of Pierus. Apollodorus says Magnes was also the father of Dictys and Polydectes of Seriphus. Another mythology says Magnes was the son of Thyia, a daughter of Deucalion.

(7) Macareus and Canace -- generally identified as a son and daughter of Aeolus who committed incest, although they are sometimes said to be the son and daughter of another Aeolus, a King of Etruria. The father sent Canace a sword, ordering her to kill herself, or she did so from shame; Macareus fled to Delphi, where he became a priest of Apollo, or else he too committed suicide. Apollodorus says in a seemingly unrelated story that Canace was loved by Poseidon, by whom she had many children, Hopleus, Nireus, Epopeus, Aloeus, and Triops.

(8) Alcyone (or Halcyone) -- daughter of Aeolus who married Ceyx, the son of Phosphor.

(9) Peisidice -- daughter of Aeolus who married Myrmidon, the son of Zeus. Their son Actor married Aegina, daughter of the Asopus.

(10) Calyce -- daughter of Aeolus, by Poseidon was the mother of Cycnus, and by Zeus or Aethlius was the mother of Endymion. The name Cycnus means

"swan," and there are at least five figures identified in this manner. This Cycnus was killed by Achilles in the first year of the Trojan War. Invulnerable to spears, Cycnus was finally smothered by Achilles, who stripped him of his armor and saw him immediately change into a beautiful white swan.

(11) Clytius -- a son of Aeolus who followed Aeneas to Italy and was killed in the war with Turnus. This Clytius is not referred to by Homer.

Aeolus (Enarete), cont.

Chart 30

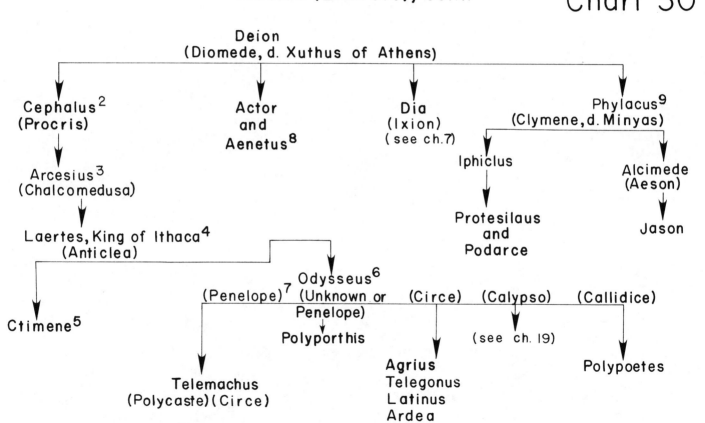

Deion
(Diomede, d. Xuthus of Athens)

Cephalus[2]
(Procris)

Actor
and
Aenetus[8]

Dia
(Ixion)
(see ch.7)

Phylacus[9]
(Clymene, d. Minyas)

Arcesius[3]
(Chalcomedusa)

Iphiclus

Alcimede
(Aeson)

Laertes, King of Ithaca[4]
(Anticlea)

Odysseus[6]
(Unknown or
Penelope)

Protesilaus
and
Podarce

Jason

(Penelope)[7]   (Circe)   (Calypso)   (Callidice)

Ctimene[5]

Polyporthis

(see ch. 19)

Telemachus
(Polycaste)(Circe)

Agrius
Telegonus
Latinus
Ardea

Polypoetes

NOTES FOR CHART 30

[1]Deion (or Deioneus)   son of Aeolus who became King
                         of Phocis. He married Diomede,
a daughter of Xuthus of Athens.   Apollodorus says they
had a daughter Asterodia, or Dia, and sons Aenetus,
Actor, Phylacus, and Cephalus.   The daughter Dia was
given in marriage to Ixion, who promised Deion a handsome prize, but instead killed him by throwing him into
a pit of burning coals.

[2]Cephalus   son of Deion who married Procris, the
             daughter of Erechtheus of Athens.   Another
mythology says Cephalus was the son of Herse and
Hermes, but Apollodorus says there were two figures
with the name Cephalus, and that it was the son of Herse
and Hermes whom Eos carried away.   The story of
Cephalus and Procris, however, is generally consistent.
Eos, having abducted Cephalus, did not win his love,
for he continually longed to return to his wife Procris.
Finally, Eos sent him away, changing his appearance
in order that Procris might not recognize him.   In the
form of a stranger, Cephalus tried to obtain the favors
of his wife and was successful.   Thereafter, he drove
her away, and she became a huntress with Artemis,
who gave her the dog Laelaps, which never missed its
prey, and a dart that never missed its target.   Procris,
dressed as a stranger, returned to Cephalus and offered
him the dog and the dart.   He accepted the gifts and
also the lady who gave them.   Procris revealed herself

to Cephalus, and they both forgave each other.   Procris,
still jealous of her husband, followed him into the woods
one day when he was hunting with the miraculous dog
and dart, and he, mistaking her footsteps for those of
a wild animal, threw the dart and killed her.

[3]Arcesius   father of Laertes, according to Homer,
            Apollodorus, Ovid, and others.   That Ar-
cesius was the son of Cephalus is remarked only by Hyginus.   Ovid says Arcesius was the son of Zeus, and
Homer calls Odysseus the "son of Laertes, sprung from
Zeus."

[4]Laertes of Ithaca   father of Odysseus in Homer, mar-
                      ried Anticlea, daughter of Hermes'
son Autolycus.   Laertes is portrayed in the Odyssey as
a grieving old man who has retired to the country in almost hopeless despair over the twenty-year absence of
his only son, Odysseus.   Apollodorus names Laertes as
one of the Argonauts, although he does not in any wise
distinguish himself during the voyage of the Argo.   Anticlea is one of the women whom Odysseus speaks with
when he visits the Underworld in the Odyssey.   He is
surprised to see his mother, "whom he had left alive"
when he went to Troy.   She tells him she died of grief
in her son's absence.   Odysseus tries to clasp her, but
her shade eludes his grasp, and moves away.

[5]Ctimene   youngest daughter of Laertes and Anticlea,
                sister to Odysseus. She is referred to in
the Odyssey as having been sent "to Same to wed. "
Same, or Samos, is a small island near Ithaca.

[6]Odysseus   son of Laertes and Anticlea, according to
                Homer. A later, discrediting, tradition,
such as Euripides followed in Iphigenia at Aulis, makes
him the son of Sisyphus, his mother having consorted
with Sisyphus before her marriage to Laertes. The
character of Odysseus is most favorably studied in Homer's Odyssey, but his role in the Iliad is considerable
also. In addition to the well-known events of the Iliad
and the Odyssey, there are many other episodes related
to Odysseus: how he feigned madness to avoid going to
the Trojan War; his responsibility in putting Philoctetes
ashore on the Island of Lemnos; his plotting the death
of Palamedes; his theft with Diomedes of the Palladium
in Troy; his role in the invention of the Wooden Horse;
and finally his adventures and death after he returned to
Ithaca in Homer's epic. Apollodorus reviews most of
these events, and some of them are described in more
detail by Quintus of Smyrna in the Posthomerica.

[7]Penelope and Others   (a) Penelope -- daughter of
                            Icarius, the son of Perieres or
Oebalus of Lacedaemon. In Homer, she is the mother
of Telemachus only, but in a later story, Apollodorus
says she became the mother of Polyporthis after Odysseus' return to Ithaca. One mythology says Telemachus
married Polycaste, the daughter of Nestor at Pylos; but
this is not established in the Odyssey, although Polycaste does bathe Telemachus when he visits Nestor to
learn the whereabouts of his father. It is generally
said that Telemachus married Circe after the death of
Odysseus in his very old age, and that she made him
and his mother Penelope immortal.

(b) Circe -- daughter of Helios, with whom
Odysseus spent some time on the Island of Aeaea after
the Fall of Troy. Homer makes no reference to children of Odysseus by Circe; however, Hesiod says
"Circe loved Odysseus and bore Agrius and Latinus and
also Telegonus. " Virgil refers to a city named Ardea
after a son or daughter of Circe and Odysseus. It is
Hyginus who says that many years later Circe sent her
son Telegonus to find his father. In Ithaca, Telegonus
accidentally killed Odysseus, and then brought his body
back to Aeaea for burial. Telegonus married Penelope,
and Telemachus married Circe.

(c) Calypso -- daughter of Atlas with whom Odysseus spent some seven years after the Fall of Troy.
Again, Homer makes no reference to children of Odysseus by Calypso; however, Hesiod says Calypso "bare
him Nausithous and Nausinous. "

(d) Callidice -- queen of the Thesprotians whom
Odysseus visited after his return to Ithaca. She urged
him to stay with her and offered him the kingdom. By
her Odysseus had a son, Polypoetes. When Callidice
died, Apollodorus says he handed over the kingdom to
his son and returned to Ithaca.

[8]Actor and Aenetus   sons of Deion and Diomede. Of
                        these two nothing further is given
by Apollodorus, who merely names them. Actor is the
name of at least a dozen figures, the best known being
the son of Peisidice and Myrmidon, the grandfather of
Patroclus.

[9]Phylacus   son of Deion of Phocis who married Cly-
                mene, a daughter of Minyas, by whom he
had Iphiclus and Alcimede. Iphiclus married a daughter
of a king of Thebes and was father of Protesilaus and
Podarce. Alcimede married Aeson, King of Iolchis,
and became the mother of Jason, according to Apollonius

Chart 30   121

of Rhodes.   Apollodorus says Aeson married Polymele,
a daughter of Autolycus.   Iphiclus went with his nephew
Jason on the Argo in search of the Golden Fleece, and
his sons Protesilaus and Podarce came from Phylace,
named for their grandfather Phylacus, to accompany
Agamemnon in his war against Troy.   According to
Homer in the Iliad, Protesilaus was the first Achaean to
fall at the hands of the Trojans.   As the elder brother,
Protesilaus was the leader of their men and ships, but
after his death Podarce took his place.   At the conclusion of the Iliad, Podarce is still alive, but is later
killed by the Amazon Penthesileia.   Quintus of Smyrna
tells of his death and funeral, "equal in honor to his
great brother."

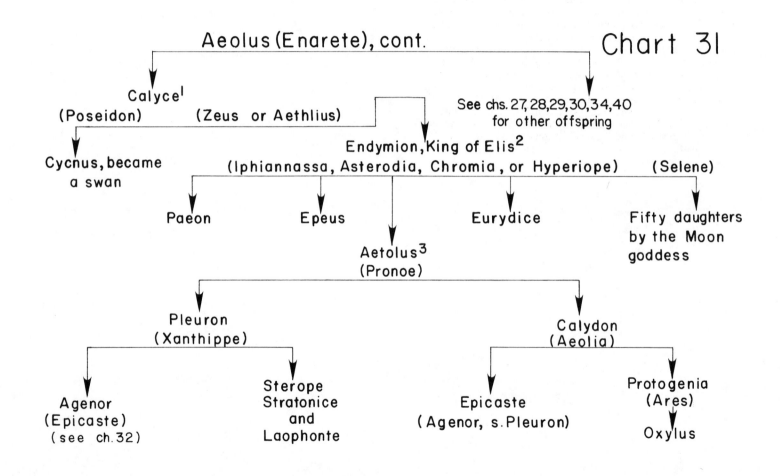

Aeolus (Enarete), cont.   Chart 31

Calyce[1]

(Poseidon)   (Zeus or Aethlius)

See chs. 27, 28, 29, 30, 34, 40
for other offspring

Cycnus, became
a swan

Endymion, King of Elis[2]
(Iphiannassa, Asterodia, Chromia, or Hyperiope)   (Selene)

Paeon   Epeus   Eurydice   Fifty daughters
by the Moon
goddess

Aetolus[3]
(Pronoe)

Pleuron
(Xanthippe)

Calydon
(Aeolia)

Agenor
(Epicaste)
(see ch. 32)

Sterope
Stratonice
and
Laophonte

Epicaste
(Agenor, s. Pleuron)

Protogenia
(Ares)

Oxylus

NOTES FOR CHART 31

[1]Calyce   daughter of Aeolus, by Poseidon was the moth-
            er of Cycnus, and by Zeus or Aethlius, a son
of Protogenia and Zeus, the mother of Endymion who became the King of Elis.

[2]Endymion   son of Calyce and Zeus or Aethlius, was
              known for his great beauty and was loved
by Selene, "the Lady Moon, Titanian goddess," as Apollonius of Rhodes calls her in the Argonautica.   Apollodorus says that Zeus offered Endymion a gift of his
own choosing, and he chose to "sleep forever, remaining deathless and ageless."   He therefore retired to a
cave on Mount Latmus, where he went to sleep for all
eternity.   Pausanias gives further details:

> The Moon was in love with Endymion and bore
> him fifty daughters.   But there exists a rather
> more likely story that Endymion married As-
> terodia--though some say it was Chromia, the
> daughter of Amphictyon's son Itonus, and some
> say it was Arcas' daughter Hyperope--and Endy-
> mion's children were Paeon and Epeus and Aeto-
> lus and a daughter Eurydice.   Endymion held a
> race for his throne between [sic] his sons at
> Olympia, and Epeus won it and became king.

This author also says that Paeon, angry at losing the
race, went as far away as possible, but Aetolus stayed
with Epeus.   The issue of Aetolus finally succeeded to
the kingdom because Epeus had no male offspring.

[3]Aetolus   eponym for the Aetolians, married Pronoe,
             daughter of Phorbus.   Apollodorus says that
Aetolus, the son of Endymion and Ephiannassa, killed
Apis, the son of Phoroneus, and fled to the Curetian
country.   There he killed his hosts, Dorus, Laodocus,
and Polypoetes, the sons of Phthia and Apollo, and
called the country Aetolia after himself.   The offspring
of the sons of Aetolus--Pleuron and Calydon--are given
here as represented in Apollodorus.   Most of these
figures have little or no mythology connected with them.
A few stories are told elsewhere in the charts.

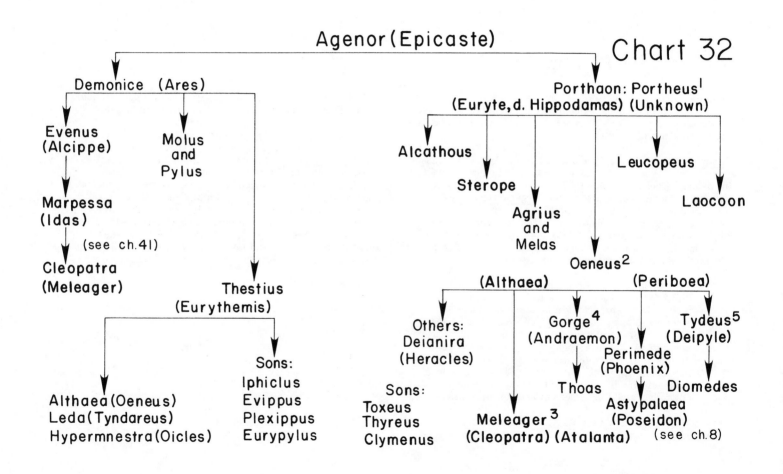

Agenor (Epicaste)

Chart 32

Demonice (Ares)

Porthaon: Portheus[1]
(Euryte, d. Hippodamas) (Unknown)

Evenus
(Alcippe)

Molus
and
Pylus

Alcathous

Leucopeus

Marpessa
(Idas)

Sterope

(see ch.41)

Laocoon

Cleopatra
(Meleager)

Agrius
and
Melas

Thestius
(Eurythemis)

Oeneus[2]

(Althaea)

(Periboea)

Others:
Deianira
(Heracles)

Gorge[4]
(Andraemon)

Tydeus[5]
(Deipyle)

Perimede
(Phoenix)

Sons:
Iphiclus
Evippus
Plexippus
Eurypylus

Sons:
Toxeus
Thyreus
Clymenus

Thoas

Diomedes

Althaea (Oeneus)
Leda (Tyndareus)
Hypermnestra (Oicles)

Meleager[3]
(Cleopatra) (Atalanta)

Astypalaea
(Poseidon)

(see ch.8)

NOTES ON CHART 32

[1]Porthaon   is called Portheus by Homer in the Iliad, in which Diomedes says, "to Portheus were born three peerless sons ... Agrius and Melas, and the third was the horseman Oeneus, that was father to my father." Apollodorus says:

> Porthaon and Euryte, daughter of Hippodamas, had sons, Oeneus, Agrius, Alcathous, Melas, Leucopeus, and a daughter Sterope, who is said to have been the mother of the Sirens by Achelous.

[2]Oeneus   son of Porthaon and Euryte, married Althaea, daughter of Thestius, by whom he had sons, Toxeus, Thyreus, Clymenus, and Meleager, and daughters, Gorge, who married Andraemon, and Deianira, who married Heracles and later caused his death. After the death of Althaea, who killed herself in remorse for causing the death of her son Meleager, Oeneus married Periboea, daughter of Hipponous, by whom he became the father of Tydeus. According to Apollodorus, Toxeus was a son of Oeneus, who was killed by his father; and Plexippus was a son of Thestius whom Meleager killed. Ovid says both Toxeus and Plexippus were sons of Thestius and were killed by their nephew Meleager.

The Calydonian Boar Hunt, one of the great events of mythology, does not survive in any extant drama or poem on the subject. There are a number of references to the event in works of the dramatists and in Homer, but the fullest account is narrated by Apollodorus. Oeneus is usually credited with having caused the Boar Hunt to take place. In sacrificing the annual crops of the country, Oeneus forgot Artemis. In great wrath, the goddess sent a boar of extraordinary size and strength to ravage the country. To attack this boar Oeneus called together all the noblest heroes of the time and promised that to him who should kill the beast he would give the skin as a prize (see Chart 33 for lists of those who participated in the Calydonian Boar Hunt).

[3]Meleager   son of Oeneus and Althaea, married Cleopatra, the daughter of Idas and Marpessa. Meleager accompanied Jason on the voyage of the Argo when he was still a very young man, and later was the principal hero of the Calydonian Boar Hunt. There are two versions of how he met his death. One story has it that when he was seven days old the Fates came and declared that Meleager should die when the brand then burning on the hearth was burned out. At this his mother Althaea snatched up the brand and hid it away for safekeeping. At the Calydonian Boar Hunt, Atalanta was the first to shoot the boar, but Meleager killed it and gave the skin to Atalanta, with whom he had fallen in love. The sons of Thestius, angry that a woman should get the prize instead of men, took it from her, and Meleager killed them. Althaea, in a rage over the death

of her brothers, kindled the brand and Meleager died immediately. The other story of Meleager's death is that war broke out between the sons of Thestius and the Calydonians over the skin of the boar. Meleager killed some of the sons of Thestius, and Althaea cursed him for killing her kinsmen. After this, Meleager would not fight, but stayed at home until the enemy approached the walls of the city. The citizens and Meleager's wife begged him to come to their rescue, and Meleager reluctantly went forth. After killing the other sons of Thestius, Meleager himself fell in battle. In both stories, Althaea and Cleopatra hanged themselves after the death of Meleager. In the Iliad, this second version of Meleager's death is told as a parallel to Achilles and his sulking refusal to go out and fight the Trojans.

[4]Gorge   daughter of Oeneus, married Andraemon, who succeeded Oeneus as the ruler of Calydon after Diomedes deposed the sons of Agrius and restored the throne to his grandfather. Thoas, the son of Gorge and Andraemon, led the Aetolians in a fleet of forty ships to Troy. At the conclusion of the Iliad, Thoas is still alive. Virgil names him as one of the Greeks in the Wooden Horse, and Apollodorus says he returned to Aetolia, where he ruled and had a son and daughter.

[5]Tydeus   son of Oeneus and Periboea. At a young age, Tydeus was banished from Calydon either for killing his own brother, Olenias, or two brothers of Oeneus, Alcathous and Melas. In either case, he fled to Argos, where he married Deipyle, a daughter of Adrastus. Tydeus fought opposite Melanippus in Polynices' War of the Seven Against Thebes. These two dealt each other a mortal wound, but Tydeus would have lived had he not disgusted the goddess Athena by eating Melanippus' brain. After this outrageous act, the goddess refused to save his life. By Deipyle, Tydeus was

the father of Diomedes, who fought in the second war against Thebes--the war of the Epigoni--and then in the war at Troy. In the Iliad, Diomedes is one of Homer's greatest heroes. He killed many Trojans, and would have killed Aeneas, except that the gods protected him; Diomedes wounded Ares and Aphrodite, and even became defiant of Apollo but did not go too far in offending this most powerful of gods. Diomedes survived the Trojan War and returned to his homeland, where he found that his wife Aegiale, another daughter of Adrastus (or, more probably, the daughter of Aegialeus, the son of Adrastus), had been unfaithful to him with Cometes, the son of Sthenelus. Diomedes then left Argos, or was exiled, and went to Italy, where he is said to have lived to a very old age. One mythology says he married the daughter of Daunus, the King of Apulia in Italy. In the Aeneid, Virgil represents Diomedes as having founded his town Argyripa, by the time Aeneas arrives in Italy and is beginning his war with Turnus. Diomedes is entreated to join the Italians in aiding Turnus, but the former great warrior will have no part in the fight against Aeneas and warns the Italians that they should "join hands in peace." Diomedes attributes all his ill-luck to the day he lost his mind and "wounded the holy hand of Venus (Aphrodite)."

Heroes of the Calydonian Boar Hunt[1] Chart 33

Meleager,[2] s. Oeneus of Calydon

Dryas, s. Ares from Calydon

Idas and Lynceus, sons of Aphareus
from Messenia

Castor and Polydeuces, sons of
Leda and Zeus-Tyndareus from Lacedaemon

Theseus, s. Aegeus from Athens

Admetus, s. Pheres from Pherae

Ancaeus and Cepheus,[3] sons of
Lycurgus from Arcadia

Jason, s. Aeson from Iolcus

Iphicles, s. Amphitryon from Thebes

Peleus, s. Aeacus from Phthia

Telamon, s. Aeacus

Eurytion,[4] s. Actor from Phthia

Atalanta,[5] d. Schoenus from
Arcadia

Amphiaraus, s. Oicles from Argos

Sons of Thestius[6]

Hyleus, killed in the hunt

NOTES FOR CHART 33

[1]Heroes of the Calydonian Boar Hunt   Although there are several other notable events in mythology, four major gathering points are referred to for the heroes of this legendary age. By following the involvement of one or more of the characters, it is possible to arrange these events in something of a chronological order: (1) The voyage of the Argo and the gathering of the Argonauts with Jason. On this voyage, Meleager, son of Oeneus, is described as hardly beyond his youth. (2) The Calydonian Boar Hunt and the gathering of the heroes at the court of Oeneus in Calydon. Meleager died as a result of this event. (3) The two wars against Thebes with Polynices, the son of Oedipus, and the Seven Against Thebes, and ten years later the Return of the Sons of the Seven, the Epigoni. Meleager's half-brother Tydeus, father of Diomedes, died with Polynices in the first war, and his son Diomedes fought with the Sons of the Seven. (4) The Trojan War, in which Diomedes fought.

The list of those who participated in the Calydonian Boar Hunt given here is from Apollodorus. From Ovid, the list is somewhat similar:

Twin sons of Tyndareus (Castor and Pollux)
Jason, who had built the first ship
Theseus and Pirithous, inseparable companions
The two sons of Thestius
Aphareus' sons, Lynceus and Idas

Caeneus, who had once been a woman
Leucippus
Acastus
Hippothous
Dryas
Phoenix, Amyntor's son
The two sons of Actor [Eurytus and Cteatus, called the Molionides after their mother Molione]
Phyleus from Elis
Telamon and Peleus, the father of great Achilles
Iolaus from Boeotia
Eurytion
Locrian Lelex
Panopeus and Hyleus
Hippasus
Nestor, then in the prime of life
Hippocoon from Amyclae
Penelope's father-in-law Laertes
Arcadian Ancaeus
The wise seer, Ampycus' son, Mopsus [Mopsus is said to have died from a snake bite at one point in the Argonautica; hence, his participation in the Boar Hunt is contradictory]
Amphiaraus
The girl warrior from Tegea [Atalanta]

In the Iliad, Homer tells through Phoenix, the friend of

Achilles, part of the Meleager story, but there are no lists of names of the participating heroes. The story is used by Phoenix as another example of "wrath" and its consequences, as Phoenix is making a futile effort to persuade Achilles to give up his quarrel and return to battle.

[2]Meleager   is said to have actually killed the wild boar, although Atalanta was first to hit the animal with an arrow. Meleager gave the skin to Atalanta, much to the displeasure of the sons of Thestius (Meleager's uncles). In the argument that followed, Meleager killed them.

[3]Ancaeus and Cepheus   were reluctant to hunt with a woman, and when Atalanta shot the boar, Ancaeus rushed in shouting, "See how far superior to woman's weapons are those of a man." Ovid says he quickly lost his life in the encounter.

[4]Eurytion   was accidentally killed by Peleus, according to Apollodorus; Ovid does not include this event.

[5]Atalanta   daughter of Schoenus, King of Scyros, or the daughter of Iasus. She is consistently called the heroine of the Calydonian Boar Hunt, and further accounts say she was finally beaten in a foot race by Hippomenes or Melanion and then married him. According to Apollodorus, she was the mother by Meleager or Melanion of Parthenopaeus, one of the Seven Against Thebes.

[6]Sons of Thestius   the names and number of these sons vary, but the context of all remarks on them would indicate a great many. Apollodorus says Toxeus was a son of Oeneus, but Ovid says both Toxeus and Plexippus were sons of Thestius and were killed by their nephew Meleager.

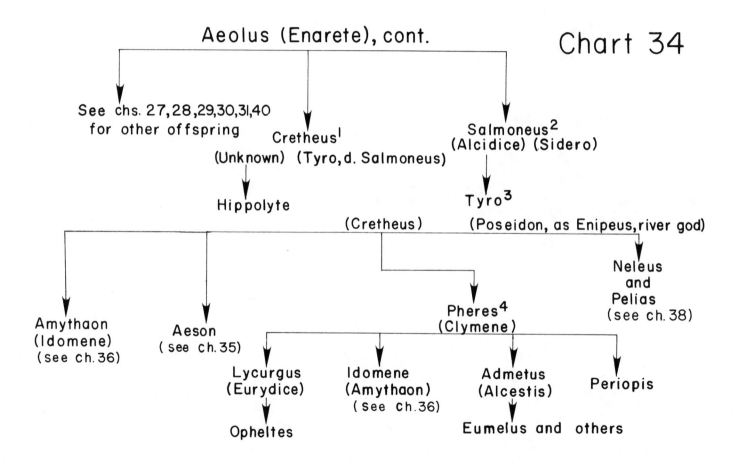

Aeolus (Enarete), cont.

Chart 34

See chs. 27,28,29,30,31,40
for other offspring

Cretheus[1]
(Unknown) (Tyro,d. Salmoneus)

Salmoneus[2]
(Alcidice) (Sidero)

Hippolyte

Tyro[3]

(Cretheus)   (Poseidon, as Enipeus,river god)

Amythaon
(Idomene)
(see ch. 36)

Aeson
(see ch. 35)

Pheres[4]
(Clymene)

Neleus
and
Pelias
(see ch. 38)

Lycurgus
(Eurydice)

Idomene
(Amythaon)
(see ch.36)

Admetus
(Alcestis)

Periopis

Opheltes

Eumelus and others

NOTES FOR CHART 34

[1]Cretheus   son of Aeolus, married Tyro, his niece,
daughter of his brother Salmoneus.

[2]Salmoneus   King of Thessaly, later King of Elis, where
he founded a city called Salmone. He first
married Alcidice, daughter of Aleus, by whom he had
his daughter Tyro.   After the death of Alcidice, who
died in childbirth, Salmoneus married Sidero, who became a cruel stepmother to Tyro.   Salmoneus was ar-
rogant and impious towards the gods, and one account
says that he and Sidero called themselves Zeus and
Hera.   Virgil has him in Tartarus, along side his brother Sisyphus, and describes the way Salmoneus acted in
life, driving his chariot through the city, dragging dried
hides and bronze drums to simulate thunder and throwing torches into the air as though they were lightening.
Zeus soon became tired of this and destroyed Salmoneus
and his entire city with real thunderbolts.

[3]Tyro   daughter of Salmoneus and Alcidice, was probably reared by her uncle Cretheus, whom she
later married.   The story is told that Poseidon, disguised as the river Enipeus, made love to Tyro, and
she conceived and bore twins in secret.   She exposed
them in a field, but they were found by a horseman and
named Pelias and Neleus.   Tyro's father and stepmother
refused to believe that a god had fathered her twins,
and so imprisoned and abused her.   Later she married

Cretheus and had three sons by him: Amythaon, Aeson,
and Pheres.   When Pelias and Neleus grew into manhood, they found their mother, and Pelias killed Sidero
for her cruelties to Tyro.   In the Odyssey, Odysseus
saw Tyro among the women when he visited the Underworld.

[4]Pheres   son of Cretheus and Tyro, and founder of
Pherae, in Thessaly, not far from Iolcus.
After Pelias, their half-brother, had usurped the throne
of Iolcus, Pheres and Amythaon left the city.   Pheres
married a daughter of Minyas, by whom he had two sons,
Admetus and Lycurgas, and two daughters, Idomene, who
married her uncle Amythaon, and Periopis, who was possibly the mother of Patroclus by Menoetius.   Pheres is
represented in Euripides' Alcestis as an old man who
nonetheless refused to volunteer as a substitute when his
son Admetus was faced with death.
    The descendants of Pheres are little known except
for Admetus, who married Alcestis, the daughter of
Pelias.   Admetus went with Jason on the Argo, and later
the cousins took part in the Calydonian Boar Hunt, according to Apollodorus.   Admetus gained the reputation
of being an extremely honorable king, and when Apollo
was sentenced by Zeus to serve a mortal for one year,
the god chose Admetus.   As a servant, Apollo found such
generosity in his master that he repaid Admetus by causing the cows to have twins, by helping win Alcestis as a

bride, and by bargaining with the Fates when it was time for Admetus to die. The Fates, however, would not be cheated, and demanded either Admetus or a substitute. It is perhaps in this last role that Admetus is best known, as the husband who allowed his wife Alcestis to die for him. This story has a happy ending, however, because Heracles visited Admetus at this time, and having drunk a quantity of good wine, went off to fight Thanatos, Death, and restored Alcestis to her husband and children.

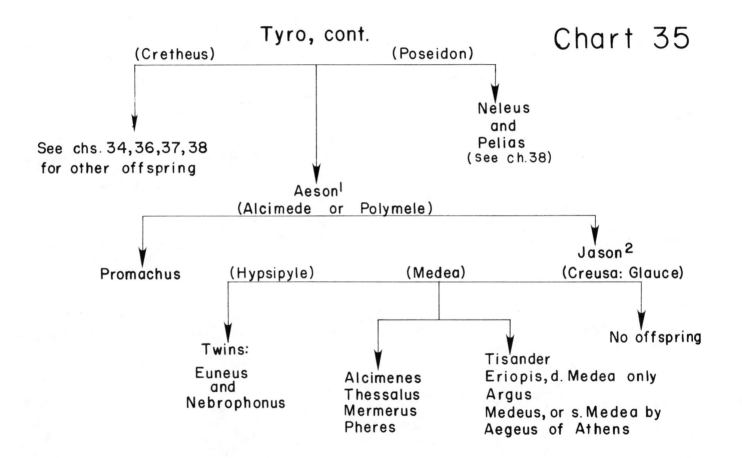

Tyro, cont.   Chart 35

(Cretheus)   (Poseidon)

See chs. 34,36,37,38
for other offspring

Neleus
and
Pelias
(see ch.38)

Aeson[1]
(Alcimede   or   Polymele)

Promachus   (Hypsipyle)   (Medea)   Jason[2]
(Creusa: Glauce)

No offspring

Twins:
Euneus
and
Nebrophonus

Alcimenes
Thessalus
Mermerus
Pheres

Tisander
Eriopis, d. Medea only
Argus
Medeus, or s. Medea by
Aegeus of Athens

NOTES FOR CHART 35

[1]Aeson   the eldest son of Tyro and Cretheus, King of Iolcus. As the eldest, Aeson should have inherited his father's kingdom, but the throne was seized by Pelias, and Aeson was sent into exile. Aeson married Alcimede, a daughter of Phylacus, according to Apollonius of Rhodes, but Apollodorus says his wife was Polymele, a daughter of Autolycus. It is generally said that Jason was the only son of Aeson, but Apollodorus says there was a younger son, Promachus. When Jason was born, his parents, fearing his life was threatened by Pelias, gave out that he was dead and sent him to Chiron the Centaur. When Jason was grown, he reappeared in Iolcus, claiming his kingdom. His uncle Pelias then sent him to Colchis to get the Golden Fleece, thinking that such an uncharted voyage would certainly end in disaster for his young nephew. During Jason's absence, Apollodorus says that Aeson was forced by Pelias to commit suicide, that the mother of Jason cursed Pelias and hanged herself, and that the infant Promachus was then put to the sword. Another story is that Aeson did not die in Jason's absence, and that when Jason returned with Medea, the ancient man was restored to youth by means of Medea's magic potions.

[2]Jason   hero son of Aeson, who led the Argonauts on the first great mythological voyage, to Colchis, where he obtained the Golden Fleece and Medea, the daughter of Aeetes, as his bride. The story of Jason's voyage is best studied in the Argonautica, by Apollonius of Rhodes, and the story of Jason's marriage to Medea and its subsequent tragedies are presented in Euripides' Medea. Ovid tells the entire story in relatively brief fashion, beginning with Jason's return to Iolcus and ending with Medea's escape to Athens in a dragon-drawn chariot. Apollodorus summarizes the Jason and Medea story, and says that after Medea went to Athens and married Aegeus, she had a son, Medeus. Afterwards Medea plotted against Theseus, the son of Aegeus, and was expelled from Athens. With her son, Medea returned to Colchis.

As to Jason's death, there are several versions. One story, not generally referred to, is that the Corinthians stoned Jason and his two sons to death after Medea killed King Creon and his daughter Glauce or Creusa. Another version is that Jason committed suicide after Medea killed their two sons and brought such general havoc to Corinth. In Euripides' Medea, Jason's death is foretold, that he will die by a falling beam of the Argo. Very little has been said of Jason's offspring, and there is no agreement as to how many or their names. Mermerus and Pheres were the two small sons Medea or the Corinthians killed. When the Argo stopped at the Island of Lemnos, Jason and Hypsipyle, the Queen of Lemnos, became lovers, and two sons were later born to Hypsipyle. Apollodorus says these sons were Nebrophonus and Euneus. No other mention is made of Nebrophonus, but in the Iliad, Homer refers to Euneus, the son of Jason, as bringing wine ships from Lemnos to the Greeks at Troy.

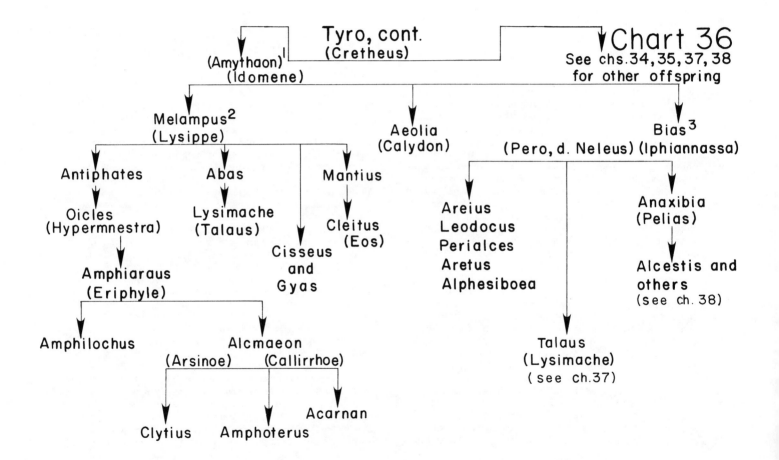

Tyro, cont.
(Cretheus)

Chart 36
See chs. 34, 35, 37, 38
for other offspring

(Amythaon)[1]
(Idomene)

Melampus[2]
(Lysippe)

Aeolia
(Calydon)

Bias[3]
(Pero, d. Neleus) (Iphiannassa)

Antiphates

Abas

Mantius

Oicles
(Hypermnestra)

Lysimache
(Talaus)

Cleitus
(Eos)

Amphiaraus
(Eriphyle)

Cisseus
and
Gyas

Areius
Leodocus
Perialces
Aretus
Alphesiboea

Anaxibia
(Pelias)

Alcestis and
others
(see ch. 38)

Amphilochus

Alcmaeon
(Arsinoe)   (Callirrhoe)

Talaus
(Lysimache)
(see ch. 37)

Clytius

Amphoterus

Acarnan

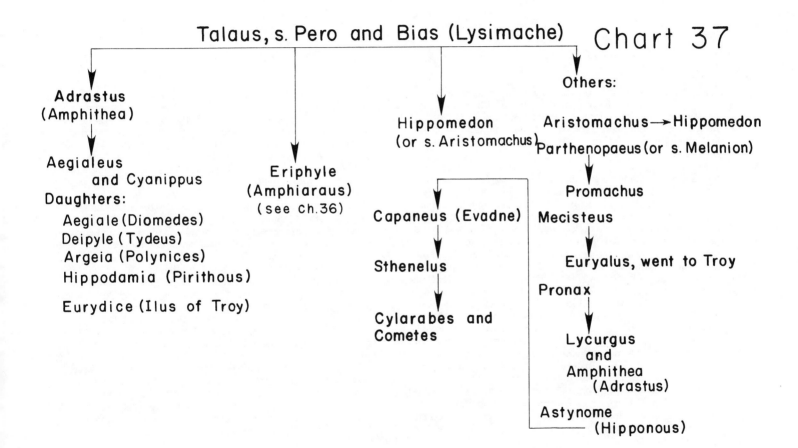

Talaus, s. Pero and Bias (Lysimache) Chart 37

Adrastus
(Amphithea)

Aegialeus
and Cyanippus
Daughters:
Aegiale (Diomedes)
Deipyle (Tydeus)
Argeia (Polynices)
Hippodamia (Pirithous)

Eurydice (Ilus of Troy)

Eriphyle
(Amphiaraus)
(see ch. 36)

Hippomedon
(or s. Aristomachus)

Capaneus (Evadne)

Sthenelus

Cylarabes and
Cometes

Others:

Aristomachus →Hippomedon
Parthenopaeus (or s. Melanion)

Promachus

Mecisteus

Euryalus, went to Troy

Pronax

Lycurgus
and
Amphithea
(Adrastus)

Astynome
(Hipponous)

NOTES FOR CHARTS 36 AND 37

[1]Amythaon   son of Cretheus and Tyro, married his
                niece Idomene, daughter of Pheres, by whom
he had two sons, Melampus and Bias, and a daughter,
Aeolia, who married Calydon.   Amythaon left Thessaly
and lived in exile at the court of his half-brother Neleus
in Pylos.

[2]Melampus   famous soothsayer, son of Amythaon and
                Idomene. He married Lysippe, daughter
of Proteus of Argos. It is said that Melempus learned
the art of divination from a brood of snakes that had
licked his ears. Among his most notable feats was the
securing of the cattle of Phylacus, which Neleus demanded of Bias as the dowry for his daughter Pero; he
also cured Iphiclus, the son of Phylacus, of impotency,
enabling him to father two sons, Podarces and Protesilaus.
Many years later, after Melampus had become a very
famous seer, he was called upon by Proetus, King of
Tiryns, to cure his three daughters of lunacy. Melampus agreed to do so, but demanded a third of Proetus'
kingdom in payment. The offer was angrily refused by
the king, and his daughters, as well as other women,
became even wilder. Proetus then hurriedly accepted
the offer, but by now Melampus had raised his price,
two-thirds of the kingdom. Proetus grudgingly accepted,
and two of his daughters, Lysippe and Iphiannassa, were
cured; the third, Iphinoe, died. Melampus then married
Lysippe, and after the death of Pero, Bias married
Iphiannassa.

As to the descendants of Melampus and Lysippe,
Amphiaraus, himself a seer, was the most famous.
Apollodorus says he was one of the hunters of the Calydonian Boar, and Aeschylus names him as one of the
Seven Against Thebes. In this war he would have been
killed, but Zeus split the earth open with a thunderbolt
and Amphiaraus disappeared. As a seer, Amphiaraus
knew that the expedition against Thebes would fail, and
that he would perish. He did not wish to go to this
war, but his wife Eriphyle, sister of Adrastus, had been
bribed with Harmonia's fatal necklace, and forced him
to go. Amphiaraus made his sons Alcmaeon and Amphilochus swear to avenge him on their mother and with
Thebes. Ten years after the War of the Seven Against
Thebes, Alcmaeon led the sons of the Seven, called the
Epigoni, in another war against Thebes. He then killed
his mother, Eriphyle, and was driven mad by the Furies
until he was purified by the river god Achelous and settled down in a new country near the delta of the Achelous River. Here he married his second wife, Callirrhoe, a daughter of the Achelous, and had two sons,
Acarnan and Amphoterus. Alcmaeon met his death at the
hands of his first wife's brothers, the sons of Phegeus.
Apparently, Alcmaeon was married to Arsinoe and Callirrhoe at the same time, since the brothers blamed their
sister for the murder and sold her into slavery. His
sons by Callirrhoe later avenged his death by killing
Phegeus and Arsinoe's brothers.

[3]Bias   son of Amythaon and Idomene, was less famous
than his brother Melampus.   Bias first married
Pero, the beautiful only daughter of Neleus and Chloris
of Pylos, by whom he was the father of Talaus and others.   After the death of Pero, Bias married Iphiannassa,
the daughter of Proetus, by whom he was father of Anaxibia, who married Pelias, King of Iolcus.   As to the
descendants of Bias, the best known are his son Talaus,
who sailed with Jason on the Argo, and his grandson
Adrastus, King of Argos and principal organizer and
leader of the Seven Against Thebes, although Polynices
had initiated the conflict in his quarrel with his brother
Eteocles.   Adrastus married Amphithea, the daughter of
Pronax, and had two sons, Aegialeus and Cyanippus, and
three daughters, Argeia, who married Polynices; Deipyle, who married Tydeus; and Aegialeia, who married
Diomedes, the son of Tydeus and Deipyle.   One mythology, however, says, more reasonably, that Aegiale
was the daughter of Aegialeus.   In the first war against
Thebes, Adrastus was the only leader who did not die,
and he was saved largely by the speed of his horse
Arion, the son of Demeter and Poseidon.   In the second
war against Thebes, Aegialeus, the son of Adrastus, was
the only leader who died.   Adrastus is one of the principal characters in Euripides' The Suppliants, a play that
depicts the aftermath of the first war against Thebes,
and the right to bury the fallen leaders of the ill-advised
expedition.   Of the other descendants of Bias, Homer
says Euryalus, the son of Mecisteus, went to Troy with
Agamemnon.   Quintus of Smyrna says he was one of the
Greeks who entered Troy in the Wooden Horse, and
there is no indication that he did not survive the war.
Sthenelus also went to Troy with Diomedes, and it was
Cometes, the son of Sthenelus, with whom Diomedes'
wife committed adultery.

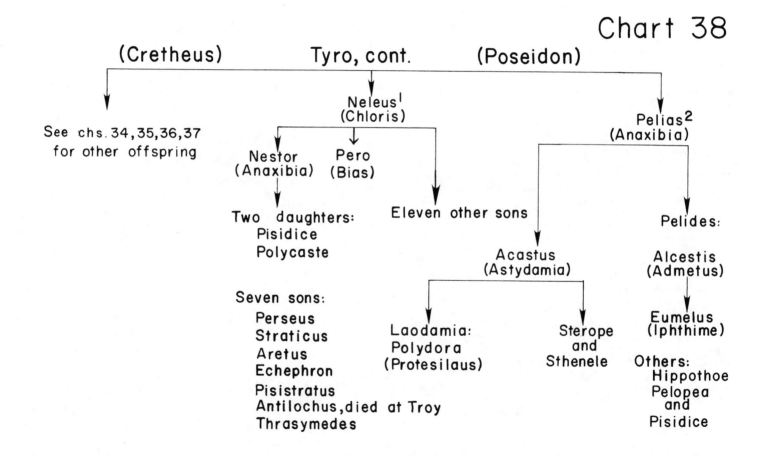

Chart 38

(Cretheus)   Tyro, cont.   (Poseidon)

See chs. 34, 35, 36, 37
for other offspring

Neleus[1]
(Chloris)

Pelias[2]
(Anaxibia)

Nestor
(Anaxibia)

Pero
(Bias)

Eleven other sons

Pelides:

Two daughters:
  Pisidice
  Polycaste

Acastus
(Astydamia)

Alcestis
(Admetus)

Seven sons:
  Perseus
  Straticus
  Aretus
  Echephron
  Pisistratus
  Antilochus, died at Troy
  Thrasymedes

Laodamia:
Polydora
(Protesilaus)

Sterope
and
Sthenele

Eumelus
(Iphthime)

Others:
  Hippothoe
  Pelopea
  and
  Pisidice

NOTES FOR CHART 38

[1]Neleus   son of Tyro and Poseidon, and brother of
            Pelias.   After Pelias assumed the throne of
Iolcus, Neleus was driven out of the land.   He went to
Messenia, where his kinsman Aphareus was king.
Aphareus gave Neleus lands along the coast, including
Pylus, which became the capital.   Here Neleus established a prosperous and well-ordered kingdom.   He married the beautiful daughter of Amphion and Niobe, Chloris, who alone of her sisters was not killed by Artemis.
In the Iliad, Nestor refers to the "twelve sons" of Neleus,
and says that he "alone was left," his eleven brothers
and father killed by Heracles when he raided Pylus.   In
the Odyssey, Odysseus sees Chloris in the Underworld,
"Queen of Pylus," who bore "glorious children" to Neleus: Nestor, Chromius, and Periclymenus.   Apollodorus names twelve sons: Taurus, Asterious, Pylaon,
Deimachus, Eurybius, Epilaus, Phrasius, Eurymenes,
Evagoras, Alastor, Nestor, and Periclymenus.   Neleus
and Chloris were also parents of the famous daughter
Pero, who married her kinsman Bias.
            Nestor, the only surviving son of Neleus, was
young when he succeeded his father as King of Pylus.
Homer says he married Eurydice, daughter of Clymenus,
but Apollodorus says he married Anaxibia, daughter of
Cratieus.   He became the father of two daughters, Pi-
sidice and Polycaste, and seven sons: Perseus, Strati-
chus, Aretus, Echephron, Pisistratus, Antilochus, and
Thrasymedes.   Nestor fought in the Calydonian Boar

Hunt and barely escaped being killed.   In his old age,
he and two sons, Antilochus and Thrasymedes, led nine-
ty ships to Troy.   In this war, Nestor and Thrasymedes
survived, but Antilochus was killed by Memnon some
time after the conclusion of the Iliad.   Thrasymedes is
said to have been one of the Greeks in the Wooden
Horse.

[2]Pelias   son of Tyro and Poseidon, twin brother of
            Neleus, and half-brother of Amythaon, Aeson,
and Pheres.   He married Anaxibia, daughter of Bias,
or Phylomache, daughter of Amphion.   Pelias had one
son, Acastus, who succeeded him as King of Iolcus,
and several daughters.   Apollodorus names four: Pisidice, Pelopia, Hippothoe, and Alcestis.   Pelias lived a
long life of extraordinary violence, and died an equally
violent death at the hands of his daughters.   One of his
first acts was to slay Sidero, Tyro's stepmother, at the
altar of Hera; later he drove his half-brothers Amythaon
and Pheres out of Iolchus, and took over the kingdom
from Aeson, whom he caused to commit suicide; twenty
or more years later, he sent Jason to get the Golden
Fleece, thinking to hear no more of his nephew.   Finally, after Jason returned from Colchis with Medea, Pelias
met his fate.   Medea, helping Jason to recover his kingdom, said she could restore Pelias to youth.   To do so,
his daughters had to consent to cutting him up and putting the dismembered body into a cauldron of boiling

water. She first demonstrated her powers by turning
an old ewe to a lamb. The daughters then eagerly killed
their father, and Medea departed, leaving them with the
hideous murder on their hands.

After the death of Pelias, Acastus became ruler,
either because Jason handed it over to him, or because
Jason and Medea had to flee the city after the murder
of Pelias. Acastus had gone with Jason and the Argonauts to Colchis, and later he went with Jason to the
Calydonian Boar Hunt. He married Astydamia, daughter
of Amyntor, or Hippolyte, a daughter of Cretheus. He
had three daughters, Laodamia, Sterope, and Sthenele,
and sons whose names are not known. After Peleus accidentally killed Eurytion at the Calydonian Boar Hunt,
he fled to Iolcus and Acastus purified him. Astydamia
fell in love with Peleus, and when her advances were
not returned, she told her husband that Peleus had attempted to seduce her. Acastus was unwilling to kill
his friend and guest, but contrived that Peleus should
be left alone on Mount Pelion, unarmed, and hoped the
Centaurs would kill him. Peleus was saved, however,
and returned to kill Astydamia and possibly Acastus.
Another story is that Peleus did not kill Acastus, but
was later driven into exile by Acastus. According to
Euripides, in The Trojan Women, this event took place
about the time that Troy fell. In this play, Neoptolemus, the grandson of Peleus, leaves Troy on short notice because of "tidings of wrong to Peleus" by Acastus.

Laodamia, the daughter of Acastus, married Protesilaus, the son of Iphiclus, who with his brother Podarce went to Troy. Protesilaus is said to be the first
Greek who died on Trojan soil. As to other descendants
of Pelias, Alcestis is the best known, and this in connection with her marriage to Admetus, the son of Pheres.
A son of Alcestis and Admetus, Eumelus, took eleven ships
to Troy and survived the war. Quintus of Smyrna says he
was one of the Greeks in the Wooden Horse; Homer says
Eumelus was married to Iphthime, a sister of Penelope.

The Crew of the Argo--Argonauts[1]
Chart 39

Orpheus, s. Calliope by Thracian Oeagrus

Asterion, s. Cometes	Tiphys, s. Hagnias [8]	Palaemonius, s. Hephaestus
Polyphemus, s. Elatus[2]	Phlias, s. Dionysus	
Iphiclus, s. Phylacus	Talaus, Areius and Leodocus, sons of Pero and Bias	Iphitus, s. Naubolis, s. Ornytus from Phocis
Admetus, King of Pherae	Heracles [9]	
	Nauplius, s. Clytoneus[10]	
Eurytus and Echion, sons of Hermes	Idmon, s. Abas or Apollo[11]	Zetes and Calais, sons of Boreas and Orithyia
Telamon and Peleus, sons of Aeacus	Castor and Polydeuces, sons of Leda and Zeus–Tyndareus	
Coronus, s. Caenus[3]	Idas and Lynceus, sons of Aphareus	Acastus, s. Pelias
Mopsus, a prophet[4]	Periclymenus, s. Neleus	Aetholides, s. Hermes
	Amphidamas and Cepheus, sons of Aleus	Dascylus, s. Lycus
Eurydamas, s. Ctimenus	Ancaeus, son of Lycurgus, the son of Aleus	Deileon, Autolycus,[12] and Phlogius, s. Deimachus.
Menoetius, s. Actor, the son of Myrmidon and Pisidice	Augeius, s. Helios	
Eurytion, s. Irus, the son of Actor (not the same as above)	Asterius and Amphion, sons of Hyperasius, s. Pelles	Sons of Phrixus, taken aboard near Colchis[13]
Eribates, s. Teleon	Euphemus, s. Europa, d. Tityos	
Butes, brother of Eribates	Erginus and Ancaeus, sons of Poseidon	
Oileus[5]	Meleager, s. Oeneus	
Canthus[6]	Laocoon, half-brother of Oeneus	
Clytius and Iphitus, sons of Erytus[7]		
Phalerus, only son of Alcon		

NOTES FOR CHART 39

[1]The Crew of the Argo   is given from Apollonius of
Rhodes, who calls them Minyae
because most of them claimed descent from the daughters
of Minyas, a king of Boeotia and son of Poseidon and
possibly one of the daughters of Aeolus.   Minyas is little more than an eponym for the inhabitants of the area
in and around Iolcus.   Apollodorus gives a similar list
of Argonauts with few changes:

Tiphys, son of Hadnias, who steered the ship
Orpheus, son of Oeagrus
Zetes and Calais, sons of Boreas
Castor and Pollux, sons of Zeus
Telamon and Peleus, sons of Aeacus
Heracles, son of Zeus
Theseus, son of Aegeus
Idas and Lynceus, sons of Aphareus
Amphiaraus, son of Oicles
Caeneus, son of Coronus
Palaemon, son of Hephaestus or of Aetolus
Cepheus, son of Aleus
Laertes, son of Arcesius
Autolycus, son of Hermes
Atalanta, daughter of Schoenus
Menoetius, son of Actor
Actor, son of Hippasus
Admetus, son of Pheres
Acastus, son of Pelias

Eurytus, son of Hermes
Meleager, son of Oeneus
Ancaeus, son of Lycurgus
Euphemus, son of Poseidon
Poeas, son of Thaumacus
Butes, son of Teleon
Phanus and Staphylus, sons of Dionysus
Erginus, son of Poseidon
Periclymenus, son of Neleus
Augeas, son of Helios
Iphiclus, son of Thestius
Argus, son of Phrixus
Euryalus, son of Mecisteus
Peneleos, son of Hippalmus
Leitus, son of Alector
Iphitus, son of Naubolus
Ascalaphus and Ialmenus, sons of Ares
Asterius, son of Cometes
Polyphemus, son of Elatus

Apollodorus gives two members whom Apollonius of
Rhodes omits and tells why he does so: Theseus and
his friend Pirithous were at this time being held prison-
ers in the Underworld; and Atalanta, who wanted to
come on the adventure but was not allowed to do so by
Jason, who felt that the lovely girl on board his ship
would stir up rivalry among the men.

[2]Polyphemus   son of Elatus and Hipseia, had fought
                with the Lapiths against the Centaurs at
the wedding of Pirithous and Hippodamia.   Now he is
described as "heavy with age," but had not lost the fighting spirit of his youth.   Polyphemus did not complete
the journey with the Argo, but was left on shore in
Mysia when Heracles left the ship to look for his squire
Hylas.   Polyphemus founded a city in Mysia, but then
became "homesick, and tramped through the Asian main-
land in search of the Argo."   He met his death in the
land of Chalybes.

[3]Coronus   son of Caenus (who had been born a woman,
             Caenis).   After being assaulted by Poseidon,
Caenis obtained power from this god to change her sex,
and she thus became Caenus, who fought with the Lapiths
and was killed by the Centaurs.   Apollonius of Rhodes
says he was "destroyed by Centaurs, yet remained
alive."   Ovid says he was changed into a bird.

[4]Mopsus   a prophet "whom Apollo had trained in the
            augury of birds."   After the death of Idmon,
Mopsus became seer for the Argonauts.   He died, however, before the ship reached home, from the bite of a
poisonous snake in the deserts of Libya.   This snake
was said to have sprung from drops of blood from the
head of Medusa when Perseus flew over Libya.   This
Mopsus should not be confused with another prophet by
the same name, a son of Apollo and Manto, a daughter
of Tiresias of Thebes.   This later Mopsus was a
prophet during the Trojan War and was somehow involved
in the death of Calchas, the famous seer of Homer's
Iliad.

[5]Oileus   a king of the Locrians, best known as the
            father of Locrian Ajax, to distinguish him
from Telamonian Ajax, both warriors in the Trojan War.

Oileus, the Argonaut, is described by Apollonius of
Rhodes as "bravest of the brave and a great man for
dashing after the enemy when their ranks were giving
away."

[6]Canthus   destined to die before the Argo reached home,
             "Fate had decided that he and the great seer
Mopsus should wander to the ends of Libya to be destroyed."   Canthus was killed in Libya by Caphaurus,
the son of Amphithemis, himself the son of Apollo and
Acacallis, a daughter of Minos of Crete.

[7]Clytius and Iphitus   sons of the "cruel" Eurytus, to
                         whom Apollo gave his bow and ar-
rows "though it did little good when he challenged the
god to a match."   Homer says in the Odyssey that Apollo killed Eurytus; however, another mythology says that
Heracles killed Eurytus for refusing to give him Iole,
the bride Heracles was bringing home when Heracles
met his death.

[8]Tiphys   son of Hagnias, was helmsman of the Argo
            until he died "of a short illness" in Bithynia.
For the remainder of the journey, Ancaeus, the son of
Poseidon and Astypalaea, was helmsman.

[9]Heracles   arrived to join the Argonauts just after com-
              pleting his Fourth Labor, capturing and de-
livering the wild boar of Erymanthus to Eurystheus.   He
was accompanied by Hylas, his "noble squire in the
first bloom of youth."   Heracles was offered the leadership of the Argonauts, but he declined, saying that no
one but Jason should lead them.   When the ship stopped
at Mysia, Hylas was drowned in a spring, and Heracles
left the journey to search for him.   Jason was accused
of jealousy and deliberately leaving Heracles behind, but
later this charge was reversed when Glaucus, a sea

Chart 39   149

deity and spokesman for Nereus, emerged from the water and told the crew that it was not the will of Zeus
that Heracles go to Colchis, that his place was in Argos,
"fated to serve his cruel Master ... to accomplish
twelve tasks," and if he succeeded in the ones that remained, to join the immortals in their home.

      The Argonauts, however, nearly met Heracles
again before their journey was over. They found the
sacred plot where, until the day before, Ladon the serpent had guarded the golden apples in the Garden of Atlas, and the Hesperides had happily taken care of the
garden. When the Argonauts arrived, the snake was
dying and the Hesperides had changed into trees: Hespere became a poplar, Erytheis an elm, and Aegle a
willow. In the Argonautica, one of the Hesperides tells
what has happened:

> There was a man here yesterday, an evil man,
> who killed the watching snake, stole our golden
> apples, and is gone.... He wore the untanned
> skin of an enormous lion and carried a great
> club of olivewood and the bows and arrows.

Some of the Argonauts immediately set out to find Heracles, but fail to do so. Lynceus reported that he
"thought he saw a lonely figure on the verge of the vast
land," but could not overtake it.

[10]Nauplius   referred to as a descendant of Danaus, is
                best known as the father of Palamedes,
who was killed by the Greeks, especially by Odysseus,
because he did not support the war against Troy. His
lineage goes back to Amymone, daughter of Danaus,
who was the mother by Poseidon of Nauplius I. Apollonius of Rhodes gives the following genealogy through
Nauplius II:

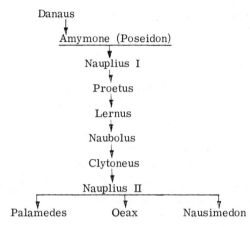

Danaus
↓
Amymone (Poseidon)
↓
Nauplius I
↓
Proetus
↓
Lernus
↓
Naubolus
↓
Clytoneus
↓
Nauplius II
↓
Palamedes   Oeax   Nausimedon

Apollodorus gives the names of the three sons, but calls
their father Nauplius I, the son of Amymone and Poseidon. It is this first Nauplius who is usually identified
as the Wrecker of Ships, the one who waited for the
ships returning from Troy and then lighted false beacons,
causing them to run aground and be destroyed on the
rocks of the shore. These actions were taken in retaliation for the murder of his son Palamedes. It is generally pointed out that Nauplius II would be more plausible
as the Wrecker of Ships, but he is not identified in this
manner.

[11]Idmon   was the last to board the Argo. He had been
         taught by Apollo to read the future from birds,
and he knew he would never return home, but he went
anyway, knowing he could not escape his fate. He was
killed by a wild boar in Bithynia just before Tiphys died.
They were both buried in the same grave.

[12]<u>Deileon, Autolycus, and Phlogius</u>   sons of Deimachus, had been living on the Assyrian coast since they lost touch with Heracles.   They were taken on board when the <u>Argo</u> passed by the region which Apollonius calls "the Assyrian coast."

[13]<u>Sons of Phrixus</u>   were taken on board when the <u>Argo</u> touched Ares' Island.   On his death-bed, Phrixus had asked his sons--Argus, Cytissorus, Phrontis, and Melas--to return to the rich lands of his father Athamas in Boeotia and claim their property. Jason found them stranded and shipwrecked, and gladly took them aboard, telling them they were kinsmen: Cretheus, a brother of Athamas, was Jason's grand-father.   Since their mother was Chalciope, a daughter of Aeetes, Jason hoped they would help in obtaining the Golden Fleece from Aeetes.

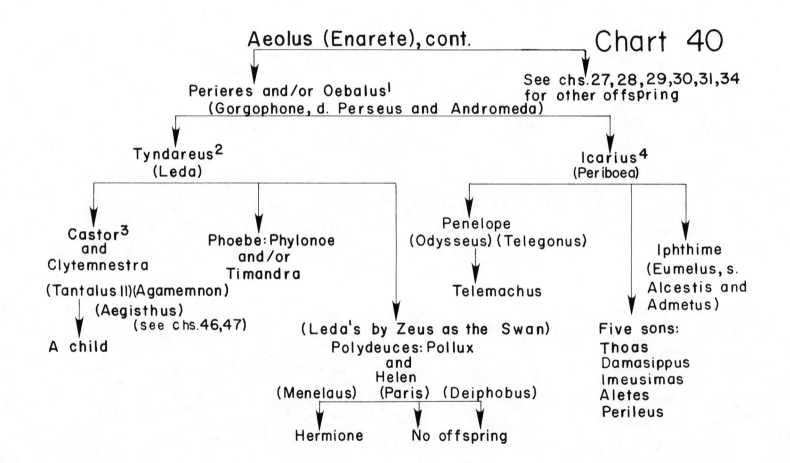

Aeolus (Enarete), cont.　　Chart 40

Perieres and/or Oebalus[1]
(Gorgophone, d. Perseus and Andromeda)

See chs.27,28,29,30,31,34
for other offspring

Tyndareus[2]
(Leda)

Icarius[4]
(Periboea)

Castor[3]
and
Clytemnestra

(Tantalus II)(Agamemnon)
(Aegisthus)
(see chs.46,47)

A child

Phoebe:Phylonoe
and/or
Timandra

Penelope
(Odysseus) (Telegonus)

Telemachus

Iphthime
(Eumelus, s.
Alcestis and
Admetus)

(Leda's by Zeus as the Swan)
Polydeuces:Pollux
and
Helen
(Menelaus)　(Paris) (Deiphobus)

Hermione　　No offspring

Five sons:
Thoas
Damasippus
Imeusimas
Aletes
Perileus

Chart 41

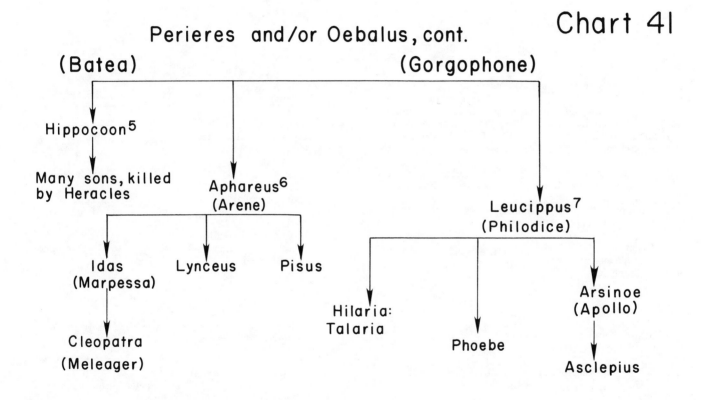

Perieres and/or Oebalus, cont.

(Batea)

(Gorgophone)

Hippocoon[5]

Many sons, killed
by Heracles

Aphareus[6]
(Arene)

Leucippus[7]
(Philodice)

Idas
(Marpessa)

Lynceus

Pisus

Hilaria:
Talaria

Phoebe

Arsinoe
(Apollo)

Cleopatra
(Meleager)

Asclepius

NOTES FOR CHARTS 40 AND 41

[1]Perieres and/or Oebalus   kings of Messenia and Spar-
                ta.   The genealogy of these
two and their descendants is almost hopelessly entangled,
and there is no tradition earlier than Apollodorus and
Pausanias to support any claim.   The following possi-
bilities are derived from Apollodorus:

(a) Aeolus   Lelex, s. Gaea,
        (Enarete)   early king of
            ↓   Laconia
     Perieres, King of Messenia   (Cleocharia)
        (Gorgophone, d. Perseus)   ↓
            ↓   Myles
     4 sons: ↓
     Aphareus   Eurotas
     Leucippus   ↓
     Tyndareus   Sparta
     Icarius

(b) Atlas, Titan son of Iapetus
        (Pleione)
            ↓
      Taygeta, one of the Pleiades
        (Zeus)
            ↓

                              Lacedaemon
                                  ↓
                              (Sparta, see inset)
                                  ↓   ┐
     Amyclas   Eurydice
     (Diomede, d. Lapithes)   (Acrisius)
         ↓   ↓
      Cynortas   Danae
         ↓   (Zeus)
      Perieres   ↓
      (Gorgophone)   Perseus
         ↓   (Andromeda)
     4 sons: ↓
     Tyndareus, Icaius   sons and
     Aphareus (Arene, d. Oebalus)   Gorgophone
     Leucippus

(c) Aeolus   Cynortas, s. Amyclas
         ↓   ↓
     Perieres   Perieres
     (Gorgophone, d.   ↓
        | Perseus)   Oebalus
         ↓   (Gorgophone) (Bates) (Unknown)
     Aphrareus (Arene)   ↓   ↓   ↓
         and   Tyndareus   Hippocoon   Arene
     Leucippus   Icarius   ↓
                                        Many sons
                                        killed by
                                        Heracles

(d) Gorgophone, d. Perseus

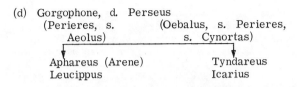

    (Perieres, s.   (Oebalus, s. Perieres,
      Aeolus)   s. Cynortas)

Aphareus (Arene)   Tyndareus
Leucippus   Icarius

[2]Tyndareus   son of Perieres or Oebalus; brother of
Icarius, and possibly half-brother of Aphareus and Leucippus. Tyndareus was driven out of Sparta by Hippocoon, another brother or half-brother, and
fled to the court of King Thestius in Aetolia. Here he
married Leda, daughter of King Thestius. Tyndareus
was later restored to the throne by Heracles, who killed
Hippocoon and his twelve sons. Leda had six children,
at least two of whom claimed Zeus as their father:
Helen and Pollux. Tyndareus was the father of Clytemnestra, and Castor is usually called the son of Tyndareus, but at his death he too became a son of Zeus
with his brother Pollux. As deities, Castor and Pollux
are called the Dioscuri, the sons of Zeus. According
to Apollodorus, Tyndareus and Leda also had other daugh-
ters--Timandra, whom Echemus married, and Phylonoe,
whom Artemis made immortal. In Hesiod's The Catalogue of Women, it is said that Tyndareus forgot to sacrifice to the goddess Aphrodite, and in anger the goddess made his daughters "twice and thrice wed and de-
serters of their husbands." Timandra deserted Echemus
and went to Phyleus, King of Dulichium.

The choosing of Helen's husband was a crucial
matter for Tyndareus, since nearly all the eligible young
princes of Greece were contending for her hand. Tyndareus feared there would be war once the decision was
made. On the advice of Odysseus, who was a suitor for
Penelope, the daughter of Icarius, Tyndareus bound all
of Helen's suitors to a sacred oath that they would support his choice of Helen's husband, and furthermore

that they would punish anyone who molested Helen in the
future. Some writers say that Helen had already been
carried off once, when she was ten years old, by Theseus of Athens. She was rescued on this occasion by
her brothers, the Dioscuri, who led a force of Spartans
and Arcadians and plundered Athens in the process.
They abducted Aethra, the mother of Theseus, to be
Helen's slave, and it is said that Helen took Aethra with
her when she later went to Troy with Paris.

Tyndareus finally chose Menelaus, the son of
Atreus, who had brought the richest gifts, and also perhaps because his daughter Clytemnestra had already married Agamemnon, the brother of Menelaus. At the deaths
of Castor and Pollux, Tyndareus made Menelaus his successor to the kingdom of Sparta.

[3]Castor and   sons of Tyndareus, according to
Polydeuces: Pollux Homer, although other writers
                         say that Polydeuces was a son of
Zeus. They went with Jason and the Argonauts to Colchis, but with the exception of Polydeuces' boxing match
with Amycus, did not especially distinguish themselves.
Ovid says they went to the Calydonian Boar Hunt, and
calls them "twin sons of Tyndareus." By the time of
the Trojan War, Castor and Polydeuces were dead.
Helen, sitting on the Wall of Troy, in the Iliad, tries
to find her brothers among the ranks, not knowing they
were already dead. The manner in which they met
death is variously given, although it always involves
their cousins, Idas and Lynceus, sons of Aphareus. One
account says that Castor and Polydeuces abducted their
cousins Hilaria and Phoebe, daughters of Leucippus,
who were already betrothed to Idas and Lynceus. In the
fight that ensued, all four brother-cousins were killed.
Another story has it that the fight came about because
Idas and Lynceus cheated Castor and Polydeuces in a
raid they all made on a herd of Arcadian cattle. One

other variation in the story is that Idas killed Castor, Polydeuces killed Lynceus, and just as Idas was about to kill Polydeuces, Zeus saved his son by killing Idas with a thunderbolt.   In any case, Polydeuces was so be-reaved over the death of Castor that he prayed to Zeus to allow him to share his immortality with his brother. They then became the Dioscuri, "sons of Zeus," minor gods who protected mariners at sea.   They also became stars, and are identified as the Gemini Twins constella-tion.   At the end of Euripides' Electra, they appear and say that Clytemnestra was wrong to kill Agamemnon, and that Orestes was equally wrong to kill Clytemnestra. Euripides ironically uses them here to pronounce a just verdict on the sorry business of blood revenge in con-trast to the great god Apollo, who had decreed that Orestes should kill his mother.

[4]Icarius   son of Perieres, or Oebalus, and Gorgophone,
          and best known as the father of Penelope, wife of Odysseus.   According to Apollodorus, Icarius married Periboea, a Naiad nymph, by whom he had five sons, Thoas, Damasippus, Imeusimas, Aletes, and Perileus, and a daughter, Penelope.   In the Odyssey, however, Homer says Penelope had a sister, Iphthime, married to Eumelus, son of Alcestis and Admetus. Perileus is said by Pausanias to have been the accuser of Orestes at his trial in Athens.   When Odysseus won the hand of Penelope, Icarius begged his daughter and son-in-law to settle in Sparta, but Odysseus refused and returned to his kingdom in Ithaca.   There are no major stories of Icarius, or accounts of his death.

[5]Hippocoon   son of Oebalus and a Naiad nymph, Batea.
          Apollodorus does not name Hippocoon's wife, but says he had sons: Dorycleus, Scaeus, Enarophorus, Eutiches, Bucolus, Lycaethus, Tebrus, Hippothous, Eurytus, Hippocorystes, Alcinus, and Alcon.   These sons and their father forced Tyndareus, and possibly Icarius,

to leave the kingdom.   Later, Heracles, having taken Pylus and killed Neleus and his sons, marched against Hippocoon and his sons.   Heracles was angry because Hippocoon had fought with Neleus, and also because the sons of Hippocoon had killed one of his kinsmen.   After mustering a considerable army, Heracles killed Hippo-coon and all his sons, and restored the kingdom to Tyndareus.

[6]Aphareus   son of Perieres and Gorgophone, who with
          his brother Leucippus inherited the king-dom of Messenia at their father's death.   Aphareus mar-ried Arene, said to be the daughter of Oebalus, his mother's second husband.   He founded a city and named it for his wife.   Apollodorus says they had three sons, Lynceus, Idas, and Pisus, but gives no further informa-tion about Pisus.   Idas and Lynceus were among those who sailed on the Argo and later hunted the Calydonian Boar.   Sometime prior to these events, apparently as a young man, Idas had abducted Marpessa, daughter of Evenus, by whom he had a daughter, Cleopatra, who married Meleager.   After the Calydonian Boar Hunt, Idas and Lynceus were both killed in a conflict with Castor and Polydeuces.   After the deaths of his sons, Aphareus left his kingdom to Neleus, to whom he had already given much land, including the city of Pylus.

[7]Leucippus   brother of Aphareus and joint ruler of
          Messenia.   He married Philodice, by whom he had only daughters, Hilaria, Phoebe, and Arsinoe. Hilaria and Phoebe were on their way to marry their cousins Idas and Lynceus, when Castor and Polydeuces carried them off.   Nothing further is said of their fate, but the two pairs of brothers were eventually killed by each other, possibly over the girls.   The third daughter, Arsinoe, is sometimes called the mother of Asclepius by Apollo, but generally Coronis, a daughter of Phlegyas, is said to be the mother.

158

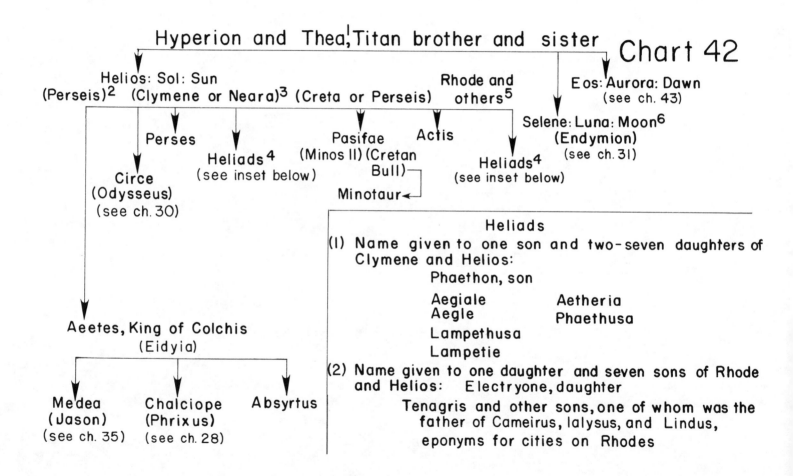

Hyperion and Thea, Titan brother and sister   Chart 42

Helios: Sol: Sun
(Perseis)[2]   (Clymene or Neara)[3]   (Creta or Perseis)   Rhode and others[5]   Eos: Aurora: Dawn
(see ch. 43)

Perses   Actis   Selene: Luna: Moon[6]
(Endymion)
(see ch. 31)

Circe
(Odysseus)
(see ch. 30)   Heliads[4]
(see inset below)   Pasifae
(Minos II)   (Cretan
Bull)   Heliads[4]
(see inset below)

Minotaur

Aeetes, King of Colchis
(Eidyia)

Medea
(Jason)
(see ch. 35)   Chalciope
(Phrixus)
(see ch. 28)   Absyrtus

Heliads
(1) Name given to one son and two-seven daughters of
Clymene and Helios:
Phaethon, son

Aegiale   Aetheria
Aegle   Phaethusa
Lampethusa
Lampetie

(2) Name given to one daughter and seven sons of Rhode
and Helios: Electryone, daughter

Tenagris and other sons, one of whom was the
father of Cameirus, Ialysus, and Lindus,
eponyms for cities on Rhodes

Eos: Aurora: Dawn[7]   Chart 43

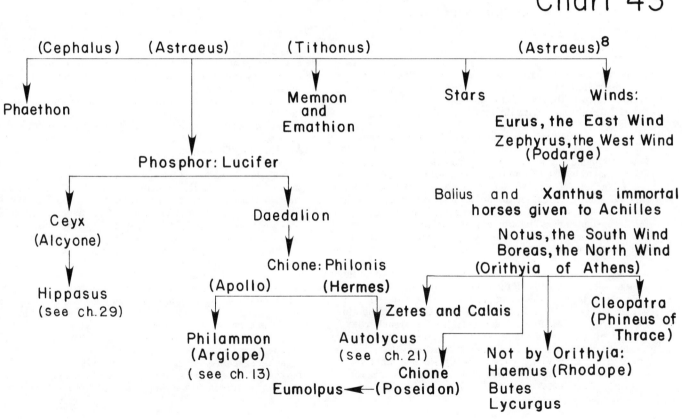

NOTES FOR CHARTS 42 AND 43

[1]<u>Hyperion and Thea</u>   Titan brother and sister, offspring of Uranus and Gaea. To them were born Helios, called Sol (the Sun) by the Romans; Selene, called Luna (the Moon) by the Romans; and Eos, called Aurora (the Dawn) by the Romans. Eos is sometimes interchanged with Hemera, the Day.

[2]<u>Perseis</u>   daughter of Oceanus and Tethys, married Helios, by whom she had three or four notable offspring: Aeetes, King of Colchis; Circe, an enchantress who left Colchis and went to live far away on the Island of Aeaea; Perses, who Apollodorus says overthrew Aeetes and assumed the throne; and Pasifae, who married Minos II of Crete and was the mother of the Minotaur and numerous other sons and daughters. Pasifae is obscurely referred to as the daughter of Helios and Creta, the sister of Minos of Crete.

Aeetes, who married Eidyia or Idyia, the youngest daughter of Oceanus and Tethys, is portrayed in the <u>Argonautica</u> as the barbaric and hostile king of the Colchians, to whom Phrixus had given the ram with the golden fleece. When Jason arrived at Colchis to obtain the fleece, it was Aeetes who set him the treacherous task of plowing the field of Ares and planting the dragon's teeth. Without the help of Aeetes' daughter Medea, Jason and his men would have thus perished at what then was almost literally the ends of the earth. Many years after the Argonauts' visit to Colchis, Aeetes was de-

posed by his brother Perses. Apollodorus further adds that Medea and her son Medeus, or Medus, by Aegeus of Athens, returned to Colchis, killed Perses, and restored the kingdom to Aeetes. At the death of Aeetes, Medeus assumed the throne in the absence of a male heir.

Absyrtus, or Apsyrtus, the only son of Aeetes, died by some brutal means at the hands of Jason and Medea. In the <u>Argonautica</u>, Apollonius of Rhodes says he was the son of Aeetes and Asterodeia, a nymph, and was called "Phaethon" by his father because he "outshone them all." He is depicted in this work as leading his father's men in pursuit of Jason and the Argonauts after they had taken the golden fleece. Later he was ambushed and killed by Jason. Apollodorus describes Absyrtus as a young child whom Medea destroyed by dismembering his body and casting the parts on the water as she and Jason fled from Colchis. Aeetes, in pursuit, was detained by gathering up the parts of his son's body, and thus Medea and Jason escaped. The death of Absyrtus is not mentioned in Euripides' <u>Medea</u>, although in this tragedy, Medea recounts several hideous deeds she has committed for Jason's sake.

Chalciope, the other daughter of Aeetes, appears in the <u>Argonautica</u> as the mother of four sons whom she is anxious to see escape Colchis with the Argonauts, fearing for their lives at the hands of Aeetes. Phrixus, the son of Athamas and Nephele, to whom Aeetes had married Chalciope, is referred to as having died by the time the Argonauts came to Colchis.

Other stories of the offspring of Helios and Perseis are found elsewhere. Circe, usually associated with Odysseus, is said by some authors to have had several children by the Ithacan, but this matter is not mentioned by Homer. Perses is referred to only in connection with usurping the kingdom of Colchis. Pasifae, as the wife of Minos of Crete, was the mother of several well-known offspring, including Phaedra, Ariadne, and the bullman Minotaur.

[3]Clymene or Neara   Clymene is identifiable only as the mother by Helios of the Heliads, and particularly of the son Phaethon. There are some ten or twelve figures called Clymene, none of which have much individuality. Ovid says this Clymene, wife of Helios, was also the wife of Merops, a king of Ethiopia. After the death of her son Phaethon, Clymene, "out of her mind with grief, roved the whole world, seeking the lifeless limbs, and later the bones of her son."

[4]Heliads   the term means "children of Helios," but in most mythology dictionaries, the reference is restricted to the daughters, from two to seven, and the son Phaethon by Clymene. The name is also given to the seven sons and one daughter whom Helios had by Rhode, a daughter of Poseidon, and eponym for the Island of Rhodes. Of these, little or nothing is known. One dictionary says, "One of these sons became the father of Cameirus, Ialysus, and Lindus, who divided the island, and gave their names to its principal cities" (Crowell's Handbook of Classical Mythology). Another book of mythology says that "by Rhode, Helios had seven sons, the Heliads, and one daughter, Electryone. One of these, Tenagris, aroused the jealousy of his brothers,

who murdered him. After the murder, they dispersed among the islands in the neighborhood of Rhodes" (Larousse, Encyclopedia of Mythology).

The only widely known story of any of the Heliads is that of Phaethon and his early tragic death. As the story is told by Ovid, Phaethon, who had been taunted by his friend Epaphus, the son of Io and Zeus, asked his mother Clymene for proof that the Sun was his father. She sent him to the East, where Helios kept his palace, and there Phaethon bargained that if Helios were really his father, he would grant any wish that the youth should make. Reluctantly, Helios gave his word and swore an irrevocable oath. Phaethon then asked that he be allowed to take the chariot of the Sun across the heavens. With much misgiving, Helios granted the request. The fierce horses quickly went out of control, and Phaethon in panic went this way and that, away from the earth, then too close to the earth, scorching the land and drying up the rivers and lakes. Zeus saw what was happening, and fearing that even Olympus was endangered, he threw a thunderbolt and struck the youth dead. His body fell into the Eridanus River. In the Argonautica, the still-smoldering body of Phaethon is passed by the crew, and its stench is commented upon. At the death of Phaethon, his sisters were so bereaved that they wept unceasingly until they were turned into poplar trees along the Eridanus River.

[5]Rhode (or Rhodos) and Others   Rhode is usually called the daughter of Poseidon and Amphitrite, or, according to one source, Aphrodite. By Helios, she was the mother of the Heliads, and also a son, Actis, who fled Rhodes and founded the city of Heliopolis in Egypt.

Of the other children of Helios, only two are generally known. Apollodorus calls Augeias a son of Helios, but does not name his mother. In his catalog of crew members, Apollodorus names Augeias as one of the Argonauts, but he is best known as the owner of the filthy stables. One of Heracles' Twelve Labors was to cleanse these stables in a single day, which he did by diverting a river through them and washing them clean of an extraordinary accumulation of dung. The other familiar story of Helios is that involving Leucothea, the daughter of King Orchamus of Persia, and Clytie.

6Selene   daughter of Hyperion and Thea, is best known
             as the Moon, who loved Endymion and offered him eternal youth. Other sources say Selene also had offspring by Zeus, a daughter Pandia, and Erse. Sometimes she is said to have had fifty daughters by Endymion, but Pausanias, for example, says this is not reasonable to suppose. Selene may have been the mother of the Nemean Lion, but this monster is usually assigned to Echidna and Orthos, and Selene is said to have suckled it. Heracles killed the Nemean Lion as his First Labor and thereafter wore its skin. Selene came to be identified with Artemis or the Roman Diana, and in some respects with Hecate, as "the night-wandering" goddess.

7Eos   the goddess of the dawn, was called Aurora by
          the Romans, and is sometimes identified as Hemera, the Day, daughter of Erebus and Nyx. As the sister of Helios, the Sun, it was her duty to announce the approach of his chariot and to accompany her brother across the heavens. Eos, says Hesiod, married Astraeus, the son of Eurybia and the Titan Crius (or Creus), and became mother of the winds and stars. Eos, however, was a notoriously amorous goddess, and her mythology consists largely of stories of other beautiful young men whom she carried off as her consorts. One of the best-known stories of Eos and her lovers is that of Cephalus, the son of Herse and Hermes, or the son of Deion (or Deioneus), King of Phocis. Apollodorus

says that there were two figures with the name Cephalus, and that it was the son of Herse and Hermes whom Eos abducted. Ovid, however, combines the two figures and tells the story as it involves Eos, Cephalus, and Procris, the wife whom Cephalus finally shot in a fatal accident. According to Hesiod, Eos and Cephalus were parents of a son, called Phaethon, whom Aphrodite carried away to be the guardian of her temple at night.

There are several versions of the parentage of Phosphor, or Lucifer, as the Romans called him, the Morning Star. One version is that he was the son of Eos by Cephalus, another that he was the son of Eos by Zeus, and still a third that he, like the other stars, was the son of Eos and Astraeus. The stories of Phosphor's sons and their progeny are mostly told by Ovid. Apollodorus accounts for Hippasus, a son of Ceyx, who fought and died in one of Heracles' wars. Ovid tells the story of Chione, or Philonis, the daughter of Daedalion, a brother of Ceyx. Chione is said to have been loved by two gods, Apollo and Hermes, within the same night and to have borne twins: Autolycus, "a true son of his crafty father," Hermes; and Philammon, a son of Apollo, "renowned for his singing and his playing of the lyre." Chione became so proud of herself that she boasted of her beauty and said it excelled even that of Artemis, whereupon the goddess took swift revenge and killed the girl. Daedalion, her father, was so bereaved at the loss of his daughter that he threw himself from the summit of Mount Parnassus. Apollo took pity and changed him into a bird, "a hawk with a hooked beak, and curving crooked talons."

Later Ovid tells the story of Ceyx and Alcyone, a daughter of Aeolus, and their transformation into kingfishers. When Ceyx was drowned at sea, Alcyone was so grief stricken that the gods again took pity, and changed them both into kingfishers. Apollodorus, however, says that Ceyx and Alcyone perished because of their pride, and because they addressed each other as Hera and Zeus, for which Zeus changed her into a kingfisher and him into a seagull.

Although Apollodorus says Tithonus was a son of Eos by Cephalus, it is generally said that Tithonus was a son of Laomedon whom Eos carried off to be her lover. In the Iliad, Eos, "rosy-fingered Dawn," is said to arise from "Tithonus' couch." In The Trojan Women, the chorus laments on the past favors that the gods had showered on the Trojans, among which was Eos' love for Tithonus, by whom she had two sons, Memnon and Emathion. Of the latter, very little is known except that, according to Apollodorus, he was a king of Arabia and was killed by Heracles. Of Memnon there is much to be said. King of Ethiopia, he is described as "swarthy Memnon," ruler of countless tribes in the "land of the black man." His story is told or at least referred to by Homer, Virgil, Apollodorus, and Ovid, but is fullest represented in the work by Quintus of Smyrna. After the death of Hector, the Trojan cause was considerably weakened. First, Penthesileia, the Amazon Queen, brought her army to Troy, but was soon defeated and killed by Achilles. Then came Memnon, a great warrior king, second to none in bravery and courage, but Achilles also killed him, after Memnon had destroyed many Greeks, including Antilochus, the favored son of old Nestor of Pylus. At Memnon's death, Eos obtained special honors for her son's body, as she had obtained the gift of immortality for her lover Tithonus. In the case of Tithonus, however, she forgot to ask also for the gift of youth, and so he grew old but could not die. One myth says that finally Eos changed Tithonus into a grasshopper or a cicada.

Of the other amors of Eos, very little has become familiar story. Orion, the giant hunter, is said by one myth to have been shot by Artemis because he lay with Eos. Cleitus, a son of Mantius and grandson of Melampus, was "snatched away by Dawn that he might dwell with the immortals," according to Homer in the Odyssey. Apollodorus says Aphrodite caused Eos to be perpetually in love because "she had bedded with Ares," who was Aphrodite's lover.

[8]Astraeus   son of the Titan Crius and Eurybia, daughter of Pontus and Gaea, the name means "starry sky." Although married to Eos, and father of the winds and stars, he does not emerge as any sort of personality, and there are no stories of conflicts between Astraeus and other lover-consorts of his wife. Hesiod says that Astraeus and Eos were parents of Notus, the South Wind; Boreas, the North Wind; and Zephyrus, the West Wind. Other winds, this writer says, are descended from Typhoeus "whose breath drives the rain." The winds were thought of as gods, although on at least two occasions such might not appear to be true. In Homer's Odyssey, their keeper Aeolus put them in a bag and gave them to the unsuspecting Odysseus; in Virgil's Aeneid, also, their keeper Aeolus is persuaded by Juno (Hera) to let "the brawlers out of their cave," in order to raise a tremendous storm against the wandering Trojans. In these two works, Aeolus is called the lord or keeper of the winds and is not referred to as their father. This Aeolus should not be confused with Aeolus, the son of Hellen, eponym of the Aeolians.

The West Wind, Zephyrus, and the North Wind, Boreas, emerge as better defined personalities than any of the other winds. This is perhaps the case because more mythology has accumulated around certain of their offspring. For example, Zephyrus by the Harpy Podarge was the father of the immortal horses Xanthus and Balius. The gods gave these horses to Peleus at his wedding to Thetis, and Peleus in turn gave them to Achilles, who took them to Troy. At the death of Patroclus, the horses weep, and Zeus regrets giving them to mortals.

Later in the Iliad, Xanthus warns Achilles of his impending fate, knowledge Achilles already has from his mother Thetis. At the death of Achilles, Xanthus and Balius will submit to being handled by no one except Neoptolemus, the son of Achilles, who later joins the Greek forces at Troy.

The most familiar story of Boreas is that he courted and abducted Orithyia, a daughter of King Erechtheus of Athens, and carried her off to his palace in Thrace. By Boreas she became the mother of Zetes and Calais, famous for their ability to fly, and two daughters, Chione and Cleopatra. Apollodorus says that Chione was seduced by Poseidon and bore a son Eumolpus. Either ashamed or afraid of her father, Chione threw the infant into the sea, but Poseidon rescued him and took him to Ethiopia, where he grew to manhood in the court of Benthesicyme, also a daughter of Poseidon. Cleopatra married Phineus, a soothsayer-king of Thrace. His parentage is variously given as either the son of Agenor or Poseidon. By Phineus, Cleopatra was the mother of two sons, whom Apollodorus calls Plexippus and Pandion. Beyond this, the different stories of Phineus and Cleopatra are much at odds with each other. Apollonius of Rhodes devotes one lengthy episode to Phineus in the Argonautica, and in this work, the former soothsayer-king has been blinded by Zeus because he presumed to reveal too much of the gods' wills to mortals. He is constantly harassed by the Harpies--filthy, incontinent bird-women in this poem--almost to the point of starvation. When the Argonauts stop by the coast of Bithynia, where Phineus is living in exile, Zetes and Calais, his brothers-in-law, rid Phineus of the Harpies, and restore the old man to a decent life. The other story of Phineus is told by Apollodorus, and is also incorporated by Sophocles in one of the Choral Odes of the Antigone. In this version of the story Phineus married a second wife, Idaea, after the death of Cleopatra. She persuaded her husband that his two sons by Cleopatra had violated her virtue, and then either she or the father blinded them and imprisoned them in a tomb. When the Argonauts put in at Bithynia, says Apollodorus, they rescued Cleopatra's two sons, who, with the help of their grandfather Boreas, blinded Phineus and otherwise punished him. This version of the story is appropriately referred to in Antigone because of the entombment motif.

Other than their role in the story of Phineus, whether it was to save him or to punish him, Zetes and Calais have little mythology. Apollonius of Rhodes says it was largely they who persuaded Jason to discontinue the search for Heracles at Mysia, and adds by way of forecast:

> Unhappy pair! A dreadful punishment was coming to them at the hands of Heracles for having thus cut short the search for him. He killed them in sea-girt Tenos on their way home from the games at Pelias' funeral, made a barrow over them and on top set a couple of pillars, one of which amazes all beholders by swaying to the breath of the roaring North Wind.

Boreas, the North Wind, was not especially given to taking mistresses, but several other children are assigned to him: Lycurgus and Butes by two different mothers; Haemus, merely the eponym for a range of mountains in Thrace, who married Rhodope, an adjacent mountain range in Thrace; and, finally, he is said to have mated with the splendid mares of Erichthonius, the son of Dardanus and Batea, and to have become the sire of the famous Trojan horses, who like their father, were as swift as the wind.

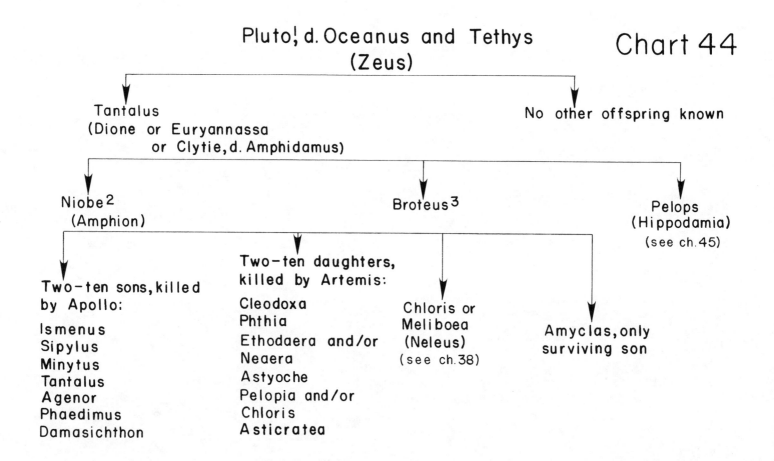

166

Pluto¦ d. Oceanus and Tethys　　Chart 44
(Zeus)

Tantalus
(Dione or Euryannassa
or Clytie, d. Amphidamus)

No other offspring known

Niobe²
(Amphion)

Broteus³

Pelops
(Hippodamia)
(see ch. 45)

Two-ten sons, killed
by Apollo:

Ismenus
Sipylus
Minytus
Tantalus
Agenor
Phaedimus
Damasichthon

Two-ten daughters,
killed by Artemis:

Cleodoxa
Phthia
Ethodaera and/or
Neaera
Astyoche
Pelopia and/or
Chloris
Asticratea

Chloris or
Meliboea
(Neleus)
(see ch. 38)

Amyclas, only
surviving son

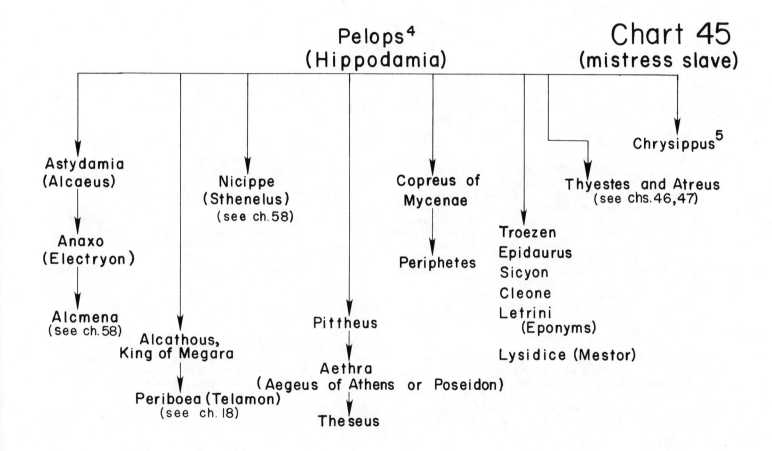

Pelops⁴
(Hippodamia)

Chart 45
(mistress slave)

Chrysippus⁵

Astydamia
(Alcaeus)

Nicippe
(Sthenelus)
(see ch.58)

Copreus of
Mycenae

Thyestes and Atreus
(see chs.46,47)

Anaxo
(Electryon)

Troezen
Epidaurus
Sicyon
Cleone
Letrini
(Eponyms)

Periphetes

Alcmena
(see ch.58)

Pittheus

Lysidice (Mestor)

Alcathous,
King of Megara

Aethra
(Aegeus of Athens or Poseidon)

Periboea (Telamon)
(see ch.18)

Theseus

NOTES FOR CHARTS 44 AND 45

[1]Pluto   one of the Oceanids, by Zeus was the mother
              of Tantalus, who became best known as one of
the extraordinary criminals thrown into Tartarus.   He
is referred to by Virgil when Aeneas is in the Underworld, and is more fully described by Homer when
Odysseus visits the Underworld:

> ... I saw Tantalus in violent torment, standing
> in a pool, and the water came nigh unto his chin.
> He seemed as one athirst, but could not take and
> drink; for as often as that old man stooped down,
> eager to drink, so often would the water be swal-
> lowed up and vanish away, and at his feet the
> black earth would appear, for some god made all
> dry.   And trees, high and leafy, let stream their
> fruits above his head, pears, and pomegranates,
> and apple trees with their bright fruit, and sweet
> figs, and luxuriant olives.   But as often as that
> old man would reach out toward these, to clutch
> them with his hands, the wind would toss them
> to the shadowy clouds.

There are several versions of the crime Tantalus committed to earn this hard punishment.   One story has it
that Tantalus, who received special favor from the gods,
repaid them by stealing their ambrosia and nectar and
telling their secrets to mortals.   A second story says
that Tantalus was involved in aiding the thief of the golden
dog of Zeus, which the god kept on guard at his temple
in Crete.   Still a third, and the most repugnant, version
of his crime is that he scorned the wisdom of the gods,
and in order to test them, murdered his own son Pelops
and served him to the gods.   The gods knew at once,
and fled in horror.   It is said that Demeter took one
bite of the shoulder before she realized what she had
done.   By Dione, one of the Oceanids, or some other
water nymph, Tantalus was the father of Pelops, the
son whom he murdered, Niobe, and Broteas.

[2]Niobe   daughter of Tantalus, should not be confused
              with another Niobe, the daughter of Phoroneus,
the first mortal woman whom Zeus loved.   The daughter
of Tantalus married Amphion, whom Homer identifies in
the Odyssey as "the son of Iasus, who once ruled might-
ily in Orchomenus of the Minyae." Homer also refers
to Amphion and Zethus of Thebes, but in no wise con-
nects this Amphion with Niobe.   The names and numbers of Niobe's children vary somewhat.   Hesiod, in
The Catalogue of Women, says she had "six daughters
and six lusty sons" all of whom perished.   Apollodorus
gives the number as seven sons and the same number
of daughters, and supplies the list of names.   In telling
the story at some length, Ovid refers to seven sons and
seven daughters, naming the sons: Ismenus, Sipylus,
Phaedimus, Tantalus, Alphenor, Damasichthon, and
Ilioneus.   He does not give any names to the daughters,

but says that all of Niobe's children perished, and that the father, Amphion, killed himself. Homer says that Niobe had six sons and six daughters, but does not name any of them. Apollodorus refers to a source that says that of the females, Chloris, the eldest, who had married Neleus of Messenia, was spared and that a son, Amyclas, survived.

As to why such disaster fell upon Niobe's children, all sources are consistent. Proud of the extraordinary number of children she had borne, Niobe boasted of herself and scorned the goddess Leto, who had but two children. Leto summoned her two children, Apollo and Artemis, who promptly killed Niobe's children. After this slaughter, Niobe wept without ceasing. Finally she returned to her father's home in Lydia, where the gods took pity on her and changed her into a fountain on Mount Sipylus.

[3]Broteas   son of Tantalus of whom very little is known.
Apollodorus says he was "a hunter, did not honor Artemis, and said that even fire could not hurt him. So he went mad and threw himself into the fire." Pausanias says it was this son of Tantalus who carved in stone the oldest image of Rhea, or Cybele, on the side of Mount Sipylus.

[4]Pelops   son of Tantalus, whose life was marked with
deeds of exceptional violence and lawlessness. First, he was the son whom Tantalus cut up and served to the gods. The gods restored him to life, however, and replaced the shoulder that Demeter had eaten with one of ivory. In his courtship of Hippodamia, the daughter of Oenomaus of Pisa, himself the son of Ares and the Pleiade Sterope, Pelops was less than honest. In order to win his daughter, Oenomaus required the suitor to compete in a chariot race, and if the suitor lost, Oenomaus lopped off his head. Before Pelops came, a

number of suitors had thus perished, and their heads were nailed over the palace doors as grim reminders. Pelops determined that he would not fall victim to this fate, and so bribed Myrtilus, Oenomaus' charioteer, to insert pins of wax in the wheels of Oenomaus' chariot. The king was thus killed, and Pelops carried his bride away. Later, he killed Myrtilus, a son of Hermes. As he died, Myrtilus invoked a curse of the gods on the House of Pelops.

Among their descendants were daughters who married kings in Argolis, sons who became powerful rulers of their own kingdoms, and many sons who founded and gave their names to great cities. Except as discussed elsewhere, there is little mythology connected with the offspring of Pelops and Hippodamia.

[5]Chrysippus   a natural son of Pelops by a nymph or a
mistress slave. There are several versions of his death, but the usual story is that he was murdered at Hippodamia's request by her sons Atreus and Thyestes because she feared Pelops would make him heir to the throne of Pisa. At the death of Chrysippus, Hippodamia either killed herself or fled from the wrath of Pelops to live with her sons Atreus or Thyestes.

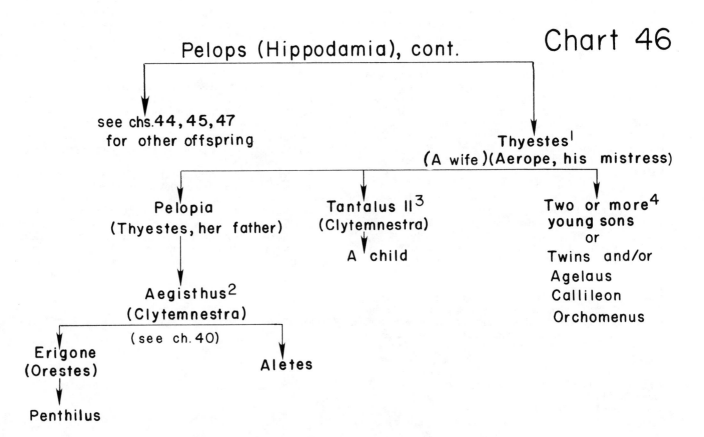

Chart 46

Pelops (Hippodamia), cont.

see chs. 44, 45, 47
for other offspring

Thyestes[1]
(A wife)(Aerope, his mistress)

Pelopia
(Thyestes, her father)

Tantalus II[3]
(Clytemnestra)

A child

Two or more[4]
young sons
or
Twins and/or
Agelaus
Callileon
Orchomenus

Aegisthus[2]
(Clytemnestra)

(see ch. 40)

Erigone
(Orestes)

Aletes

Penthilus

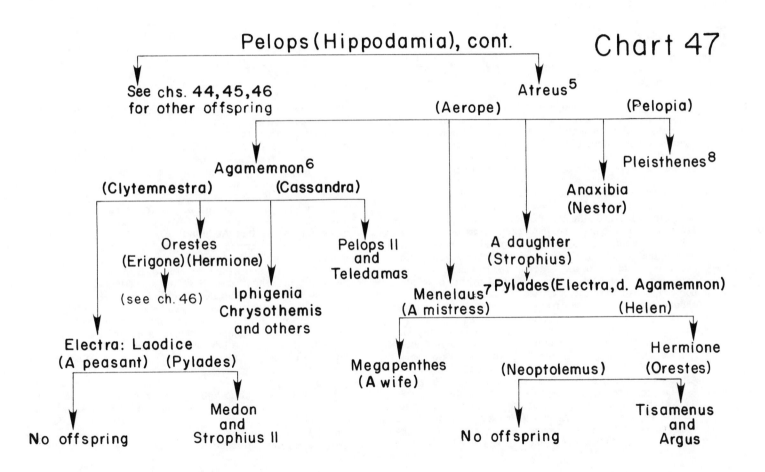

Pelops (Hippodamia), cont.   Chart 47

NOTES FOR CHARTS 46 AND 47

[1]Thyestes   son of Pelops and Hippodamia and brother of Atreus, with whom his life was horribly entangled. Atreus married Aerope, the daughter of a Cretan king, Catreus, who had sold her because she committed adultery with one of the slaves. As the wife of Atreus, she continued to commit adultery with Thyestes. Furthermore, she stole from her husband a golden fleece that Atreus had failed to sacrifice to Artemis, and gave it to her lover. After the deaths of both Sthenelus and his son Eurystheus, the throne of Mycenae was vacant, and the oracle gave out that the new king should be Thyestes or Atreus. Thyestes suggested that the throne should go to the one who could produce a golden fleece. Atreus readily agreed, only to discover that he had been betrayed by his wife and no longer had the golden fleece. Atreus, acting on orders from Zeus, then proposed that the throne should go to the one who could produce a reversal in the sun's course. Thyestes now readily consented, thinking his brother had no chance of bringing off such a phenomenon. It nonetheless happened, and thus Atreus became king, immediately banishing his brother, who fled the city. After he learned of Aerope's unfaithfulness with Thyestes, Atreus regretted that he had exiled his brother beyond the reach of vengeance, and pretended to be reconciled. At this reconciliation, Atreus killed at least two of the young sons of Thyestes and served them to their father, who ate, and did not know until it was too late. When Atreus revealed the truth of the matter, Thyestes once more fled and began plans for further retaliation. An oracle told Thyestes that he could avenge himself by having a child by his own daughter Pelopia. This event subsequently took place, and the child was Aegisthus. In the meantime, however, Atreus had taken Pelopia for his mistress, and when her child was born, Atreus adopted it as his own. In due time Thyestes was seized and brought back to Mycenae, where Atreus imprisoned him and sent Aegisthus to kill him. Thyestes recognized the sword that Aegisthus carried as his own, and thus was able to recognize his son. Pelopia was summoned, and when she realized that she had borne a child by her father, she killed herself with the sword. Aegisthus took the bloody sword as evidence that the hated brother (Thyestes) was dead, and catching Atreus off-guard, killed him instantly. Thyestes once again was on the throne, but soon the kingdom was invaded by Agamemnon and Menelaus, the sons of Atreus, and Thyestes fled for the last time. There is no information as to when or how he died; however, Apollodorus says he went to Cytheria.

[2]Aegisthus   son of Pelopia and Thyestes, as explained above. When the throne of Mycenae was assumed by Agamemnon, Aegisthus went into exile. While Agamemnon was engaged in the ten-year Trojan War, Aegisthus returned to Mycenae, where he and

Clytemnestra, Agamemnon's queen, became lovers and planned to kill the king upon his return home. Aeschylus, Sophocles, Euripides, and Homer before them, each gave his own version of the role Aegisthus played in the murder of Agamemnon, ranging from total guilt (in Homer) to merely acting as a pawn for Clytemnestra. Some years later, Agamemnon's son Orestes returned from exile and killed Aegisthus and his own mother Clytemnestra. According to Sophocles, Clytemnestra and Aegisthus had children of their own, but they are not named. A daughter Erigone is named by Pausanias, and she is said to have borne a son by Orestes.

[3]Tantalus   son of Thyestes, is said by one source to have perished at the hands of Atreus at the infamous banquet; however, Euripides, in Iphigenia in Aulis, says Tantalus was the first husband of Clytemnestra. Agamemnon killed Tantalus and a child, and married Clytemnestra himself.

[4]Two or More Young Sons   the names and number of whom vary. Apollodorus says they were Agalaus, Callileon, and Orchomenus, whom Thyestes had by a Naiad nymph. Aeschylus says there were two of them, but gives no names. Still another source gives them as Tantalus and Pleisthenes. Whatever their names or numbers, they were slaughtered by Atreus and served at a banquet to their father Thyestes.

[5]Atreus   son of Pelops and Hippodamia, and brother of Thyestes. Apart from this brother, Atreus has no mythology.

[6]Agamemnon   son of Atreus, according to Homer, although another tradition says Agamemnon

and Menelaus were sons of Atreus' son Pleisthenes. After killing Tantalus, a son of Thyestes, Agamemnon married Clytemnestra, daughter of Tyndareus and Leda, and worked on behalf of his brother Menelaus to receive the hand of Helen, the daughter of Leda and Zeus. By Clytemnestra, Agamemnon had at least four children: Electra, called Laodice by Homer; Iphigenia, perhaps the same as Iphiannassa, named by Homer; Chrysothemis, named by Homer and Sophocles; and Orestes, the youngest child and only son.

After winning the Trojan War, Agamemnon returned to Mycenae with the Trojan princess Cassandra, where they were both killed by Clytemnestra and Aegisthus. As to Agamemnon's children, Iphigenia was sacrificed on the altar of Artemis at Aulis; Orestes, after growing to young manhood in exile, returned to Mycenae with his cousin-friend Pylades, and killed Clytemnestra and Aegisthus. For killing his mother, Orestes was beset by Clytemnestra's Furies until he was exonerated by a jury trial in Athens. Eventually, he returned to become King of Mycenae. At the death of Menelaus, Orestes also became King of Sparta. At some point in his career, Orestes either killed, or ordered killed, Neoptolemus, the son of Achilles, who married Hermione and had two sons by her. Orestes is generally thought to have died at a very old age, and Apollodorus says he "was killed by the bite of a snake at Oresteum in Arcadia." He was succeeded on the thrones of Mycenae and Sparta by his son Tisamenus.

Laodice, or Electra as she was called by the playwrights, aided her brother in the murder of their mother, and according to Euripides, in the Electra, she was ordered to marry Pylades and go into permanent exile with him. Chrysothemis is merely named by Homer in the Iliad, and in Sophocles' Electra she has the role of weakly opposing Electra in the murderous designs against their mother.

Cassandra's twin sons by Agamemnon, Pelops and Teledamas, are mentioned only by Pausanias, who says they were slaughtered by Aegisthus along with their parents. The sons of Electra and Pylades, Medon and Strophius, are also named by Pausanias, but no story is given about them.

[7]<u>Menelaus</u>   son of Atreus, according to Homer, and brother to Agamemnon. As a suitor to Helen, Menelaus had much competition, and, finally, when she and her father made the choice, all the rejected suitors took an oath that if anything happened to her, they would band together and fight for her honor. Some ten years after Helen married Menelaus, her rejected suitors had a chance to prove their loyalty. Paris, the son of Trojan King Priam, visited Sparta. During this visit, Menelaus was called away to attend the funeral of his maternal grandfather, King Catreus of Crete. Before Menelaus returned, Paris, either forceably or with her consent, abducted Helen and carried her with him to Troy. Paris, after choosing Aphrodite as the "fairest," was promised the world's most beautiful woman, and so his fate was fulfilled.

After Menelaus returned to find Helen gone, he appealed to his brother to aid him in recovering Helen and to make war against the Trojans. Agamemnon then mustered all the heroes and leaders of the day, and, after some delay at Aulis, sailed for Troy. At the end of the ten-year war, Menelaus recovered Helen, threatened to execute her, but instead returned to Sparta, where they resumed their royal lives. In the <u>Odyssey</u>, Telemachus visits Helen and Menelaus in Sparta some ten years after their return from Troy.

Although Helen was reputed to be the world's most beautiful woman and was favored by Aphrodite, she was remarkably barren, having only one child, the daughter Hermione. By slave mistresses, Menelaus had several other children, notably Megapenthes, who would have succeeded to the Spartan throne except that the people preferred Orestes, who in the meantime had married Hermione. At the death of Orestes, his son Tisamenus inherited the thrones of Mycenae and Sparta. Later, however, Tisamenus was driven into exile by the sons of Heracles, who claimed that their father had twice been wrongfully cheated out of the kingdom, first by Eurystheus and again when Atreus and Thyestes assumed the throne. One myth says that Tisamenus was killed in Argos in a battle with the Heraclids, or in Achaea, where he and his people had fled to escape the invaders.

[8]<u>Pleisthenes</u>   a son of Atreus and Aerope, or one of the sons of Thyestes who was killed by Atreus for the banquet. A third version of his parentage is that Pleisthenes was a son of Atreus whom Thyestes took into exile with him. Later, Pleisthenes attempted to murder Atreus, thinking him to be his hated uncle. Instead, Atreus killed Pleisthenes, and then learned that it was his own son. In this version of the story, Agamemnon and Menelaus are infant sons of Pleisthenes who were taken by Atreus and reared as his own sons. This genealogy is referred to by Clytemnestra in Aeschylus' <u>Agamemnon</u>.

Heroes of the Trojan War Chart 48

1 From the Iliad, Book II, the "Catalog of Ships." of which Homer says he will give the "Captains of the Danaans and their Lords. But the common folk I could not tell or name, nay, not though ten tongues were mine and ten mouths, and a voice unwearying." A.T. Murray's note in this translation says that Homer lists 1186 ships, on which there could have been 100,000 to 120,000 troops.

2 From Apollodorus, The Library, "Epitome III," there is a considerable list. He says "The armament mustered in Aulis. The men who went to Troy were as follows....."

3 From Euripides' "Iphigenia in Aulis," there is a long choral ode in which the women of Aulis enumerate the army leaders who have assembled in their city before going to Troy.

4 From the Iliad in its entirety, an extensive list of Greeks and Trojans who fought and died at Troy.

5 From Quintus of Smyrna in The War at Troy, still other figures are reported to have fought and died or survived. Most of the heroes whom Virgil names in the Aeneid are also mentioned in the work by Quintus.

6 From Virgil's Aeneid and the work by Quintus, a list of those who entered the Wooden Horse may be compiled.

NOTES FOR CHART 48

[1]Homer, "The Catalog of Ships":

(1) From Boeotia -- Peneleos, Leitus, Arcesilaus, Protheonor, and Clonius (50 ships).

(2) From Aspledon and Orchomenus of the Minyae -- Ascalaphus and Ialmenus, sons of Ares (30 ships).

(3) From Phocis -- Schedius and Epistrophus, sons of Iphitus, the son of Naubolus (40 ships).

(4) From Locris -- Ajax, son of Oileus (40 ships).

(5) From Euboea, etc. -- Elephenor, son of Chalcodon (40 ships).

(6) From Athens -- Menestheus, son of Peteus (50 ships).

(7) From Salamis -- Ajax, son of Telamon (12 ships).

(8) From Argos, Tiryns, etc. -- Diomedes, son of Tydeus, and Sthenelus, son of Capaneus; also Euryalus, son of Mecisteus, the son of Talaus (80 ships).

(9) From Mycenae, etc. -- Agamemnon, son of Atreus (100 ships).

(10) From Lacedaemon, Sparta, etc. -- Menelaus, son of Atreus (60 ships).

(11) From Pylus, etc. -- Nestor of Gerenia (90 ships).

(12) From Arcadia, etc. -- Agapenor, son of Ancaeus (60 ships).

(13) From Buprasium, Elis, etc. -- Amphimachus, son of Cteatus; Thalpius, son of Eurytus; and Diores, son of Amarynceus; and Polyxeinus, son of Agasthenes, the son of Augeias (40 ships).

(14) From Dulichium and the Echinae -- Meges, son of Phyleus (40 ships).

(15) From Ithaca, etc. -- Odysseus, son of Laertes (12 ships).

(16) From Aetolia, Calydon, etc. -- Thoas, son of Andraemon (40 ships).

(17) From Crete, etc. -- Idomeneus and Meriones (80 ships).

(18) From Rhodes -- Tlepolemus, son of Heracles by Astyoche (9 ships).

(19) From Syme -- Nireus, son of Aglaia and King
Charops (3 ships).

(20) From Nisyrus, etc. -- Pheidippus and Antiphus,
son of King Thessalus, son of Heracles (30 ships).

(21) From Pelasgian Argos -- Achilles, son of Peleus
(50 ships).

(22) From Phylace, etc. -- Protesilaus, son of Iphiclus,
who died when the troops first reached Troy;
Podarces, son of Iphiclus, succeeded his older
brother (40 ships).

(23) From Pherae -- Eumelus, son of Admetus and
Alcestis (11 ships).

(24) From Methone, etc. -- Philoctetes, who was left
wounded on the Island of Lemnos; his place was
taken by Medon, the natural son of Oileus (7 ships).

(25) From Oechalia, etc. -- Podalirius and Machaon,
physician sons of Asclepius, the son of Apollo (30
ships).

(26) From Ormenius, etc. -- Eurypylus, son of Euaemon (40 ships).

(27) From Argissa, etc. -- Polypoetes, son of Pirithous and Hippodamia; and Leonteus, son of Coronus, the son of Caenus (40 ships).

(28) From Cyphus, near Dodona -- Guneus, son of
Ocytus (22 ships).

(29) From Peneius and Pelion -- Prothous, son of
Tenthredon (40 ships).

[2]Apollodorus, "Catalog of Ships":

(1) Boeotians, ten leaders, 40 ships.

(2) Orchomenians, four leaders, 30 ships.

(3) Phocians, four leaders, 40 ships.

(4) Locrians, Ajax, son of Oileus, 40 ships.

(5) Euboeans, Elephenor, son of Chalcodon and Alcyone, 40 ships.

(6) Athenians, Menestheus, 50 ships.

(7) Salaminians, Ajax, son of Telamon, 12 ships.

(8) Argives, Diomedes, son of Tydeus, 80 ships.

(9) Mycenaeans, Agamemnon, son of Atreus and
Aerope, 100 ships.

(10) Lacedaemonians, Menelaus, son of Atreus and
Aerope, 60 ships.

(11) Pylians, Nestor, son of Neleus and Chloris, 40
ships.

(12) Arcadians, Agapenor, 7 ships.

(13) Eleans, Amphimachus, 40 ships.

(14) Dulichians, Meges, son of Phyleus, 40 ships.

(15) Cephallenians, Odysseus, son of Laertes and Anticlea, 12 ships.

Chart 48   179

(16) Aetolians, Thoas, son of Andraemon and Gorge, 40 ships.

(17) Cretans, Idomeneus, son of Deucalion II, 40 ships.

(18) Rhodians, Tlepolemus, son of Heracles and Astyoche, 9 ships.

(19) Symaeans, Nireus, son of Charopus, 3 ships.

(20) Coans, Phidippus and Antiphus, sons of Thessalus, 30 ships.

(21) Myrmidons, Achilles, son of Peleus and Thetis, 50 ships.

(22) From Phylace, Protesilaus, son of Iphiclus, 40 ships.

(23) Pheraeans, Eumelus, son of Admetus and Alcestis, 11 ships.

(24) Olizonians, Philoctetes, son of Poas, 7 ships.

(25) Aeanianians, Guneus, son of Ocytus, 22 ships.

(26) Triccaeans, Podalirius, 30 ships.

(27) Ormenians, Eurypylus, 40 ships.

(28) Gyrtonians, Polypoetes, son of Pirithous, 30 ships.

(29) Magnesians, Prothous, son of Tenthredon, 40 ships.

(Total number of ships, 1,013)

[3]Euripides, "Catalog of Ships" (the following Chorus, spoken by women of Chalcis in Euboea who have crossed over to Aulis to see the fleet, is quoted in its entirety from Iphigenia in Aulis, lines 160-302, translated by Moses Hadas and John McLean):

I came to the sandy shore of Aulis by the sea. Through the pouring waters of Euripus' narrow channel I plied my boat, leaving behind me my own city Chalcis, nurse of famous Arethusa whose waters join the sea. To see the Achaean host I came, and the sea-faring ships of the Achaean heroes. These heroes, our husbands tell us, with a fleet of a thousand vessels, are led by fair-haired Menelaus and noble Agamemnon in quest of Helen. Cowherd Paris took her from reedy Eurotas, a gift of Aphrodite when at the fountain dews the Cyprian held contest of beauty with Hera and Pallas.

Through Artemis' grove of many sacrifices I came in haste, and my cheeks were dyed with blushes of youthful shyness, for I wished to see the army's stronghold and the tents of the Danaan warriors, and the crowd of horses. I saw the two Ajaxes sitting talking together, Oileus' son, and Telamon's, the pride of Salamis. Protesilaus I saw and Palamedes whom Poseidon's daughter bore, sitting on seats and taking their pleasure in the complicated moves of the draught-board; and Diomedes delighting in the joy of the discus; and near him Meriones, scion of Ares, a marvel to mortals; and Laertes' son from the island hills; and Nireus too, handsomest of the Achaeans.

And swift-running Achilles I saw, whose feet are like the wind, him that Thetis bore and Chiron trained; he was running a race in full armor on the shingle by the seashore. He ran hard, racing a four-horse chariot, lap after lap, straining for victory. The charioteer kept shouting; he was Eumelus of Pheres' race, and I saw his beautiful horses, and their elaborate bridles of gold. He was urging them on with a goad. The middle horses at the yoke were dappled with white-flecked hairs, while the trace-horses on the outside were bays, and at the ankles of their whole hooves their fetlocks were dappled. They ran close to the turns of the course, and beside them sprinted Peleus' son, fully armed, keeping alongside the chariot rail by the wheels of the car.

I came to the host of ships; it was a marvelous spectacle to satisfy the sight of a woman's eyes, a pleasure honey-sweet. The right wing of the fleet was held by the Myrmidon armament from Phthia, fifty dashing vessels. In golden images the Nereid goddesses stood at the sterns, the insignia of the forces of Achilles.

A like number of oared ships of the Argive stood hard by. The commander of these was Mecisteus' son (Euryalus) whose foster-father was Talaus, and with him was Sthenelus, son of Capaneus. The next station Theseus' son (Acamas) held, leading sixty Attic ships. Their ensign was Pallas riding on winged steeds, a sight to cheer the sailors.

I saw the Boeotian naval armament of fifty vessels, equipped with their ensigns; this was Cadmus holding a golden dragon at the curved sterns. Earth-born Leitus commanded their naval host. And there were vessels from the land of Phocis and also ships of Locris equal to them in number, led by Oileus' son, who came from the famous city of Thronium.

From Cyclopean Mycenae Atreus' son sent a hundred vessels and their men. With him was the chieftain Adrastus, standing by his friend, in order that Hellas might take righteous vengeance on the one who forsook her home for the sake of barbarian bridals. I saw the ensign of the prows of Gerenian Nestor of Pylus: the river Alpheus, his neighbor, represented with bull's feet.

Of the Aenians there were twelve ships, which King Guneus commanded. Not far from these were the chiefs of Elis, whom all the folk called Epeians. Eurytus commanded these and also led the armament of the Taphians with white oars, whose King was Meges; he was the son of Pyleus and came from the islands of Echinae which sailors avoid.

We had passed along the line from right to left, and there at the end, close beside the neighboring ships, was the fleet of Ajax, nurseling of Salamis, twelve of the trimmest ships, completing the line.

[4]The following names, Greek and Trojan, killed at Troy, are derived from the Iliad:

(1) Abas, Troj., s. Eurydamas -- killed by Diomedes, s. Tydeus.
(2) Ablerus, Troj., -- killed by Antilochus, s. Nestor.
(3) Acamas, Troj., s. Eussorus -- killed by Ajax, s. Telamon.
(4) Acamas, Troj. -- killed by Meriones.
(5) Adamas, Troj. -- killed by Meriones.
(6) Adrastus, Troj. -- killed by Patroclus.
(7) Adrastus, Troj., captured by Menelaus who would have spared him -- killed by Agamemnon.
(8) Aenius, Troj. -- killed by Achilles.

Chart 48   181

(9) Aesepus and Pedasus, Troj. twins, sons of Bu-
colion, s. Laomedon -- killed by Euryalus,
s. Mecisteus.

(10) Aesymnus, Gr. -- killed by Hector.

(11) Agastrophus, Troj., s. Paeon -- killed by
Diomedes.

(12) Agelaus, Gr. -- killed by Hector.

(13) Agelaus, Troj., s. Phadmon -- killed by Diomedes.

(14) Alastor, Troj. -- killed by Odysseus.

(15) Alcandrus, Troj. -- killed by Odysseus.

(16) Alcathous, Troj., s. Aesyetes -- killed by Idomeneus.

(17) Alcmaeon, Gr., s. Thestor -- killed by Sarpedon,
Troj. ally.

(18) Amopaon, Troj. -- killed by Teucer, s. Telamon.

(19) Amphiclus, Troj. -- killed by Meges, s. Phyleus.

(20) Amphimachus, Gr., s. Cteatus, s. Poseidon --
killed by Hector.

(21) Amphius, Troj. ally, s. Merops -- killed by
Diomedes.

(22) Amphius, Troj. ally, s. Selagus -- killed by
Ajax, s. Telamon.

(23) Amphoterus, Troj. -- killed by Patroclus.

(24) Anchialus, Gr. -- killed by Hector.

(25) Antiphates, Troj. -- killed by Leontus.

(26) Antiphus, Troj., s. Priam -- killed by Agamemnon.

(27) Aphareus, Gr., s. Caletor -- killed by Aeneas.

(28) Apisaon, Troj., s. Phausius -- killed by Eurypylus, s. Euaemon.

(29) Apisaon, Troj., s. Hippasus -- killed by Lycomedes.

(30) Arcesilaus, Gr. -- killed by Hector.

(31) Archelochus, Troj., s. Antenor -- killed by
Ajax, s. Telamon.

(32) Archeptolemus, Troj. -- killed by Teucer.

(33) Areilycus, Troj. -- killed by Patroclus.

(34) Areithous, Troj. -- killed by Achilles.

(35) Aretaon, Troj. -- killed by Teucer.

(36) Aretus, Troj., s. Priam -- killed by Automedon.

(37) Asaeus, Gr. -- killed by Hector.

(38) Ascalaphus, Gr., s. Ares -- killed by Deiphobus,
s. Priam.

(39) Asius, Troj., s. Hyrtacus -- killed by Idomeneus,
s. Deucalion.

(40) Asteropaeus, Troj. ally -- killed by Achilles.

(41) Astyalus, Troj. -- killed by Polypoetes, s. Pirithous.

(42) Astynous, Troj. -- killed by Diomedes.

(43) Astypylus, Troj. -- killed by Achilles.

(44) Atymnius, Troj., s. Amisodarus -- killed by
Antilochus, s. Nestor.

(45) Autonous, Gr. -- killed by Hector.

(46) Autonous, Troj. -- killed by Patroclus.

(47) Axylus, Troj., s. Teuthras -- killed by Diomedes.

(48) Bathycles, Gr., s. Chalcon -- killed by Glaucus,
Troj. ally.

(49) Bienor, Troj. -- killed by Agamemnon.

(50) Calesius, Troj. -- killed by Diomedes.

(51) Caletor, Troj. -- killed by Ajax, s. Telamon.

(52) Cebriones, Troj., s. Priam -- killed by Patroclus.

(53) Charops, Troj., s. Hippasus -- killed by Odysseus.

(54) Chersidamas, Troj. -- killed by Odysseus.

(55) Chromius, Troj., s. Priam -- killed by Diomedes.

(56) Chromius, Troj. -- killed by Odysseus.

(57) Chromius, Troj. -- killed by Teucer.

(58) Cleitus, Troj., s. Peisenor -- killed by Teucer.

(59) Cleobulus, Troj. -- killed by Ajax, s. Oileus.

(60) Clonius, Gr. -- killed by Agenor.

(61) Coeranus, Gr. -- killed by Hector.
(62) Coeranus, Troj. -- killed by Odysseus.
(63) Coon, Troj., s. Antenor -- killed by Agamemnon.
(64) Crethon, Gr., s. Diocles, s. Orsilochus -- killed by Aeneas.
(65) Croesmus, Troj. -- killed by Meges, s. Phyleus.

(66) Daetor, Troj. -- killed by Teucer.
(67) Damasus, Troj. -- killed by Polypoetes.
(68) Dardanus, Troj., s. Bias -- killed by Achilles.
(69) Deicoon, Troj., s. Pergasus -- killed by Agamemnon.
(70) Deiochus, Gr. -- killed by Paris.
(71) Deiopites, Troj. -- killed by Odysseus.
(72) Deipyrus, Gr. -- killed by Helenus, s. Priam.
(73) Democoon, Troj., s. Priam -- killed by Odysseus.
(74) Demoleon, Troj., s. Antenor -- killed by Achilles.
(75) Demuchus, Troj., s. Philetor -- killed by Achilles.
(76) Deucalion, Troj. -- killed by Achilles.
(77) Diores, Gr., s. Amarynceus -- killed by Peiros, s. Imbrasus, from Thrace.
(78) Dolon, Troj. ally, s. Eumedes -- captured, then killed by Diomedes and Odysseus.
(79) Dolops, Troj., s. Lampus, s. Laomedon -- killed by Menelaus.
(80) Dolops, Gr., s. Clytius -- killed by Hector.
(81) Doryclus, Troj., s. Priam -- killed by Ajax, s. Telamon.
(82) Dresus, Troj. -- killed by Euryalus, s. Mecistus.
(83) Dryops, Troj. -- killed by Achilles.

(84) Echelus, Troj., s. Agenor -- killed by Achilles.
(85) Echelus, Troj. -- killed by Patroclus.

(86) Echemmon, Troj., s. Priam -- killed by Diomedes.
(87) Echepolis, Troj., s. Thalysius -- killed by Antilochus, s. Nestor.
(88) Echius, Gr. -- killed by Polites, s. Priam.
(89) Echius, Troj. -- killed by Patroclus.
(90) Eioneus, Gr. -- killed by Hector.
(91) Elasus, Troj. -- killed by Patroclus.
(92) Elatus, Troj. -- killed by Agamemnon.
(93) Elephenor, Gr., s. Chalcodon -- killed by Agenor, s. Antenor.
(94) Eniopeus, Troj., s. Thebaeus -- killed by Diomedes.
(95) Ennomus, Troj. ally -- killed by Achilles.
(96) Ennomus, Troj. -- killed by Odysseus.
(97) Epaltes, Troj. ally -- killed by Patroclus.
(98) Epeigeus, Gr. -- killed by Hector.
(99) Epicles, Troj. ally -- killed by Ajax, s. Telamon.
(100) Epistor, Troj. -- killed by Patroclus.
(101) Epistrophus, Troj. ally -- killed by Achilles.
(102) Erylaus, Troj. -- killed by Patroclus.
(103) Erymas, Troj. -- killed by Patroclus.
(104) Erymas, Troj. -- killed by Idomeneus.
(105) Euchenor, Gr., s. Polidus -- killed by Paris, s. Priam.
(106) Eunomus, Troj. -- killed by Odysseus.
(107) Euippus, Troj. ally -- killed by Patroclus.
(108) Euphorbus, Troj., s. Panthous -- killed by Menelaus.

(109) Gorgythion, Troj., s. Priam and Castianeira -- killed by Teucer.

(110) Halius, Troj. ally -- killed by Odysseus.
(111) Harpalion, Troj. ally, s. Pylaemenes -- killed by Meriones.
(112) Hector, Troj., s. Priam -- killed by Achilles.

Chart 48   183

(113) Helenus, Gr., s. Oenops -- killed by Hector.
(114) Hippodamus, Troj. -- killed by Achilles.
(115) Hippodamus, Troj. -- killed by Odysseus.
(116) Hippolochus, Troj., s. Antimachus -- killed by
       Agamemnon.
(117) Hippomachus, Troj. -- killed by Leonteus.
(118) Hipponous, Gr. -- killed by Hector.
(119) Hippothous, Troj. ally -- killed by Ajax, s. Tela-
       mon.
(120) Hippotion, Troj. -- killed by Meriones.
(121) Hypeirochus, Troj. -- killed by Odysseus.
(122) Hypeiron, Troj. -- killed by Diomedes.
(123) Hyperenor, Troj., s. Panthous -- killed by Mene-
       laus.
(124) Hypsenor, Gr., s. Hippasus -- killed by Deipho-
       bus.
(125) Hypsenor, Troj., s. Dolopion -- killed by Eury-
       pylus.
(126) Hyrtius, Troj., s. Gyrtius -- killed by Ajax, s.
       Telamon.

(127) Iamenus, Troj. -- killed by Leonteus.
(128) Iasus, Gr., s. Sphelus, s. Bucolus -- killed by
       Aeneas.
(129) Idaeus, Troj., s. Dares -- captured by Diomedes,
       rescued by Hephaestus.
(130) Ilioneus, Troj., s. Phorbas -- killed by Peneleos.
(131) Imbrius, Troj., s. Mentor -- killed by Teucer.
(132) Ipheus, Troj. ally -- killed by Patroclus.
(133) Iphidamas, Troj., s. Antenor -- killed by Aga-
       memnon.
(134) Iphinous, Gr., s. Dexios -- killed by Glaucus,
       Troj. ally.
(135) Iphition, Troj. ally, s. Otrynteus -- killed by
       Achilles.
(136) Isus, Troj., s. Priam -- killed by Agamemnon.

(137) Laodamas, Troj., s. Antenor -- killed by Ajax,
       s. Telamon.
(138) Laogonus, Troj., brother of Dardanus, sons of
       Bias -- killed by Achilles.
(139) Laogonus, Troj., s. Onetor -- killed by Meriones.
(140) Leucas, Gr. -- killed by Antiphus, s. Priam.
(141) Lycaon, Troj., s. Priam -- killed by Achilles.
(142) Lycon, Troj. -- killed by Peneleos.
(143) Lycophontes, Troj. -- killed by Teucer.
(144) Lycophron, Gr., s. Mastor -- killed by Hector.
(145) Lysander, Troj. -- killed by Ajax, s. Telamon.

(146) Maris, Troj., brother Atymnius -- killed by
       Thrasymedes, s. Nestor.
(147) Mecisteus, Gr. -- killed by Polydamas, s. Priam.
(148) Medon, Gr., s. Oileus -- killed by Aeneas.
(149) Melanippus, Troj. -- killed by Patroclus.
(150) Melanippus, Troj., s. Hicetaon -- killed by Anti-
       lochus.
(151) Melanippus, Troj. -- killed by Teucer.
(152) Melanthius, Troj. -- killed by Eurypylus.
(153) Menesthes, Gr. -- killed by Hector.
(154) Menon, Troj. -- killed by Leon
(155) Mermerus, Troj. -- killed by Antilochus.
(156) Mnesus, Troj. ally -- killed by Achilles.
(157) Morys, Troj. -- killed by Meriones, s. Molos.
(158) Mulius, Troj. -- killed by Patroclus.
(159) Mulius, Troj. -- killed by Achilles.
(160) Mydon, Troj. -- killed by Antilochus.
(161) Mydon, Troj. -- killed by Achilles.

(162) Nastes, Troj. ally -- killed by Achilles.
(163) Noemon, Troj. ally -- killed by Odysseus.

(164) Odius, Troj. -- killed by Agamemnon.
(165) Oenomaus, Gr. -- killed by Hector.
(166) Oenomaus, Troj. -- killed by Idomeneus.

(167) Oileus, Troj. -- killed by Agamemnon.
(168) Ophelestes, Troj. -- killed by Teucer.
(169) Ophelestes, Troj. ally -- killed by Achilles.
(170) Opheltius, Gr. -- killed by Hector.
(171) Opheltius, Troj. -- killed by Euryalus, s. Mecisteus.
(172) Oresbius, Gr. -- killed by Hector.
(173) Orestes, Gr. -- killed by Hector.
(174) Orestes, Troj. -- killed by Leonteus.
(175) Ormenus, Troj. -- killed by Teucer.
(176) Ormenus, Troj. -- killed by Polypoetes.
(177) Orsilochus, Gr., s. Diocles, s. Orsilochus -- killed by Aeneas.
(178) Orsilochus, Troj. -- killed by Teucer.
(179) Orus, Gr. -- killed by Hector.
(180) Othryoneus, Troj. ally, had asked for Cassandra in marriage -- killed by Idomeneus.
(181) Otus, Gr. -- killed by Polydamas, s. Priam.

(182) Pandarus, Troj. -- killed by Diomedes.
(183) Pandocus, Troj. -- killed by Ajax, s. Telamon.
(184) Patroclus, Gr., s. Menoetius -- killed by Hector and Apollo.
(185) Pedaeus, Troj., s. Antenor -- killed by Meges, s. Phyleus.
(186) Pedacus, Troj. -- killed by Euryalus.
(187) Peiros, Troj. ally, s. Imbrasus -- killed by Thoas of Aetolia.
(188) Peisander, Troj., s. Antimachus -- killed by Agamemnon.
(189) Peisander, Troj. -- killed by Menelaus.
(190) Perimus, Troj., s. Megas -- killed by Patroclus.
(191) Periphas, Gr., s. Ochesius -- killed by Hector and Ares.
(192) Periphetes, Gr., s. Copreus -- killed by Hector.
(193) Periphetes, Troj. -- killed by Teucer.
(194) Phaestus, Troj., s. Borus -- killed by Idomeneus.

(195) Phalces, Troj. -- killed by Antilochus.
(196) Phegeus, Troj., s. Dares -- killed by Diomedes.
(197) Phereclus, Troj., s. Tecton, s. Harmon -- killed by Meriones.
(198) Phorcup, Troj., s. Phaenops -- killed by Ajax, s. Telamon.
(199) Phylacus, Troj. -- killed by Leitus.
(200) Pidytes, Troj. ally -- killed by Odysseus.
(201) Pites, Gr. -- killed by Hector.
(202) Polidus, Troj., s. Eurydamas -- killed by Diomedes.
(203) Polyaemon, Troj. -- killed by Teucer.
(204) Polydorus, Troj., s. Priam -- killed by Achilles.
(205) Polymelus, Troj., s. Argeas -- killed by Patroclus.
(206) Promachus, Gr., s. Alegenor -- killed by Acamas, s. Antenor.
(207) Pronous, Troj. -- killed by Patroclus.
(208) Prothoenor, Gr., s. Areilycus -- killed by Polydamas, s. Panthous.
(209) Prothoon, Troj. -- killed by Teucer.
(210) Prytanis, Troj. -- killed by Odysseus.
(211) Pylaemenes, Troj. ally, s. Atymnius -- killed by Antilochus and Menelaus.
(212) Pylartes, Troj. -- killed by Patroclus.
(213) Pylartes, Troj. -- killed by Ajax, s. Telamon.
(214) Pylon, Troj. -- killed by Polypoetes.
(215) Pyraechmes, Troj. ally -- killed by Patroclus.
(216) Pyrasus, Troj. -- killed by Ajax, s. Telamon.
(217) Pyris, Troj. -- killed by Patroclus.

(218) Rhesus, Troj. ally, King of Thracians -- killed by Diomedes and Odysseus.
(219) Rhigmus, Troj. ally, s. Peires -- killed by Achilles.

(220) Sarpedon, Troj. ally, s. Zeus -- killed by Patroclus.

Chart 48   185

(221) Satnius, Troj., s. Enops -- killed by Ajax, s.
       Oileus.
(222) Scamandrius, Troj., s. Strophius -- killed by
       Menelaus.
(223) Schedius and/or Perimedes, Gr., sons of Iphitos
       -- one or both killed by Hector.
(224) Simoeisus, Troj., s. Anthemion -- killed by Ajax,
       s. Telamon.
(225) Socus, Troj., s. Hippasus -- killed by Odysseus.
(226) Sthenelaus, Troj., s. Ithaemenes -- killed by
       Patroclus.
(227) Stichius, Gr. -- killed by Hector.

(228) Teuthras, Gr. -- killed by Hector.
(229) Thersilochus, Troj. ally -- killed by Achilles.
(230) Thestor, Troj., s. Enops -- killed by Patroclus.
(231) Thoas, Troj. -- killed by Menelaus.
(232) Thoon, Troj., s. Phaenops -- killed by Diomedes.
(233) Thoon, Troj. -- killed by Antilochus.
(234) Thoon, Troj. -- killed by Odysseus.
(235) Thrasius, Troj. -- killed by Achilles.
(236) Thrasymelus, Troj., squire to Sarpedon -- killed
       by Patroclus.
(237) Thymbraeus, Troj. -- killed by Diomedes.
(238) Tlepolemus, Gr., s. Heracles, s. Zeus -- killed
       by Sarpedon, s. Zeus.
(239) Tlepolemus, Troj. ally -- killed by Patroclus.
(240) Trechus, Gr. -- killed by Hector.
(241) Troilus, Troj., s. Priam -- killed by Achilles,
       some time prior to the Iliad.
(242) Tros, Troj., s. Alastor -- killed by Achilles.

(243) Xanthus, Troj., s. Phaenops -- killed by Diom-
       edes.

[5]Quintus of Smyrna: Those who fought and died
or survived at Troy after Hector's death:

(1)   Acamas, Troj., s. Antenor, killed by Philoctetes.
(2)   Achilles, Gr., killed by Paris and Apollo.
(3)   Aeneas, Troj., s. Anchises, survived.
(4)   Agamemnon, Gr. leader, survived the war; later
      murdered by his wife Clytemnestra upon return
      home.
(5)   Agenor, Troj., killed by Neoptolemus, s. Achilles.
(6)   Ajax, Gr., s. Oileus, drowned by Poseidon.
(7)   Ajax, Gr., s. Telamon, committed suicide over
      Achilles' armor, which was awarded to Odys-
      seus.
(8)   Amazons: Trojan allies:
      Alcibie, killed by Diomedes
      Antandre, killed by Achilles
      Antibrote, killed by Achilles
      Bremousa, killed by Idomeneus
      Clonie, killed by Podarces, s. Iphicles
      Derimacheia, killed by Diomedes
      Derinoe, killed by Ajax, s. Oileus
      Evandre, killed by Meriones
      Harmothoe, killed by Achilles
      Hippothoe, killed by Achilles
      Penthesileia, leader and Queen of the Amazons,
        killed by Achilles
      Polemous, killed by Achilles
      Thermodosa, killed by Meriones.
(9)   Anchises, father of Aeneas, carried by his son to
      survival.
(10) Andromache, Hector's widow, captive of Neoptolem-
      us, later married to Helenus, s. Priam.
(11) Antenor, Troj., survived, was spared by the Greeks.
(12) Antilochus, s. Nestor, killed by Memnon.
(13) Astyanax, infant son of Hector, thrown from the
      wall of Troy.
(14) Cassandra, d. Priam, captive of Agamemnon, killed
      by Clytemnestra.
(15) Deiphobus, Troj., s. Priam, killed by Menelaus.
(16) Diomedes, Gr., s. Tydeus, survived.

(17) Eurypylus, Troj. ally, s. Telephus, s. Heracles and Astyoche, Priam's sister; killed by Neoptolemus.
(18) Glaucus, Troj. ally, killed by Ajax, s. Telamon.
(19) Hecuba, Queen of Troy, captive of Odysseus, changed into a dog before Odysseus sailed for Ithaca.
(20) Helen, returned to Sparta with Menelaus.
(21) Helenus, Troj., s. Priam, survived as captive of Neoptolemus.
(22) Ilioneus, Troj. elder, killed by Diomedes.
(23) Idomeneus, Gr. ally from Crete, survived only to return home and find his kingdom usurped, and his wife and children murdered by the usurper.
(24) Machaon, Gr., s. Asclepius, killed by Eurypylus.
(25) Memnon, Troj. ally from Ethiopia, s. Eos and Tithonus, killed by Achilles.
(26) Menelaus, returned to Sparta.
(27) Meriones, Gr. ally from Crete, survived.
(28) Nireus, Gr., killed by Eurypylus.
(29) Neoptolemus, s. Achilles, survived, was later killed by Orestes, s. Agamemnon.
(30) Nestor, Gr., survived, returned to Pylus.
(31) Odysseus, survived, returned to Ithaca after ten years of wandering.
(32) Oenone, first wife of Paris, died with him after refusing to cure his wound.
(33) Pammon, Troj., s. Priam, killed by Neoptolemus.
(34) Paris, s. Priam, mortally wounded by Philoctetes and died.
(35) Peneleos, Gr., killed by Eurypylus.
(36) Philoctetes, Gr., s. Poeas, survived.
(37) Podalirius, Gr., s. Asclepius, survived.
(38) Podarces, Gr., brother of Protesilaus, s. Iphicles, killed by Penthesileia.
(39) Polites, Troj., s. Priam, killed by Neoptolemus.
(40) Polypoetes, Gr., survived.
(41) Polyxena, d. Priam, sacrificed on Achilles' tomb.
(42) Priam, King of Troy, killed by Neoptolemus.
(43) Sthenelus, Gr. survived.
(44) Teucer, s. Telamon, half-brother of Ajax, survived, was later exiled by his father for failure to avenge the honor of Ajax.
(45) Thoas, Gr., survived.
(46) Thrasymedes, s. Nestor, survived, returned to Pylus with his father.

[6]Those who entered the Wooden Horse:

(a) Virgil:

Sthenelus
Ulysses (Odysseus)
Thessandrus
Acamas
Neoptolemus
Thoas
Machaon
Epeos
Menelaus
Agamemnon
Peneleos, and others ...

(b) Quintus of Smyrna:

Neoptolemus	Thoas
Menelaus	Polypoetes
Odysseus	Ajax, s. Oileus
Sthenelus	Eurypylus
Diomedes	Meriones
Philoctetes	Idomeneus
Antilochus	Podalirius
Menestheus	Eurymachus

Chart 48   187

Teucer	Demophoon
Ialmenus	Amphimachus
Thalpius	Agapenor
Antimachus	Meges
Leontius	Epeos, and "all the others
Eumelus	too, that the polished
Euryalus	horse could contain."

(c) Apollodorus: does not name any of those who entered the Horse, but says, "Into this horse Odysseus persuaded fifty (or according to the author of
the Little Iliad, three thousand) of the doughtiest to
enter...."

Kings of Athens[1]

Chart 49

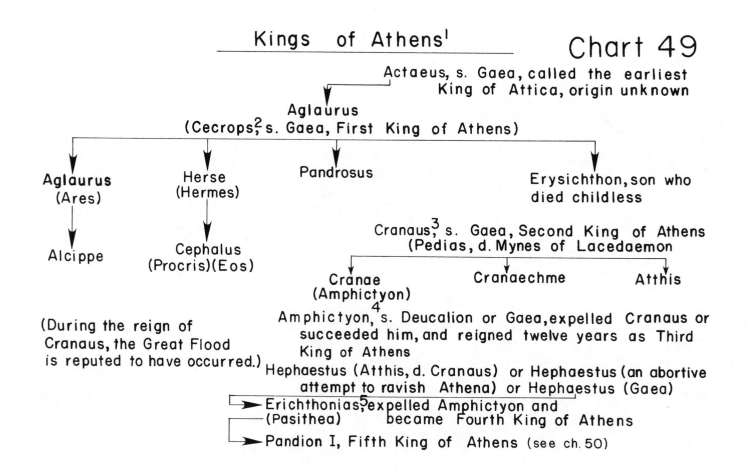

Actaeus, s. Gaea, called the earliest King of Attica, origin unknown

Aglaurus
(Cecrops,[2] s. Gaea, First King of Athens)

Aglaurus
(Ares)

Herse
(Hermes)

Pandrosus

Erysichthon, son who died childless

Alcippe

Cephalus
(Procris)(Eos)

Cranaus,[3] s. Gaea, Second King of Athens
(Pedias, d. Mynes of Lacedaemon

Cranae
(Amphictyon)

Cranaechme

Atthis

(During the reign of Cranaus, the Great Flood is reputed to have occurred.)

Amphictyon,[4] s. Deucalion or Gaea, expelled Cranaus or succeeded him, and reigned twelve years as Third King of Athens

Hephaestus (Atthis, d. Cranaus) or Hephaestus (an abortive attempt to ravish Athena) or Hephaestus (Gaea)

Erichthonias,[5] expelled Amphictyon and
(Pasithea)   became Fourth King of Athens

Pandion I, Fifth King of Athens (see ch. 50)

NOTES FOR CHART 49

[1]Kings of Athens   Actaeus, whom Pausanias says was
                     the first ruler of Attica, was of un-
known origin, hence was called a son of Gaea, or Earth.
Nothing is known of him except that he had a daughter,
Aglarus or Agraulus, who married Cecrops, also a son
of Gaea, who became the second ruler, or first king of
Athens.

[2]Cecrops   described by Apollodorus as "a son of the
            soil, with a body compounded of man and
serpent." He became the first king of Athens, and the
country that was formerly called Acte became Cecropia.
By Aglaurus, the daughter of Actaeus, Cecrops became
the father of three daughters, Aglaurus, Herse, and
Pandrosus; and a son, Erysichthon, "who departed this
life childless." The story of Alcippe, daughter of Aglaurus and Ares, has been told elsewhere (see Chart 7).
Cephalus as the son of Herse and Hermes is not generally known, as most sources call him the son of Deion
(or Deioneus). As to the fates of the three daughters
of Cecrops, see below, note 5. During the reign of
Cecrops, it is said that the gods decided to take possession of cities in which each of them would receive special worship. Athena and Poseidon struggled for possession of Athens, but the city was awarded to Athena because Cecrops bore witness that she was first to plant
the olive tree. Henceforth, the city was called Athens
after the goddess.

[3]Cranaus   the second king of Athens. The son of
            Cecrops having died young, the rule passed
to another line. Cranaus was a son of the soil, and it
was during his reign that the Great Flood is reputed to
have taken place. By Pedias, a daughter of Mynes of
Lacedaemon, Cranaus was the father of three daughters,
Cranae, Cranaechme, and Atthis. Apollodorus says
"when Atthis died a maid, Cranaus called the country
Atthis."

[4]Amphictyon   the third king of Athens, was either the
               son of Deucalion, who survived the Flood,
or he was a son of the soil. Pausanias says he married one of the daughters of Cranaus, but nonetheless deposed his father-in-law and seized the throne for himself. He reigned twelve years and was expelled by
Erichthonias.

[5]Erichthonias   after expelling Amphictyon, became the
                 fourth king of Athens. Apollodorus says
he was the son of Hephaestus and Atthis, daughter of
Cranaus, who was also said to have died as a maid.
Erichthonias is also called the son of Athena and Hephaestus, and Pausanias says he was the son of Hephaestus
and Gaea. As to Athena's role in his parentage, the
story is told that Hephaestus pursued her, and finally
attempted to embrace her. Athena, determined to remain a maiden, repulsed him, and "he dropped his seed

on the leg of the goddess. In disgust, she wiped off the
seed with a piece of wool and threw it to the ground. "
Erichthonias sprang up from this seed, and the story
continues that Athena brought him up unknown to the other gods, wishing to make him immortal. She put him
in a chest, and entrusted it to the daughters of Cecrops,
forbidding them to open the chest. Aglaurus and Herse
opened the chest out of curiosity and saw either a snake,
a child with a snake's tail, or a snake coiled about a
child. For breaking Athena's order, Aglaurus and Herse
were driven mad and jumped from the Acropolis. Pandrosus was honored on the Acropolis with an enclosure
in which Athena planted her olive tree. During this
reign, Erichthonias set up the wooden image of Athena
in the Acropolis and initiated the Panathenaic Festival.
Another source credits him with inventing the chariot,
perhaps for the purpose of concealing his serpent lower
body. At his death, Erichthonias was succeeded on the
throne of Athens by his only son, Pandion, who became
the fifth king of Athens.

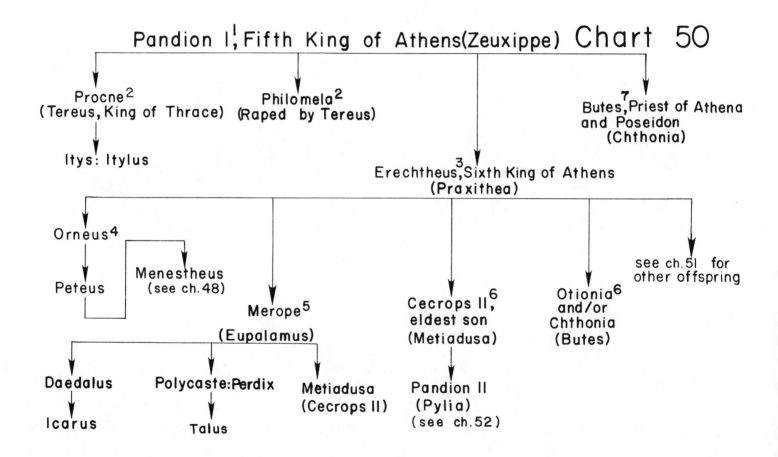

192

Pandion I, Fifth King of Athens (Zeuxippe) Chart 50

Procne[2]
(Tereus, King of Thrace)

Philomela[2]
(Raped by Tereus)

Butes,[7] Priest of Athena
and Poseidon
(Chthonia)

Itys: Itylus

Erechtheus,[3] Sixth King of Athens
(Praxithea)

Orneus[4]

Peteus

Menestheus
(see ch. 48)

Merope[5]

(Eupalamus)

see ch. 51 for
other offspring

Cecrops II,[6]
eldest son
(Metiadusa)

Otionia[6]
and/or
Chthonia
(Butes)

Daedalus

Icarus

Polycaste: Perdix

Talus

Metiadusa
(Cecrops II)

Pandion II
(Pylia)
(see ch. 52)

Chart 51

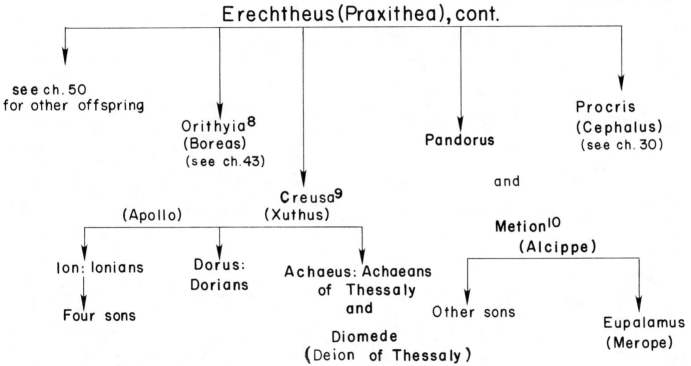

Erechtheus(Praxithea), cont.

see ch. 50
for other offspring

Orithyia[8]
(Boreas)
(see ch.43)

Pandorus

Procris
(Cephalus)
(see ch. 30)

Creusa[9]
(Xuthus)

and

(Apollo)

Metion[10]
(Alcippe)

Ion: Ionians

Dorus:
Dorians

Achaeus: Achaeans
of Thessaly
and

Other sons

Four sons

Diomede
(Deion of Thessaly)

Eupalamus
(Merope)

NOTES FOR CHARTS 50 AND 51

[1]Pandion I son of Erichthonias and the Naiad nymph Pasithea, became the fifth king of Athens at his father's death. By Zeuxippe, Pasithea's sister, Pandion had four children: Procne, Philomela, Erechtheus, and Butes. (The practice of marrying one's niece has been referred to several times, but marriage to an aunt was not common.) During the reign of Pandion, war broke out with Labdacus, the king of Thebes, and the Thracian king Tereus, a son of Ares, was asked for help. After a successful conclusion of the war, Pandion gave Tereus the hand of his daughter Procne. At his death, Pandion was succeeded on the throne by Erechtheus.

[2]Procne and Philomela sisters, daughters of Pandion, whose fates were among the most horrible in Greek mythology. Ovid tells the story with great detail and embellishment; Apollodorus states directly what happened; but there is little difference in the line of events. Procne, married to Tereus, bore a son, Itys or Itylus, and was happy until her husband fell in love with her sister Philomela. Tereus then raped Philomela, cut out her tongue to prevent her talking and imprisoned her. Finally, Philomela succeeded in weaving her story into a robe and sent it to her sister. Procne, taking perhaps the most outrageous vengeance ever thought of, killed her son, dismembered his body, and served him to Tereus. When he was told what he had eaten, he took up an axe and would have killed them both, but according to Apollodorus, "they prayed the gods to be turned into birds, and Procne became a nightingale and Philomela a swallow. Tereus was also changed into a bird and became a hoopoe." In a note to his translation of Apollodorus, Sir James Frazer points out that "later Roman mythographers somewhat absurdly inverted the transformation of the two sisters, making Procne the swallow and the tongueless Philomela the nightingale." Robert Graves says that Tereus cut out Procne's tongue and confined her to slave quarters, telling Philomela that her sister was dead. In this version, then, Procne would be the swallow, having no tongue, and Philomela the nightingale.

[3]Erechtheus son of Pandion and Zeuxippe, became the sixth king of Athens when his father died of grief over Procne and Philomela. Erechtheus married Praxithea, and according to Apollodorus, had three sons: Cecrops, Pandorus, and Metion; and four daughters: Procris, Creusa, Chthonia, and Orithyia. Ovid says Erechtheus had "four young sons and as many daughters." Based on a composite list of sources, Robert Graves says he had "four sons, among them his successor Cecrops; also seven daughters: namely, Protogonia, Pandora, Procris, wife of Cephalus, Creusa, Orithyia, Chthonia, who married her uncle Butes, and Otionia, the youngest." Pausanias also names Orneus, who

founded the city of Ornea, as the son of Erechtheus. As
to the parents of Daedalus, it is generally said that he
was the son of Eupalamus, a son of Metion, but his
mother varies: Iphinoe, Alcippe, or Merope, a daughter
of Erechtheus, according to a source cited by Plutarch,
although no other source has named Merope as one of
Erechtheus' daughters.

During the reign of Erechtheus, war broke out between the Athenians and the Eleusinians. When the king
inquired of the oracle how he might win the war, he was
told that he must sacrifice one of his daughters. Apollodorus says that "he slaughtered his youngest, and others also slaughtered themselves; for, as some said,
they had taken an oath among themselves to perish together." In the war that followed, Erechtheus won and
killed Emolpus, the son of Poseidon and Chione, daughter of Boreas and Orithyia. Poseidon then destroyed
Erechtheus, or Zeus killed him with a thunderbolt at the
request of Poseidon, who was enraged at the Athenians
for killing his son. According to Pausanias, it was not
Eumolpus, but a son of Eumolpus, Ismarus, who was
killed by Erechtheus, and Erechtheus himself perished
in battle.

[4]Orneus   son of Erechtheus, and eponym for the city
             of Ornea. His son Peteus was father of
Menestheus, who was one of Helen's suitors and later
took fifty ships to Troy as leader of the Athenians.
Homer says in the Iliad that no one was his equal in
"the marshalling of chariots and of warriors that bear
the shield." It is not said whether Menestheus died in
the Trojan War, but Quintus of Smyrna says he was one
of the Greeks who entered Troy in the Wooden Horse.

[5]Merope   daughter of Erechtheus, and given as the
            mother of Daedalus by one source. Eupal-
amus, a son of Metion, is generally named as the father
of Daedalus. There were also two daughters: Metiadusa, who married Cecrops, the eldest son of Erechtheus, and became the mother of Pandion II; and Perdix
or Polycaste, who became the mother of Talus or Calus.
Sometimes Talus is also called Perdix. Talus served
as an apprentice to his uncle Daedalus, who, Apollodorus
says, "was an excellent architect and the first inventor
of images." Talus is said to have invented the saw by
imitating the teeth in a serpent's jawbone. Deadalus
became jealous and afraid that Talus would surpass himself, and so threw the boy down from the Acropolis.
Daedalus was tried for murder in the Areopagus and
condemned. He fled from Athens and found asylum at
the court of Minos and Pasifae in Crete. Here he engaged in at least two unusual building projects: Queen
Pasifae had fallen in love with the handsome Marathonian bull, and Daedalus contrived a wooden cow in which
Pasifae hid herself in order for the bull to mount. The
creation deceived even the bull, with the result that
Pasifae later gave birth to the monstrous Minotaur with
a man's body and a bull's head. This project led to the
second feat: Minos commissioned Daedalus to build the
Labyrinth, in which he could hide the evidence of his
wife's shameful passion. This Labyrinth was so intri-
cate that anyone who went in never found the way out,
and was destroyed by the fierce Minotaur. Finally,
Theseus of Athens came to kill the monster, and with
the help of Ariadne, Minos' daughter, and Daedalus, he
found his way in, unwinding a ball of thread as he went,
and then out again by following the thread back. Minos
imprisoned Daedalus and his son Icarus, for their roles
in helping Theseus, and would have killed them except
they escaped by devising wings of feathers held together
by wax. Daedalus escaped and made his way to Sicily,
but Icarus flew too high, and the sun melted the wax
in his wings. He dropped into the sea which was henceforth called the Icarian Sea.

[6]Cecrops II, Otionia, etc.   Cecrops II, eldest son of Erechtheus, succeeded to the throne of Athens at his father's death.   He married his niece Metiadusa, and had one son, Pandion, who later became king of Athens.   The sons of Metion overthrew Pandion and expelled him from the city.   He went to Megara, where he married Pylia, daughter of King Pylus, and later became ruler of his father-in-law's kingdom.   By Pylia, Pandion was the father of four sons.

Otionia was the daughter of Erechtheus who gave herself for a sacrifice to aid her father in his war with the Eleusinians.   Chthonia, if there was another daughter with this name, married her uncle Butes.

[7]Butes   twin brother of Erechtheus.   At the death of their father, Pandion I, Butes received the priesthood of Athena and Poseidon, and Erechthus received the kingdom.   Butes married his niece Chthonia. One source suggests that this Butes may be the same as the Argonaut Butes, who was the son of Poseidon and Zeuxippe.

[8]Orithyia   daughter of Erechtheus who was carried away by Boreas, the North Wind, who found her while she was dancing and gathering flowers on the banks of the Ilissus River.

[9]Creusa   married Xuthus, son of Hellen and Orseis, or the son of Aeolus, a son of Hellen.   He went to Athens, where he became the leader of mercenary troops for Erechtheus.   Later, the Athenian king rewarded Xuthus by giving him Creusa as his wife.   She bore him three sons, and perhaps a daughter, Diomede, although the latter's mother is not specifically known. Euripides, however, in his play Ion, says that Ion was the son of Apollo, and Xuthus adopted him as his own. The same source also says that Dorus was the son of Xuthus, and not his brother, as Apollodorus says.   Other than the dramatic story Euripides tells in Ion, the descendants of Creusa and Xuthus have little or no mythology, and are mostly eponyms.

[10]Pandorus and Metion   sons of Erechtheus, opposed the succession of Cecrops at their father's death.   During the reign of Pandion II, the sons of Metion seized the throne, but later the four sons of Pandion--Aegeus, Pallas, Nisus, and Lycus-- marched against Athens, drove the Metionids out, and divided the kingdom among themselves.

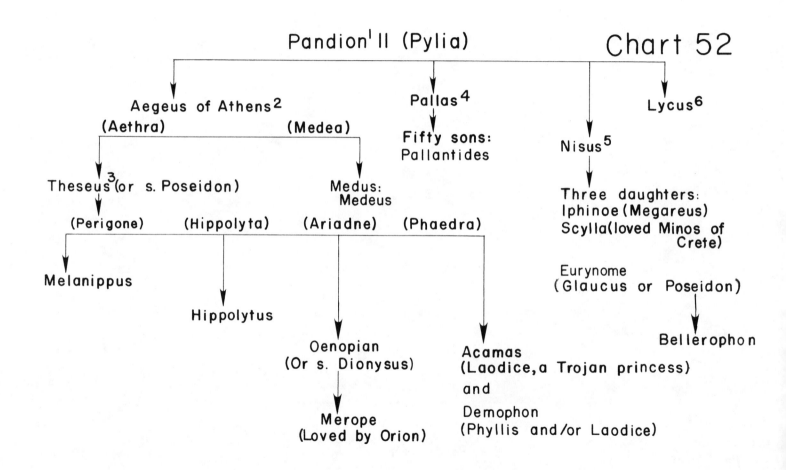

Pandion'II (Pylia)   Chart 52

Aegeus of Athens[2]

(Aethra)   (Medea)

Pallas[4]

Fifty sons:
Pallantides

Lycus[6]

Nisus[5]

Theseus[3](or s. Poseidon)

Medus:
Medeus

Three daughters:
Iphinoe (Megareus)
Scylla(loved Minos of
      Crete)

(Perigone)   (Hippolyta)   (Ariadne)   (Phaedra)

Eurynome
(Glaucus or Poseidon)

Melanippus

Hippolytus

Oenopian
(Or s. Dionysus)

Acamas
(Laodice, a Trojan princess)

and

Demophon
(Phyllis and/or Laodice)

Bellerophon

Merope
(Loved by Orion)

NOTES FOR CHART 52

[1]Pandion II   son of Cecrops and Metiadusa, succeeded
his father in the rule of Athens, but was
soon overthrown by the sons of Metion.   Pandion fled to
Megara, where he married Pylia, the daughter of King
Pylus.   Sometime later, King Pylus killed his father's
brother and had to flee the city, leaving the kingdom to
Pandion.   After the death of Pandion at Megara, his son
Nisus ruled, and the other sons returned to Athens and
drove out the sons of Metion.

[2]Aegeus   son of Pylia and Pandion, although Apollodorus says that he "was a son of Scyrius, epo-
nym of the island of Scyrus, but was passed off by Pandion as his own."   At Pandion's death, Aegeus, Pallas,
and Lycus marched against Athens, and took the throne
that had been usurped by the sons of Metion.   The kingdom was divided among them, but Aegeus alone was the
king.   First, he married Meta, daughter of Hoples, then
Chalcioppe, daughter of Rhexenor, but neither wife bore
children.   He then consulted the oracle at Delphi as to
how he might have children and was told not to open the
wineskin until he reached Athens.   Passing through
Corinth, he encountered Medea, wife of Jason, and she
promised to use her powers of sorcery to help him
have children if he would give her asylum in Athens.
At this time, Medea was plotting her terrible revenge
on Jason, and King Creon of Corinth had already passed
sentence of banishment on her.   Aegeus promised to aid

her and went his way.   He next stopped by the court of
Pittheus, son of Pelops, who was king of Troezen.   Pittheus understood what the oracle had said, and arranged
for Aegeus to lay with his daughter Aethra.   It is said
that Poseidon also lay with Aethra that night, and so the
parentage of Theseus was disputed.   Aegeus, however,
must have fully expected the child to be his because he
left a sword and a pair of sandals under a huge rock,
and told Aethra that when the boy was old enough to lift
the stone she should send him to Athens.
    In the meantime, Medea had caused the deaths of
Creon and the princess of Corinth, had killed her own
children in vengeance on Jason, and had escaped to
Athens.   Aegeus not only welcomed her, but married
her, according to Apollodorus, and she bore him a son,
Medus or Medeus.   Years later, when Theseus had
grown to young manhood, he arrived in Athens carrying
the sword Aegeus had left under the rock.   Medea,
jealous of her own son's inheritance, plotted against
Theseus and would have poisoned him, except that Aegeus recognized his own sword and received his son,
driving Medea and her son out of Athens.   Aegeus is
said to have died by suicide when Theseus forgot to
change the black flag to a white flag of victory on the
ship that brought him home from success in killing the
Minotaur in Crete.   Seeing the black flag, Aegeus
thought his son dead, and so plunged from the Acropolis
into the sea, which thereafter was called Aegean.   The-

seus joyfully arrived home only to find his father dead, and himself the successor to the throne.

3 Theseus   son of Aegeus (or Poseidon) and Aethra, became the most famous of all legendary kings and heroes of Athens. For the most part, the stories of Theseus center about either his exploits in killing certain monsters or evil-doers or his marital adventures. There are also a number of instances in which Theseus came to the rescue of the oppressed and ordered justice in their cause.

At an early age, even before he came to his father in Athens, Theseus established a wide reputation for ridding the road to Athens of a number of lawless renegades. First, he killed Periphetes, son of Hephaestus and Anticlea, who was called the Clubman because of an iron club with which he killed travelers. Theseus took the club and continued to carry it about. Next, he killed Sinis the Pinebender, about whose method of killing are several versions. One version has it that Sinis bent two pine trees to the ground, tied his victim's extremities to the two trees, and then let go, tearing the body in two. Theseus killed him in a similar manner; by Perigone, the beautiful daughter of Sinis, he had a son, Melanippus. Third, Theseus slew the Crommyon Sow, the offspring of Echidna and Typhon. Fourth, he killed Sciron, who held the territory named after him, and forced passers-by to wash his feet, and as they knelt to do so, he kicked them into the sea to be eaten by a huge turtle. Theseus killed Sciron in a similar manner. Fifth, he killed Cercyon, who forced travelers to wrestle with him, and so killed them. Theseus lifted him up and dashed him to the ground. Sixth, he killed Danastes, also known as Procrustes, or the Stretcher. This malefactor lived beside the road and offered hospitality to those who passed by. Apollodorus says he put the short guests in a long bed and stretched them

to fit the bed; the tall guests he put in a short bed and sawed off the parts that did not fit. Theseus dispatched him in a comparable manner, and continued on his way to Athens. At this time, Theseus is said to be only seventeen years old.

Once in Athens, Theseus nearly lost his life at the hands of Medea, who recognized him and was jealous that he would inherit his father's kingdom. She contrived to persuade Aegeus that the young man was an enemy and should be disposed of. He was therefore sent out to kill the Marathonian bull, which had ravaged the country ever since Heracles brought it from Crete years earlier. Aegeus had used the same plan years before to dispose of Androgeus, the son of Minos. This time, however, the bull perished, and Theseus gave it to Aegeus to sacrifice. Medea then tried to poison Theseus, but in this she failed, because Aegeus recognized Theseus' sword as his own, and so recognized his son. Medea was banished, and Aegeus received his son with great rejoicing.

Theseus' next service consisted of waging war against his father's brother Pallas and his fifty sons (who were contending for the throne) and of ridding the kingdom of factions that were seeking to overthrow Aegeus. A more serious endeavor arose, however, when it was time once again for the Athenians to pay tribute to Minos of Crete. This practice had begun eighteen years earlier when Androgeus, the son of Minos, had been killed. A plague had followed, and the oracle gave out that only by paying Minos the tribute he demanded could the land be free of the plague. Minos declared that every nine years, seven young girls and seven boys should be sent to Crete to be sacrificed to the Minotaur. Two bloody sacrifices had already been made, and for this third sacrifice, Theseus either volunteered or was chosen by lot to go with the young Athenians, intending to kill the Minotaur and put an end

Chart 52   201

to the hideous tributes. The stories of Theseus' Cretan adventures vary somewhat, but one version is fairly standard. As Apollodorus says, Ariadne, the daughter of Minos, fell in love with Theseus and offered to help him if he would carry her to Athens and marry her. He agreed, and she then gave Theseus a ball of thread, which he unwound as he entered the Labyrinth where Minos kept the monster. Theseus found the Minotaur at the very center of the Labyrinth, killed him with his fists, and followed the thread back out again. He thus escaped from Crete, taking Ariadne and the Athenian youths with him. What happened after they reached the island of Naxos is variously told: Apollodorus says Dionysus fell in love with Ariadne and carried her off; in the Odyssey, Homer says she was killed by Artemis; other sources say Theseus deserted Ariadne, and she hanged herself, or else Dionysus came to Naxos and married her. By the god she was the mother of several sons, Thoas, Staphylus, Oenopion, and Peparethus, according to Apollodorus; Oenopion, however, is sometimes called Theseus' son.

Theseus continued to Athens, and as he came nearer shore he forgot to change the black flag of the ship to a white flag, and his father, believing his son and heir dead, threw himself into the sea and died. Theseus reached home only to find his father dead and himself king of Athens. As king of Athens, Theseus was involved in at least two familiar events used by the playwrights: Sophocles, in Oedipus at Colonus, makes Theseus the final witness to the death of Oedipus, and in The Suppliants Euripides gives Theseus the judgment of ordering that the dead bodies of the Argives who perished in Polynices' war against Thebes be buried. Theseus is said by some writers to have been one of the Argonauts, although Apollonius of Rhodes says he was not one of those who sailed with Jason because at that time Theseus and his friend Pirithous were being held

in the Underworld. A more reasonable explanation would be that Theseus is in no wise related to the time period in which Jason is said to have made his voyage, as indicated in the story of Aegeus, who promised Medea sanctuary in Athens before Theseus was born, and long after the voyage of the Argo was finished. Ovid includes Theseus as one of those who participated in the Calydonian Boar Hunt.

One of the more clearly defined events in Theseus' life was that involving the Amazons. On this expedition, he either went with Heracles, or with the aid of his friend Pirithous fitted out a campaign of his own. One of the Amazon queens either fell in love with Theseus or he abducted her by force. Her name was probably Hippolyte, since her son by Theseus was named Hippolytus. After the Amazon died, Theseus was formally married to Phaedra, another daughter of Minos of Crete, by whom he had two sons, Demophon and Acamus, who fought in the Trojan War. The story of Phaedra and Hippolytus is one of the most tragic in the life of Theseus. Best told in Euripides' play Hippolytus, the events center around Phaedra's uncontrolled passion for her stepson and the disastrous consequences of the affair. Believing his son guilty of a lawless rape of Phaedra, Theseus banished him at once, and called on Poseidon to destroy him. This the god did, seemingly all too quickly, and Theseus learned too late that Hippolytus was totally innocent.

As to some of Theseus' later escapades, two of the most daring involve his friend Pirithous, at whose wedding Theseus had fought in the war against the Centaurs. Both Theseus and Pirithous declared that they would marry daughters of Zeus. First they abducted Helen, who was to be Theseus' bride, and at that time was only a child, and left her with Theseus' mother Aethra. Then they went about the business of getting a bride for Pirithous, who declared that he would have no less than Persephone, the Queen of Hades. This proved to be very dangerous, and according to Homer was fatal. When Odysseus visited the Underworld in the Odyssey, Pirithous and Theseus were among the dead; Virgil in the Aeneid is even more explicit: Pirithous and Theseus are among those in Tartarus. A more favorable story, however, is that Heracles rescued Theseus when he went to the Underworld on his Labor of getting the dog Cerberus, but was unable to rescue Pirithous.

While Theseus was away from Athens, the brothers of Helen, Castor and Pollux, had invaded the city and taken their sister home, along with Aethra, who thereafter was a slave to Helen and went to Troy with the Spartan queen when she was abducted by Paris. When Theseus returned to Athens, his people no longer wanted him as their king, and the throne was now occupied by Menestheus, a direct descendent of Erechtheus. Theseus sent his sons Demophon and Acamas to his friend Elephenor in Euboea, and himself took leave of Athens. Perhaps he sailed for Crete, but was forced off course and landed on the island of Scyrus, at that time ruled by Lycomedes. While there, Theseus was either pushed or fell off a cliff and so met his death.

There is some confusion as to the surviving sons of Theseus, Acamus and Demophon. Homer says nothing about them, but he does name Menestheus and Elephenor in the Catalog of Ships and Leaders. Quintus of Smyrna tells in some detail that they rescued their grandmother Aethra when the Greeks sacked Troy. In The Sons of Heracles, Euripides portrays Demophon as King of Athens, defending the sons of Heracles against Eurystheus. Apollodorus, however, tells that Demophon married Phyllis, a Thracian princess, whom he later deserted and died by reason of a curse that Phyllis had placed on him. The same story is also told of Acamus and Laodice, a Trojan princess.

[4]Pallas   son of Pandion and Pylia, who at first supported Aegeus in his claim to the Athenian throne, thinking that Aegeus would have no heirs, and that his own sons would eventually inherit the kingdom. Later, when it was apparent that the line of Aegeus had been preserved and that Theseus would be king, Pallas and his fifty sons, the Pallantides, rebelled and tried to seize the throne. They were defeated and killed by Theseus. After shedding his kinsmen's blood, Theseus went into exile at Troezen for a year.

[5]Nisus   possibly a son of Ares, but usually said to be the son of Pandion, exiled king of Athens, who ruled Megara after the banishment of his father-in-law Pylus. When Pandion died, his son Nisus succeeded him. Nisus had three daughters: Eurynome, mother of Bellerophon by Poseidon or Glaucus, King of Corinth; Iphinoe, who married Megareus, a king of Onchestus in Boeotia; and Scylla, who betrayed her father for love of King Minos of Crete. Ovid tells the story of Scylla in detail, and other writers, Aeschylus, for example, use the incident as an allusion to the depths of infamy a woman is capable of. Minos of Crete was waging war against Megara, and might not have taken the city except that Scylla, falling in love with Minos, knew that her father's strength lay in a single purple hair that grew in his forehead. While Nisus slept, Scylla cut it off and went to Minos, expecting him to make her his wife. Instead he either drowned her, or she drowned herself, and was transformed into a bird, "called Ciris," Ovid says, "or Shearer, a name she owes to the cutting off of her father's hair." Nisus meanwhile had been changed into a sea-eagle, and when he saw his daughter as a bird, he tried to tear her flesh to pieces with his talons. After the death of Nisus, his son-in-law Megareus succeeded to the throne.

Chart 52   203

[6]Lycus   son of Pandion and Pylia, should not be con-
          fused with several others of the same name.
This Lycus with his brothers drove the sons of Metion
out of Athens, where Aegeus became ruler.   Later, however, Lycus seems to have sided with the brother Pallas
and his rebellion against Aegeus.   In this war with Theseus, Pallas and his sons were killed, and Lycus was
exiled.   He fled to a region on the southern coast of
Asia Minor, where Sarpedon, the exiled brother of
Minos I, was living.   Later, the area was called Lycia.
Whether Lycus established the line of kings there is not
known, but it was for Iobates, a king of Lycia, that
Bellerophon killed the Chimera; he later married Philonoe, the daughter of Iobates.   Glaucus, who fought in
the Trojan War against the Greeks, came from this line.

Chart 53

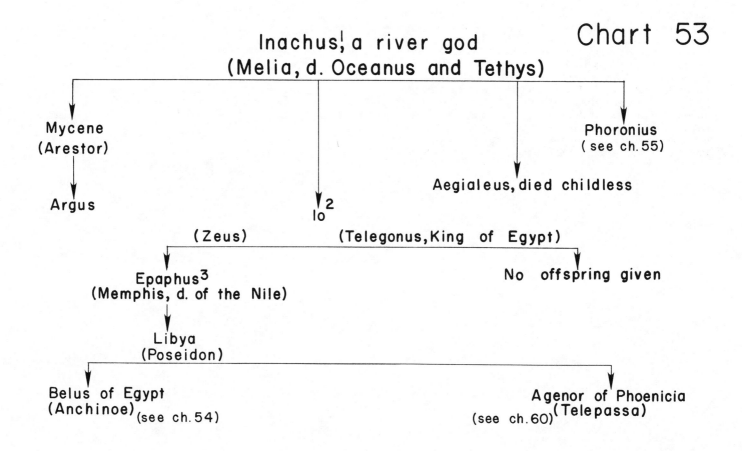

Inachus, a river god
(Melia, d. Oceanus and Tethys)

Mycene
(Arestor)

Argus

Io²

Phoronius
(see ch. 55)

Aegialeus, died childless

(Zeus)   (Telegonus, King of Egypt)

Epaphus³
(Memphis, d. of the Nile)

No offspring given

Libya
(Poseidon)

Belus of Egypt
(Anchinoe) (see ch. 54)

Agenor of Phoenicia
(see ch. 60) (Telepassa)

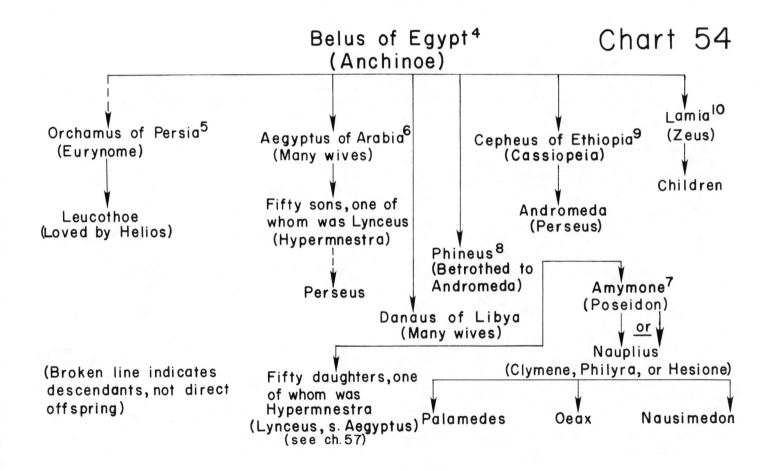

Belus of Egypt[4]
(Anchinoe)

Chart 54

Orchamus of Persia[5]
(Eurynome)

Leucothoe
(Loved by Helios)

Aegyptus of Arabia[6]
(Many wives)

Fifty sons, one of
whom was Lynceus
(Hypermnestra)

Perseus

Cepheus of Ethiopia[9]
(Cassiopeia)

Andromeda
(Perseus)

Lamia[10]
(Zeus)

Children

Phineus[8]
(Betrothed to
Andromeda)

Danaus of Libya
(Many wives)

Amymone[7]
(Poseidon)

_or_

Nauplius
(Clymene, Philyra, or Hesione)

(Broken line indicates
descendants, not direct
offspring)

Fifty daughters, one
of whom was
Hypermnestra
(Lynceus, s. Aegyptus)
(see ch. 57)

Palamedes

Oeax

Nausimedon

NOTES FOR CHARTS 53 AND 54

[1]Inachus   a river god, son of Oceanus and Tethys, who gave his name to a river in Argolis. By Melia, a daughter of Oceanus, Inachus had only two sons, Phoroneus and Aegialeus, according to Apollodorus. Other writers--Ovid, Euripides, and Aeschylus--say that Io was the daughter of Inachus. In the Odyssey, Homer speaks of "Mycene of the lovely crown," who is identified by Pausanias as a daughter of Inachus who married Arestor, and may be the eponym for the city of Mycenae. Aegialeus died childless, and the country was called Aegialia after him. Phoroneus reigned over the whole land and afterwards named it Peloponnese.

[2]Io   daughter of Inachus, is referred to as "Mother Io," and is described as "Half woman and half cow ... a monster to behold," in Aeschylus' The Suppliant Maidens. In Prometheus Bound, Aeschylus uses Io as a minor character who wanders near the rock where Prometheus is chained. She tells her story, how Zeus loved her, how she was transformed into a cow, the wandering, and torture by the gadfly sent by Hera, with no end of her suffering in sight. Prometheus, able to foresee the future, tells her that her wanderings will cease, and that she will bear a son, Epaphus, by Zeus. Apollodorus says that at least, after traveling over "great tracts of land in Europe and Asia," she came to Egypt, where she recovered her original form and gave birth to Epaphus, beside the river Nile. Later, Io married Telegonus, a king of Egypt.

[3]Epaphus   son of Zeus and Io, married Memphis, a daughter of the Nile who gave her name to the city founded by Epaphus. Libya, their daughter, gave her name to that region. By Poseidon, Libya was the mother of twins, Agenor, who migrated to Phoenicia, and Belus, who remained in Egypt.

[4]Belus   son of Libya and Poseidon, remained in Egypt, reigned over the country, and married Anchinoe, a daughter of the Nile, by whom he had twin sons, Aegyptus and Danaus. Apollodorus also says that Cepheus of Ethiopia and Phineus were sons of Belus.

[5]Orchamus of Persia   whom Ovid calls a descendant, not a son, of Belus, and he tells the story of Leucothoe, Clytie, and Helios.

[6]Aegyptus of Arabia and Danaus of Libya   the story of whom is fairly consistent in its main outlines, although opinions differ as to its outcome. Aegyptus and Danaus, twin brothers, quarreled over their inheritance. To settle the dispute and to gain his brother's wealth by dowry, Aegyptus wanted his sons to marry the daughters of Danaus, which the daughters strongly opposed. Danaus fled to Argos, where he and his daughters became suppliants to the King for help and protection. Later the daughters of Danaus agreed to marry their cousins and were instructed

by their father to murder their grooms on their wedding night. The mass carnage took place as planned, except that the daughter Hypermnestra did not murder her husband Lynceus, but instead defied her father and established a well-known family line, which eventually bore Heracles.

There are several accounts of what happened after the murder: Lynceus killed Danaus and all the daughters except Hypermnestra, and became king and ancestor of the Argive line; Danaus married the other daughters to victors in a footrace contest, and when he died at an old age was succeeded by Lynceus; the daughters were purified of their crimes by Athena and Hermes; and the daughters were punished in Tartarus by being set to eternally fill leaky jars with water. Of Danaus' daughters only two have any identity, Hypermnestra and Amymone. Of Aegyptus' sons only Lynceus has a mythology. The following account and lists are derived from Apollodorus:

> ... Danaus was settled by Belus in Libya, Egyptus in Arabia; but Egyptus subjugated the country of the Melampods and named it Egypt after himself. Both had children by many wives; Egyptus had fifty sons and Danaus fifty daughters. As they afterwards quarrelled concerning the kingdom, Danaus feared the sons of Egyptus, and by the advise of Athena he built a ship, being the first to do so, and having put his daughters on board he fled. And touching at Rhodes he set up the image of Lindian Athena. Thence he came to Argos and the reigning king Gelanor surrendered the kingdom to him; and having made himself master of the country he named the inhabitants Danai after himself. But the country being waterless, because Poseidon had dried up even the springs out of anger at Inachus for tes-

tifying that the land belonged to Hera, Danaus sent his daughters to draw water. One of them, Amymone, in her search for water threw a dart at a deer and hit a sleeping satyr, and he, starting up, desired to force her; but Poseidon appearing on the scene, the satyr fled, and Amymone lay with Poseidon, and he revealed to her the springs at Lerna.

But the sons of Egypt came to Argos, and exhorted Danaus to lay aside his enmity, and begged to marry his daughters. Now Danaus distrusted their professions and bore them a grudge on account of the exile; nevertheless he consented to the marriage and allotted the damsels among them. First they picked out Hypermnestra as the eldest to be the wife of Lynceus, and Gorgophone to be the wife of Proteus; for Lynceus and Proteus had been borne to Egypt by a woman of royal blood, Argyphia; but the rest Busiris, Enceladus, Lycus, and Daiphron obtained by lot the daughters that had been borne to Danaus by Europe, to wit, Automate, Amymone, Agave, and Scaea. These daughters were borne to Danaus by a queen; but Gorgophone and Hypermnestra were borne to him by Elephantis. And Istrus got Hippodamia; Chalcodon got Rhodia; Agenor got Cleopatra; Chaetus got Asteria; Diocorystes got Hippodamia; Alces got Glauce; Alcmenor got Hippomedusa; Hippothous got Gorge; Euchenor got Iphimedusa; Hippolytus got Rhode. These ten sons were begotten on an Arabian woman; but the maidens were begotten on Hamadryad nymphs, some being daughters of Atlantia, and others of Phoebe. Agaptolemus got Pirene; Cercetes got Dorium; Eurydamas got Phartis; Aegius got Mnestra; Argius got Evippe; Archelous got Anaxibia; Menemachus got Nelo. These seven sons were begotten on a Phoenician woman, and the maidens on an Ethiopian woman. The sons of Egypt by Tyria got as their wives, without drawing lots, the daughters of Danaus by Memphis in virtue of the similarity of their names; thus Clitus got Clite; Sthenelus got Sthenele; Chrysippus got Chrysippe. The twelve sons of Egypt by the Naiad nymph Caliadne cast lots for the daughters of Danaus by the Naiad nymph Polyxo: the sons were Eurylochus, Phantes, Peristhenes, Hermus, Dryas, Potamon, Cisseus, Lixus, Imbrus, Bromius, Polyctor, Chthonius; and the damsels were Autonoe, Theano, Electra, Cleopatra, Eurydice, Glaucippe, Anthelia, Cleodore, Evippe, Erato, Stygne, Bryce. The sons of Egypt by Gorgo, cast lots for the daughters of Danaus by Pieria, and Periphas got Actaea, Oneus got Podarce, Egyptus got Dioxippe, Menalces got Adite, Lampus got Ocypete, Idmon got Pylarge. The youngest sons of Egypt were these: Idas got Hippodice; Daiphron got Adiante (the mother who bore these damsels was Herse); Pandion got Callidice; Arbelus got Oeme; Hyperbius got Celaeno; Hippocorystes got Hyperippe; the mother of these men was Hephaestine, and the mother of these damsels was Crino.

When they got their brides by lot, Danaus made a feast and gave his daughters daggers; and they slew their bridegrooms as they slept; all but Hypermnestra, for she saved Lynceus because he had respected her virginity: Wherefore Danaus shut her up and kept her under ward. But the rest of the daughters of Danaus buried the heads of their bridegrooms in Lerna and paid funeral honors to their bodies in front of the city; and Athena and Hermes purified them at the command of Zeus. Danaus afterwards united Hypermnestra

to Lynceus; and bestowed his other daughters on the victors in an athletic contest.

[7]Amymone   daughter of Danaus, who became the mother of Nauplius by Poseidon. Apollonius of Rhodes gives the following account of Nauplius, who sailed on the Argo:

> ... Nauplius, whose lineage we can trace to King Danaus himself. For his father was Clytoneus son of Naubolus; Naubolus was the son of Lernus; and we know that Lernus was the son of Proetus, himself the son of an earlier Nauplius, who proved to be the finest sailor of his time, offspring as he was of one of Danaus' daughters, the lady Amymone, and her lover the Sea-god.

However, Apollodorus gives a less detailed genealogy, and a much less favorable reputation to Nauplius, and does not distinguish two figures with the same name:

> Amymone had a son Nauplius by Poseidon. This Nauplius lived to a great age, and sailing the sea he used by beacon lights to lure to death such as he fell in with. It came to pass, therefore, that he himself died by that very death.

This Nauplius married Clymene, daughter of Castreus, and became the father of Palamedes, Oeax, and Nausimedon. Of these sons, only Palamedes is well-known by reason of his infamous death. The story is told that Odysseus and/or Diomedes was responsible for the Greek army stoning him to death because he opposed going to the war. Apollodorus tells how Nauplius avenged his son's death by lighting a beacon on Mount Caphereus, and when the Greek ships tried to land, thinking it a port of safety, they were wrecked on the rocks and many perished.

[8]Phineus   brother of Cepheus of Ethiopia, has no myth-
            ology other than that related to Andromeda
and the story of Perseus.   See Note 9, below.

[9]Cepheus of Ethiopia   the story of Cepheus, his wife
                          Cassiopeia, and their daughter
Andromeda is a familiar one, told by Ovid, Apollodorus,
Euripides, and Sophocles, and referred to many times
by still other writers.   Cassiopeia, too confident in her
own beauty, angered Poseidon and the daughters of
Nereus, who caused a great flood and a sea monster to
invade the land.   The oracle gave out that the monster
could be appeased only if Andromeda were bound to a
rock and exposed to the sea.   The hero Perseus, just
come from slaying the Gorgon Medusa, arrived in time
to save Andromeda from the monster, and then claimed
her as his wife.   The king's brother, Phineus, had been
betrothed to Andromeda, and when Perseus claimed her,
he objected and would have led his followers in a great
fight, but Perseus showed the head of Medusa and turned
Phineus and the others into stone statues.

[10]Lamia   a queen of Libya, variously called a daugh-
            ter of Poseidon or Belus of Egypt.   By Zeus,
she was the mother of children, whom Hera destroyed.
Lamia, driven mad with grief, went up and down the
land snatching babies from their mother's arms and devouring them.   According to one mythology, Lamia was
the mother of Scylla.

Chart 55

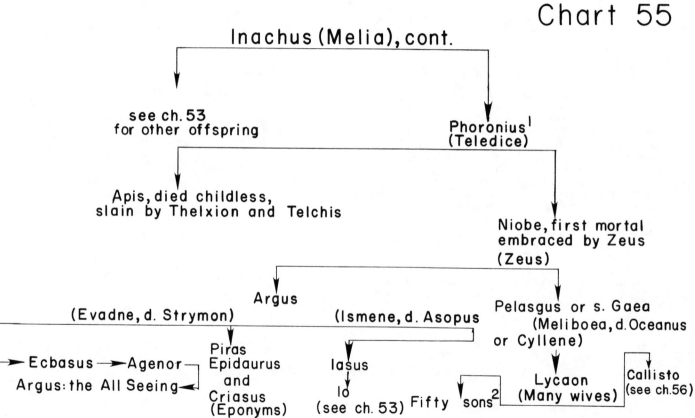

Inachus (Melia), cont.

see ch. 53
for other offspring

Phoronius[1]
(Teledice)

Apis, died childless,
slain by Thelxion and Telchis

Niobe, first mortal
embraced by Zeus
(Zeus)

Argus

(Evadne, d. Strymon)

(Ismene, d. Asopus

Pelasgus or s. Gaea
(Meliboea, d. Oceanus
or Cyllene)

Ecbasus → Agenor
Argus: the All Seeing

Piras
Epidaurus
and
Criasus
(Eponyms)

Iasus

Io
(see ch. 53)

Fifty sons[2]

Lycaon
(Many wives)

Callisto
(see ch. 56)

NOTES FOR CHART 55

[1]Phoronius   son of Inachus and Melia, daughter of
Oceanus.   All names on this genealogy
chart are derived from Apollodorus, whose lineage for
Io differs from all other writers.

[2]Sons of Lycaon   who exceeded all mortals in pride
and impiety.   The story is told that
to test the divinity of Zeus, they or their father slaughtered a human being and served it to the god.   In disgust, Zeus fled from the table and blasted Lycaon and
his sons with thunderbolts, all but the youngest, Nyctimus, who succeeded to the kingdom.   Ovid says that
Lycaon was changed into a wolf, as befitting his savage
nature.   During the reign of Lycaon, there occurred
the Great Flood, which was thought to have been caused
by the savagery and impiety of Lycaon's sons.   The
names given here are from Apollodorus:

>   Melaeneus, Thesprotus, Helix, Nyctimus,
>   Peucetius, Caucon, Mecisteus, Hopleus,
>   Macareus, Macednus, Horus, Polichus, Acontes,
>   Evaemon, Ancyor, Archebates, Carteron,
>   Aegaeon, Pallas, Eumon, Canethus, Prothous,
>   Linus, Coretho, Maenalus, Teleboas, Physius,
>   Phassus, Phthius, Lycius, Halipherus, Genetor,
>   Bucolion, Socleus, Phineus, Eumetes, Harpaleus,
>   Portheus, Plato, Haemo, Cynaethus, Leo,
>   Harpalycus, Heraeus, Titanas, Mantineus, Clitor,
>   Stymphalus, and Orchomenus.

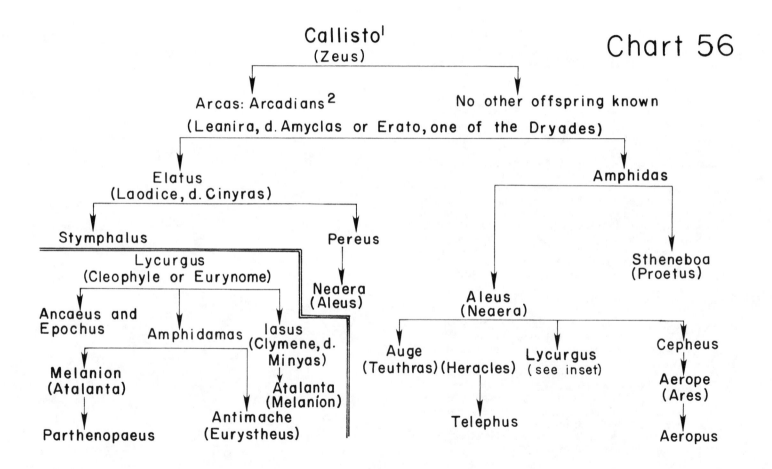

Callisto[1]
(Zeus)

Chart 56

Arcas: Arcadians[2]
(Leanira, d. Amyclas or Erato, one of the Dryades)

No other offspring known

Elatus
(Laodice, d. Cinyras)

Amphidas

Stymphalus

Pereus

Sthenebœa
(Proetus)

Lycurgus
(Cleophyle or Eurynome)

Neaera
(Aleus)

Aleus
(Neaera)

Ancaeus and
Epochus

Amphidamas

Iasus
(Clymene, d.
Minyas)

Auge
(Teuthras)

(Heracles)

Lycurgus
(see inset)

Cepheus

Melanion
(Atalanta)

Atalanta
(Melanion)

Telephus

Aerope
(Ares)

Parthenopaeus

Antimache
(Eurystheus)

Aeropus

NOTES FOR CHART 56

[1]Callisto   generally referred to as the daughter of Lycaon, the Arcadian king destroyed by Zeus
or turned into a wolf, according to some stories.   The
details of Callisto's fate vary, but the main events are
usually the same.   As a huntress, and devotee of Artemis, Callisto took a vow of chastity that was violated
by Zeus.   At this point, she became transformed into a
bear, although there are several versions of why this
change took place: Zeus transformed her in order to
conceal her from Hera; Hera, in outraged jealousy, af-
fected the change; or that Artemis changed her because
the girl broke her vow of chastity.   In any event, the
bear was eventually shot, although Hermes rescued
Zeus' baby from Callisto's dying womb and gave it to
his mother, Maia, who raised it as a near brother to
the god.   Eventually, Zeus made Callisto immortal in the
constellation Arctos, the Great Bear, and at the end of
his life, Arcas, her son, became the lesser constellation that guards the bear.

[2]Arcas: Arcadians   son of Zeus and Callisto, was
reared by Maia, the mother of
Hermes, and later succeeded his uncle Nyctimus, the
only survivor of Lycaon's sons, on the throne of Arcadia.   He taught his people the art of weaving cloth
and cultivation of crops, which he had learned from
Triptolemus.   Arcas eventually gave his name to the inhabitants of the region, hitherto called Pelasgians, and

continued the work of bringing the arts of civilization to
the primitive, savage-like people.   At his death, the
kingdom was divided among his sons, and the line of
Arcas continued to rule for many generations.   Arcas
is said to have become a constellation and guards the
Great Bear, who had been his mother Callisto.

214

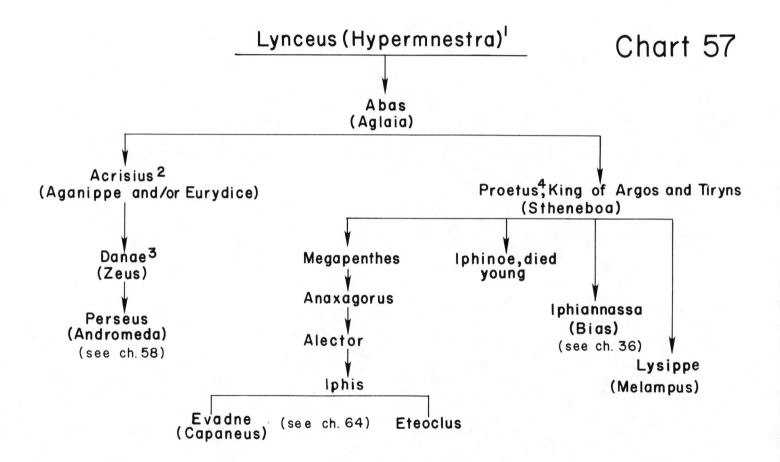

Lynceus (Hypermnestra)[1]

Chart 57

Abas
(Aglaia)

Acrisius[2]
(Aganippe and/or Eurydice)

Proetus,[4] King of Argos and Tiryns
(Stheneboa)

Danae[3]
(Zeus)

Megapenthes

Iphinoe, died
young

Perseus
(Andromeda)
(see ch. 58)

Anaxagorus

Iphiannassa
(Bias)
(see ch. 36)

Alector

Lysippe
(Melampus)

Iphis

Evadne
(Capaneus)

(see ch. 64)

Eteoclus

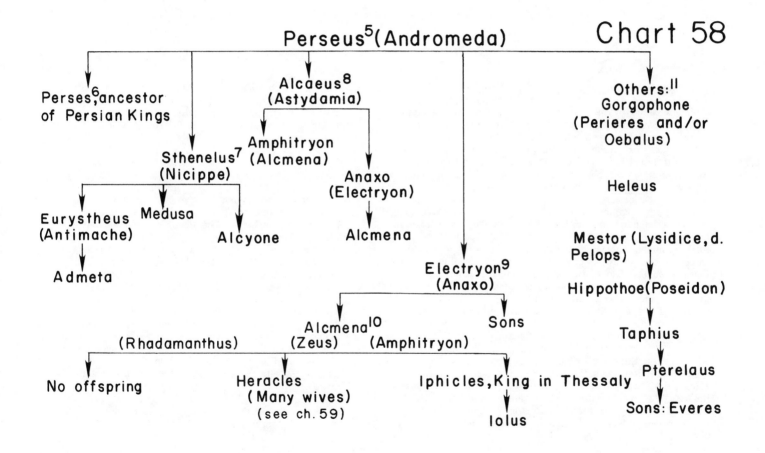

Chart 58

Perseus[5](Andromeda)

Perses,[6]ancestor of Persian Kings

Alcaeus[8] (Astydamia)

Others:[11] Gorgophone (Perieres and/or Oebalus)

Sthenelus[7] (Nicippe)

Amphitryon (Alcmena)

Anaxo (Electryon)

Heleus

Eurystheus (Antimache)

Medusa

Alcyone

Alcmena

Admeta

Mestor (Lysidice, d. Pelops)

Electryon[9] (Anaxo)

Hippothoe(Poseidon)

Alcmena[10] (Zeus)

Sons

Taphius

(Rhadamanthus) (Amphitryon)

No offspring

Heracles (Many wives) (see ch. 59)

Iphicles,King in Thessaly

Pterelaus

Iolus

Sons: Everes

NOTES FOR CHARTS 57 AND 58

[1]Lynceus-Hypermnestra   only son of Aegyptus to survive the mass slaughter of their husbands by the daughters of Danaus; and the only daughter of Danaus who did not kill her husband. In refusing to kill her husband, Hypermnestra had to disobey her father, for which she was punished, imprisoned, and tried for her life.   The events of this story are treated in a trilogy by Aeschylus, of which only the first part, The Suppliant Women, is extant.   Hypermnestra was tried for the crime of disobedience to her father, and was acquitted on the grounds that a wife owed more loyalty to a husband than to a father.   Lynceus and Hypermnestra had one son, Abas, according to Apollodorus. Abas married Aglaia, daughter of Mantineus, and they were parents of twin sons, Acrisius and Proetus. Apollodorus says, "These two quarrelled with each other while they were still in the womb, and when they were grown up they waged war for the kingdom, and in the course of the war they were the first to invent shields."

[2]Acrisius   gained mastery of the kingdom and drove his twin brother Proetus from Argos.   By Aganippe or Eurydice, daughter of Lacedaemon and Sparta, Acrisius was the father of the beautiful daughter Danae, but had no sons.   The oracle told Acrisius that his daughter would give birth to a son who would kill him.   Fearing for his life, Acrisius locked Danae in an underground prison and guarded her day and night.   Nonetheless, Zeus obtained her in the shape of a stream of gold, which came through the roof of the prison.   Afterwards, she bore the son Perseus.   Years later, Acrisius' death came at the hands of Perseus, who accidentally killed him in a game of quoits, not knowing who he was.

[3]Danae   daughter of Acrisius, was persecuted by her father before the birth of her son and afterwards because he did not believe her child was the son of Zeus.   He therefore put Danae and her child in a chest and set it afloat.   The chest washed ashore at Seriphus.   Here Danae and her son were protected and given a home by Dictys, a brother of King Polydectes of Seriphus.   The king fell in love with Danae, and would have violated her, but Perseus had become a man and protected his mother's honor.   The king devised a means of getting rid of Perseus by ordering him to fetch the Gorgon's head, thinking he would perish, and Danae would be available for his pleasure.   Perseus, however, did not perish and eventually returned to take his mother back to Argos.   Virgil says in the Aeneid that "Danae and Acrisian settlers" later came to Italy and founded a city called Ardea, the capital of the Rutulians.

[4]Proetus   twin brother of Acrisius, sons of Abas and Aglaia of Argos.   At the death of Abas, the

kingdom was inherited jointly, but the brothers fought until Proetus was driven from the country. He fled to the court of Iobates in Lycia, where he married the king's daughter Stheneboa (or Anteia). Iobates championed his son-in-law's cause and sent an army against Acrisius. Nothing conclusive was decided by this battle, and the two brothers then divided the kingdom. Acrisius remained in Argos, and Proetus established the city of Tiryns. At the death of Proetus, his son Megapenthes became ruler, and it was during this time that Perseus, ashamed of having accidentally killed his grandfather, Acrisius, changed kingdoms, and became ruler of Tiryns.

By Stheneboa, Proetus had three daughters-- Iphinoe, Iphiannassa, and Lysippe--who went mad, because they insulted either Hera or perhaps Dionysus. Melampus, the seer from Messina, cured two of them, whom he and his brother Bias married. In the process, Melampus bargained Proetus out of at least two-thirds of his kingdom (see Chart 36).

The other familiar story of Proetus is the one involving Bellerophon. Stheneboa fell in love with Bellerophon when he visited her husband's court, and when he would not return her advances, she told Proetus that their guest had assaulted her. Proetus, not wanting to violate the law of the guest, sent Bellerophon to Iobates, king of Lycia, with a sealed letter for his own destruction. However, Iobates, failing at first to kill Bellerophon, took a great liking to him, and gave him his daughter Philonoe. When Stheneboa heard that instead of being killed, Bellerophon had married her sister, she hanged herself. Another source says Bellerophon killed her.

[5]Perseus   son of Danae and Zeus, is perhaps most familiar as the hero who killed the Gorgon Medusa, cut off her head, and gave it to Athena, who placed it on the Aegis. In this dangerous exploit with the Gorgons, Perseus was aided by two gods: Athena, who supported him in the endeavor, and Hermes, who supplied him with a special wallet in which to put the Gorgon's head, a pair of winged sandals that enabled him to fly, and the cap of Hades, which rendered him invisible. After killing Medusa and cutting off her head, Perseus flew eastward until he came to the land of King Cepheus, which was on the seacoast of Ethiopia or Syria. Here he found that the wife of Cepheus, Cassiopeia, had boasted of her beauty over that of the Nereids, and that the land was being ravaged by a sea monster. To appease the monster, Cepheus had exposed his daughter Andromeda as an offering. Perseus saw the beautiful girl naked, chained to a rocky cliff, and loved her at once. He stopped only long enough to ask Cepheus for her hand and a kingdom, and then quickly attacked the monster. After a bloody battle, he killed it, and there was great rejoicing. Soon, however, Andromeda's uncle, Phineus, claimed that he was betrothed to his niece, and another battle ensued. Perseus defeated Phineus and his followers by holding up the Gorgon's head and turning them to stone.

After a long while, Perseus returned to Seriphus with Andromeda. Here he found that King Polydectes had been openly pursuing Danae. Once again Perseus opened the wallet and produced the terrible head of the Gorgon. Polydectes and his court were turned instantly to stone. Leaving Dictys on the throne, Perseus sailed for Argos with Andromeda and Danae. Acrisius, fearing that his grandson was returning to seek revenge, fled to the town of Larisa, but Perseus followed, bearing no ill-will. At Larisa, the king was holding funeral games for his father, Abas, and Perseus came just in time to enter the discus throwing. In this game the discus went astray and killed Acrisius. In this way, the oracle was fulfilled, and Acrisius died at the hands of

Danae's son. Ashamed to inherit the throne of the man he had killed, Perseus traded the kingdom of Argos for the city of Tiryns, which was then ruled by his cousin Megapenthes, the son of Proetus. Here Perseus ruled the rest of his life, and was the father of six sons and one daughter.

6Perses eldest son of Perseus and Andromeda, was born while his parents were still with Cepheus. When they returned to Seriphus, Perses remained with his grandfather and later inherited the throne because Cepheus had no sons. One source says this Perses was the ancestor and eponym of the Persians.

7Sthenelus son of Perseus and Andromeda, married Nicippe, a daughter of Pelops, by whom he had one son, Eurystheus, and two daughters, Alcyone and Medusa. At the death of his brother Electryon, Sthenelus seized the throne and drove Amphitryon (son of Alcaeus), his nephew and rightful heir, into exile. Eurystheus, the son of Sthenelus, succeeded his father only by a narrow chance. Heracles, as the son of Alcmena and Amphitryon, should have become king of Argos, but the story is told that Hera, angry because Zeus had lain with Alcmena, held back the birth of Heracles until after Eurystheus was born. Thus, the older became king. In the course of time, Heracles killed his wife and children in a fit of madness, and was ordered to serve Eurystheus for a period of some twelve years. Eurystheus continually tried to get rid of his great rival by setting him impossible and dangerous Labors to do. This was the will of the gods, however, and Heracles did all that was assigned to him, eventually achieving immortality. Eurystheus was killed in a conflict with the sons of Heracles, and the rule of Argos succeeded to Atreus and Thyestes, sons of Pelops.

8Alcaeus son of Perseus and Andromeda, was father of a son, Amphitryon, and a daughter, Anaxo, by Astydamia, another daughter of Pelops; or, according to Apollodorus, "he had them by Laonome, daughter of Guneus, or by Hipponome, daughter of Menoeceus." Anaxo married her father's brother Electryon, and had Alcmena and many sons. Amphitryon married his sister's daughter, Alcmena.

9Electryon son of Perseus and Andromeda, married his niece Anaxo, by whom he had one daughter, Alcmena, and many sons, named by Apollodrus as: Stratobates, Gorgophonus, Phylonomus, Celaeneus, Amphimachus, Lysinomus, Chirimachus, Anactor, and Archelaus. By a Phrygian woman named Midea, he also had a natural son, Licymnius. Electryon succeeded his father in the kingdom and reigned until his death. During his reign, the sons of Pterelaus and a crew of Taphians invaded the kingdom and claimed their share as descendants of Mestor, Electryon's brother. A battle ensued, and only Licymnius and Everes, a son of Pterelaus, survived. Electryon was killed some time later by his son-in-law Amphitryon. Apollodorus says Electryon was accidentally killed while Amphitryon was trying to turn back charging cattle; others say that the two men were quarreling over cattle, and Amphitryon killed his father-in-law in a fit of hot temper. At any rate, after the death of Electryon, his brother Sthenelus seized the throne and drove Amphitryon out.

10Alcmena daughter of Electryon and Anaxo, married her mother's brother, Amphitryon, and by him and Zeus had two sons, Iphicles and Heracles. While Amphitryon was waging war against the Taphians, to avenge Alcmena's brothers, Zeus "assumed the likeness of Amphitryon and bedded with Alcmena," according to Apollodorus and the Roman playwright Plautus in his comedy Amphitryon. Later, Amphitryon learned from Tiresias what events had taken place, and when the twins were born, it was assumed that Heracles was the son of Zeus because he was one day older than Iphicles, and because at the age of eight months he had strangled two huge serpents to death.

Iphicles, as the lesser of the two brothers, has little mythology. Apollodorus says he had a son, Iolus, by Automedusa, daughter of Alcathous of Megara. Later, after Heracles and Iphicles had successfully fought against the Minyans in their war against Thebes, Creon of Thebes gave Iphicles his youngest daughter to wife. Iphicles died while fighting with Heracles against Hippocoon of Lacedaemon.

Amphitryon is said to have died in the war that Heracles fought against the Minyans. After the death of Amphitryon, Alcmena married Rhadamanthus, son of Zeus and Europa, according to Apollodorus and Pausanias, but in the play by Euripides, The Sons of Heracles, she appears as an old woman, and nothing is said of her marriage to Rhadamanthus. She is referred to several times in Homer, and particularly in the Odyssey, as one of the women whom Odysseus meets in his trip to the Underworld. It is generally thought that she outlived her famous son, Heracles, and at her death went to the Isles of the Blessed.

11Others   offspring of Perseus and Andromeda, of whom very little is known. (1) Gorgophone, the only daughter, married Perieres, a son of Aeolus, and had two sons, Aphareus and Leucippus. At the death of Perieres, she apparently married Oebalus, a king of Sparta, by whom she had Tyndareus and Icarius. Hippocoon, a son of Oebalus, is not, however, the son of Gorgophone. (2) Heleus, founder of the city Helos, became one of the rulers of the Taphian Islands, after

Amphitryon raided the islands and gave the rule to his uncle. (3) Mestor married Lysidice, a daughter of Pelops, by whom he had a daughter, Hippothoe. Apollodorus says, "This Hippothoe was carried off by Poseidon to the Echinadian Islands where she became the mother of Taphius, who colonized Taphus. And Taphius had a son Pterelaus, whom Poseidon made immortal by implanting a golden hair in his head." The sons of Pterelaus--Chromius, Tyrannus, Antiochus, Chersidamas, Mestor, and Everes--were those who invaded Mycenae and made war against Electryon.

Children and Wives of Heracles[1]

Chart 59

By Deianira, daughter of Oeneus:[2]
- Hyllas (Iole)
- Ctesippus
- Glenus
- Onites
- Macaria, only daughter[3]

By Megara, daughter of Creon
of Thebes (not Jocasta's brother):
- Therimachus
- Deicoon
- Creontides

By Omphale, Queen of Lydia:
- Agelaus———►Family of Croesus
- Lymon or Lamus
- Alcaeus

By Chalcioppe, daughter of Eurypylus:
- Thettalus———►Two sons

By Epicaste, daughter of Augeas:
- Thestalus

By Parthenope, daughter of Stymphalus (see ch.56)
- Everes

By Auge, daughter of Aleus:
- Telephus (Astyoche, d. Laomedon)
  ↓
- Eurypylus, died at Troy

By Astyoche, daughter of
Phylas or Laomedon of
Troy, or Astydamia, daughter
of Amyntor:
- Tlepolemus, died at Troy
  (Polyxo)

By Astydamia, daughter of Amyntor:
- Ctesippus

By Autonoe, daughter of Pireus:
- Palaemon

By the fifty daughters of Thespius:[4]
- Fifty-one sons

By Hebe, daughter of Hera and Zeus:[5]
- Alexiares
- Anicetus

By Echidna, daughter of Phorcys and
Ceto:[6]
- Agathyrus
- Gelonus
- Scythes ———► Scythian Kings

NOTES FOR CHART 59

[1]Heracles son of Zeus and Alcmena, is more commonly called by his Roman name, Hercules. Most of the mythology connected with Heracles consists of (1) his great achievements in physical prowess, ridding the land of certain destructive monsters and the like; (2) wars that Heracles made against his or his friend's enemies; (3) the many wives or mistresses he had and their nearly countless offspring; and (4) the Labors he undertook in service to Eurystheus. Much difference of opinion exists as to the order of events in his life; however, there is general agreement as to how he was born and how he died. As early as Hesiod in the Theogony it was said of Heracles: "He accomplished his great work and now lives forever with the immortals, where neither sorrow nor old age can touch him."

There are numerous references to Heracles throughout Homer, and a number of extant plays, Greek and Roman, on various aspects of the hero, but the longest overall account of his life is given by Apollodorus in The Library. As to the plays, the following contain stories of or substantial references to Heracles: (1) Aeschylus' Prometheus Bound contains a prophecy that eventually a descendant of Io, a powerful bowman, will free Prometheus. (2) Sophocles' The Trachinean Women deals with the tragic events leading up to the death of Heracles. (3) Seneca's Hercules on Oeta is a very long play that deals, as does Sophocles' play, with events leading up to the death of Hercules, and continues with the death, and the hero's transfiguration into the heavens. (4) At the end of Sophocles' Philoctetes, Heracles appearing as a ghost and bidding the angry Philoctetes go with the Greeks to Troy and aid them in their conquest of the Trojans. (5) Euripides' Alcestis makes comic use of Heracles as he half-drunkenly goes off to do battle with Thanatos and brings back the dead wife Alcestis. (6) Euripides' The Madness of Heracles depicts the madness of Heracles and the ensuing murder of his wife and sons. (7) Seneca's Mad Hercules follows the basic story in Euripides' play. Both of these plays portray the madness of Heracles as occurring after he completed his Twelve Labors, whereas most sources say the madness and murders came first, and the Labors were done in expiation of the crime. (8) Euripides' The Children of Heracles takes place after the death of Heracles and depicts the continuing persecution of Heracles' sons by Eurystheus, who had set the Twelve Labors for their father. (9) Plautus' Amphitryon details the seduction of Alcmena by Jupiter (Zeus), the resulting confusion of Amphitryon, and finally the birth of Alcmena's twins, one of whom was Jupiter's son. (10) In Aristophanes' The Frogs, the god Dionysus, wishing to return the dead poet Euripides to life, consults with Heracles as to the best way to descend into the Underworld, and is told that getting down there is no problem; the getting back is the difficulty.

In addition to the plays, Heracles is also a figure in the Argonautica, but soon drops out of this work.

Perhaps the most familiar reference to Heracles
is in relation to the Ten (or Twelve) Labors. Apollodorus accounts for these Labors and the events that
preceded them:

> Now it came to pass that after the battle with the
> Minyans Hercules was driven mad through the
> jealousy of Hera, and flung his own children,
> whom he had by Megara, and two children of
> Iphicles into the fire; wherefore he condemned
> himself to exile, and was purified by Thespius,
> and repairing to Delphi he inquired of the god
> where he should dwell.... And she [the priest-
> ess] told him to dwell in Tiryns, serving Eurys-
> theus for twelve years and to perform the ten
> labours imposed on him....

The Labors are generally given as the following:

(1) To kill and bring back the skin of the Nemean Lion.

(2) To kill the Lernaean Hydra.

(3) To bring the Cerynitian Hind alive to Mycenae.

(4) To bring the Erymanthian Boar alive to
Eurystheus.

(5) To carry out the dung of the cattle of Augeas in a single day.

(6) To chase away the Stymphalian Birds.

(7) To bring the Cretan Bull to Tiryns.

(8) To bring the mares of Diomedes, the Thracian, to Mycenae.

(9) To bring the belt of Hippolyte, the Amazon
queen, to Admeta, the daughter of Eurystheus.

(10) To get the kine of Geryon from Erythia.

(11) To get the Golden Apples from the Hesperides.

(12) To bring Cerberus from the Underworld.

Labors 11 and 12 were imposed because Eurystheus did
not recognize killing the Lernaean Hydra or cleaning out
the stables of Augeas.

[2]Sons of Heracles   the names given here, through
                          Autonoe, are derived from Apol-
lodorus.

[3]Macaria   the only daughter of Heracles, offered her-
                 self as a sacrifice to gain favor of the gods
when her brothers fought against the sons of Eurystheus.
Her impending death is willingly accepted by Macaria in
Euripides' The Children of Heracles, but there is no
further reference to the sacrifice in the play.

[4]Daughters of Thespius   mothers of at least fifty sons
                               of Heracles. Apollodorus tells
this story as follows:

> While he was with the herds and had reached his
> eighteenth year he slew the lion of Cithaeron, for
> that animal harried the kine of Amphitryon and

Chart 59   223

Thespius.   Now this Thespius was king of Thes-
piae, and Heracles went to him when he wished
to catch the lion.   The king entertained him for
fifty days, and each night Thespius bedded one
of his daughters with him; for he was anxious
that all of them should have children by Heracles,
though Heracles thought his bedfellow was always
the same.

A less believable version of the story is that all this
was accomplished in one night, a feat that one comic
referred to as his "thirteenth Labor."   Afterward, he
went to Mount Cithaeron, killed the lion, and "dressed
himself in the skin."   Another source, however, says
his well-known lion's skin was that of the Nemean Lion,
the killing of which was his first Labor.   Apollodorus
names the fifty daughters of Thespius and the fifty-one
sons (one set of twins) they bore; however, none of the
daughters or sons have any history beyond this context.

[5]Hebe   daughter of Hera and Zeus.   At his death, ac-
           cording to Apollodorus, "a cloud passed under
Heracles and with a peal of thunder wafted him up to
heaven."   He was thus received by the gods, and being
reconciled to Hera, married her daughter Hebe, by
whom he had two sons, Alexiares and Anicetus, of whom
nothing further is known.   The marriage is referred to
by Homer in the Odyssey, and in Euripides' play The
Children of Heracles, Hebe and Heracles are referred
to as "two stars."

[6]Echidna   daughter of Phorcys and Ceto, described by
            Herodotus as a "creature that was half-
maiden, half-serpent, being a woman from the buttocks
upward, and below them a snake."   This description of
Echidna is rather standard, but the mating of Heracles
with Echidna seems to be limited to Herodotus, who

tells the story as a part of the legendary history of the
Scythians.   When Heracles was on his tenth Labor, to
get the kine of Geryon, he "entered the country now
called Scythia; and being overtaken there by winter and
frost, he wrapped himself in his lion's skin and fell
asleep."   When he awoke, his chariot mares were gone,
and he looked all over the country for them.   Finally,
he came upon the cave in which Echidna lived.   She ad-
mitted to stealing the mares, but would not return them
until he had slept with her.   This he did, and finally
she gave up the mares.   When the sons borne by her
were grown to manhood, she gave names to them, calling them Agathyrus, Gelonus, and Scythes.   The first
two proved to be unequal to the strength and skill of
their father, and so they were sent out of the country,
but Scythes was as great as his father and so stayed
there and from him the whole line of the kings of Scythia.

224

Chart 60

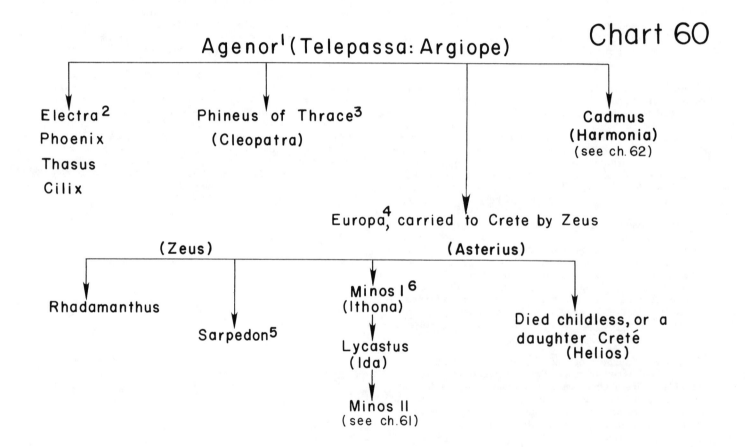

Agenor[1] (Telepassa: Argiope)

Electra[2]
Phoenix
Thasus
Cilix

Phineus of Thrace[3]
(Cleopatra)

Cadmus
(Harmonia)
(see ch. 62)

Europa[4], carried to Crete by Zeus

(Zeus)   (Asterius)

Rhadamanthus

Sarpedon[5]

Minos I[6]
(Ithona)

Lycastus
(Ida)

Minos II
(see ch. 61)

Died childless, or a
daughter Creté
(Helios)

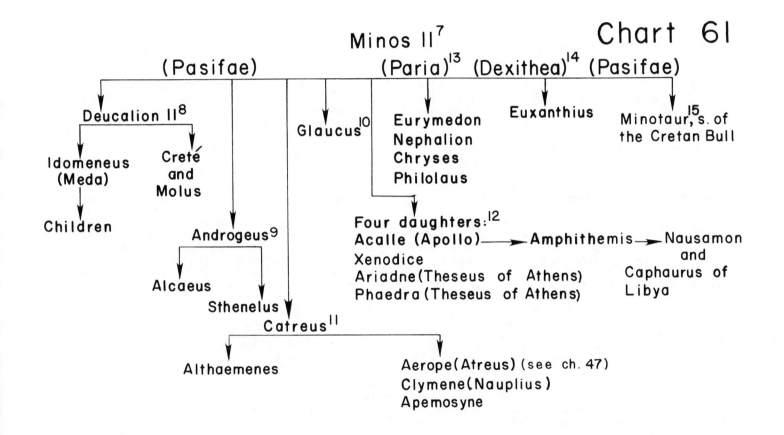

Chart 61

Minos II[7]
(Pasifae) (Paria)[13] (Dexithea)[14] (Pasifae)

Deucalion II[8]   Euxanthius   Minotaur,[15] s. of
                                                                 the Cretan Bull
Idomeneus   Creté   Glaucus[10]   Eurymedon
(Meda)   and   Nephalion
             Molus   Chryses
                                         Philolaus
Children
                Androgeus[9]   Four daughters:[12]
                                Acalle (Apollo) ——→ Amphithemis ——→ Nausamon
                                Xenodice   and
          Alcaeus   Ariadne(Theseus of Athens)   Caphaurus of
                              Phaedra(Theseus of Athens)   Libya
              Sthenelus
                   Catreus[11]

       Althaemenes   Aerope(Atreus) (see ch. 47)
                                Clymene(Nauplius)
                                Apemosyne

NOTES FOR CHARTS 60 AND 61

[1]Agenor twin brother of Belus, sons of Poseidon and Libya. Agenor left his brother to rule Egypt, and migrated to Phoenicia. Here he married Telepassa (or Argiope), by whom he had several sons: Phoenix, Thasus, Cilix, Phineus, and Cadmus; and one or two daughters: Europa and an obscure Electra. When Europa was abducted by Zeus, Agenor ordered his sons to go find her, or never return. Their mother Telepassa went with them, and remained with her son Cadmus until she died and was buried in Thrace.

[2]Electra, Phoenix, Thasus, and Cilix lesser-known offspring of Agenor and Telepassa. Electra is identified by Pausanias as a sister of Cadmus for whom Electra's Gate in Thebes was named. Phoenix, son of Agenor, left home in search of Europa, but did not go far before he settled down and ruled the land that he called Phoenicia. Thasus, another son of Agenor, sailed in search of Europa with Cadmus and founded a colony on the large island in the Aegean Sea to which he gave the name Thasus. Cilix, son of Agenor, gave up the search for Europa, and founded Cilicia, on the southeast coast of Asia Minor, north of Cyprus.

[3]Phineus son of Agenor, is usually identified as the blind king-soothsayer of Salmydessus in Thrace. He married Cleopatra, daughter of Boreas and Orithyia of Thrace.

[4]Europa beautiful daughter of Agenor who was loved by Zeus, although Homer says she was the daughter of Agenor's son Phoenix. The story is uniformly told that Zeus, either assuming the form of a white bull, or sending a white bull to do his bidding, lured Europa to climb onto his back and swam away to the island of Crete. Here she became the mother of three sons. Later she was married to Asterius, a king of Crete, by whom she was either childless or had a daughter, Creté, mother of Pasifae by Helios. Her sons by Zeus were all famous. Rhadamanthus became known for his great concern for justice and lawgiving. He and his brother Minos, together with Aeacus, the son of Zeus and Aegina, became the three judges of the dead in the Underworld. One account, by Apollodorus, says Rhadamanthus married Alcmena at the death of Amphitryon, and they ruled over the Isles of the Blessed.

[5]Sarpedon the name given to two different figures, one the grandfather of the other, or perhaps, as Apollodorus says, there was only one Sarpedon whom Zeus allowed to live for three generations. After a quarrel with his brother Minos, Sarpedon fled Crete and settled in the land ruled by Lycus, the exiled brother of Aegeus. The kingdom was eventually called Lycia, and Sarpedon and Lycus ruled jointly. If there were two figures named Sarpedon, the genealogy is as follows:

Sarpedon, s. Europa and Zeus
  (Laodamia)

    ↓

Evander or Zeus (Deidamia)

    ↓

Sarpedon, died at Troy

Both Laodamia and Deidamia were daughters of Bellerophon and Philonoe.

In the Iliad, Homer says nothing about two Sarpedons, but identifies his hero as the leader of the Lycian troops in the Trojan War, the son of Zeus and Laodamia. Early in the Iliad, Sarpedon nearly died after being wounded by Tlepotemus, a son of Heracles, but Boreas, the North Wind, blew breath into him again. Later, Sarpedon is killed by Patroclus, much to the regret of Zeus. Apollo is sent to rescue the body, and Hypnos (Sleep) and Thanatos (Death) carry it back to Lycia.

[6]Minos I   son of Europa and Zeus, became king of Crete after he drove his two brothers into exile. Some mythologists say that Minos I and II are the same figures, or that the word "Minos" like "Pharoah" in Egypt, was the name of the office. Others say that there were two figures of an entirely different character. Minos I is generally identified with his sense of justice and moderation, which earned the favor of the gods, who made him one of the judges in the Underworld. The other figure is generally associated with one of his offspring or one of his numerous wives or mistresses.

[7]Minos II   son of the nymph of Mount Ida and Lycastus, the son of Minos I, if there were two figures. By Pasifae, daughter of Helios and Perseis, or Helios and Creté, Minos had many children, and by mistresses he had many others. Most of the stories associated with this figure involve one or more of his children or some adventure with one of his mistresses.

[8]Deucalion II   eldest son of Minos and Pasifae, who succeeded to the throne at his father's death. Apollodorus says, "To Deucalion were born Idomeneus and Creté, and a natural son Molus," but does not give the name of a wife. Homer says Idomeneus took eighty ships to the Trojan War, and Virgil and Apollodorus tell the remainder of the story. After surviving the war, Idomeneus returned to Crete only to find that his wife Meda had been unfaithful with one Leucus, who had then murdered Meda and her children, including a daughter, Clisithyra. Leucus "made himself tyrant of ten cities in Crete; and when, after the Trojan War, Idomeneus landed in Crete, Leucus drove him out." Virgil says that Idomeneus then sailed with his followers and settled in Italy.

[9]Androgeus   son of Minos and Pasifae, who was murdered in some manner by Aegeus of Athens, or by a band of conspirators as he traveled to Thebes. He distinguished himself as the winner of the Panathenaic games, and one story says he died at the hands of a band of those he defeated. The most usual story, however, is that he died fighting the Marathonian bull, which had been brought from Crete by Heracles on his seventh Labor, and that Aegeus of Athens was to blame for Androgeus' death. At any rate, the boy's father, Minos, King of Crete, declared war against Athens. After a long and bitter struggle, the war came to an end with Minos exacting the terrible tribute of young Athenians to be sacrificed to the Minotaur. Androgeus was survived by two sons, Alcaeus and Sthenelus, whom Heracles took with him on his Labor of securing the belt of Hippolyta, the Amazon. Later,

Heracles fought and conquered the island of Thasus, and left Alcaeus and Sthenelus to rule.

10Glaucus   a son of Minos and Pasifae. Apollodorus says that Glaucus "while yet a child, in chasing a mouse, fell into a jar of honey and was drowned." Polyidus, a diviner, found the body and was ordered by Minos to restore his son alive. While he was shut up with the dead body, a serpent appeared, and Polyidus threw a stone and killed it, fearing to be killed himself if any harm came to the body. Then another serpent came, and seeing the first serpent dead, went away and came back with an herb which brought the dead serpent back to life. Polyidus placed the same herb on the dead body of Glaucus and raised him from the dead. Thereafter, Polyidus was forced against his will by Minos to teach Glaucus the art of divination, but "as he was sailing away, he bade Glaucus spit into his mouth. Glaucus did so and forgot the art of divination."

11Catreus   son of Minos and Pasifae, was the father of three daughters and one son, Althaemenes. An oracle told Catreus that one of his children would kill him. After this, Catreus and his children tried to avoid such a fate. Aerope and Clymene were given to Nauplius to sell in foreign lands. Aerope was bought by Atreus for his wife, and Nauplius himself married Clymene. Apemosyne migrated with her brother to Rhodes, but shortly thereafter she was murdered by her brother. Apollodorus says that "he kicked her to death," because she said the god Hermes had lain with her.

When Catreus was very old, he went to Rhodes, wanting to leave his kingdom to his son. Upon landing, Althaemenes thought Catreus and his men were raiders, and so killed him with one cast of a javelin. When he learned whom he had killed, Apollodorus says that "he prayed and disappeared in a chasm." It was to the funeral of Catreus that Aerope's son Menelaus was called away while the Trojan prince, Paris, was a guest in his home.

12Acalle, etc.   daughters of Minos and Pasifae. By Acalle, Apollo had a son, Amphithemis, and then Minos banished his daughter and her son to Libya. Xenodice is named by Apollodorus, but nothing is said about her. As to Ariadne and Phaedra, their stories are told in relation to Theseus.

13Paria   eponym for the island of Paros, on which her four sons by Minos were rulers. When Heracles was on his way to the Amazons, on his ninth Labor, he put in at the island of Paros. Fighting ensued, and two of Heracles' men were killed. After this, Heracles killed the sons of Minos--Eurymedon, Nephalion, Chryses, and Philolaus.

14Dexithea   mistress of Minos, by whom she had the son Euxanthius, or the daughter Euxanthia. Apollodorus names these members of Minos' family, but gives no information about them.

15Minotaur   monster offspring of Pasifae and the Cretan Bull. Minos kept the Minotaur in the Labyrinth at Cnossus until the creature was eventually killed by Theseus of Athens.

Chart 62

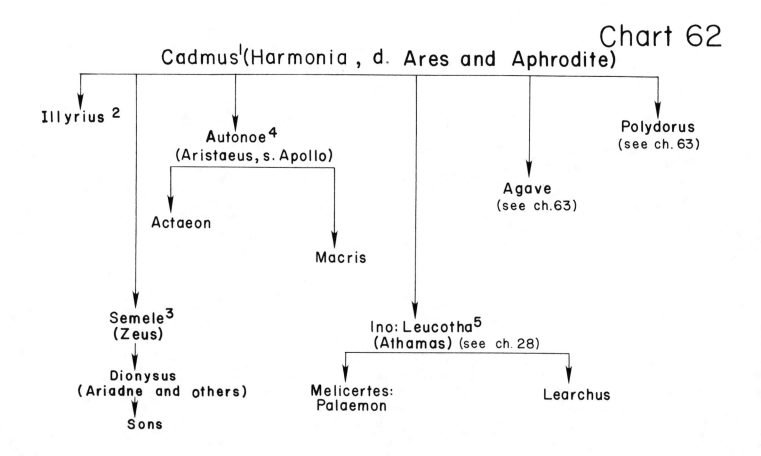

Cadmus[1](Harmonia , d. Ares and Aphrodite)

Illyrius [2]

Autonoe[4]
(Aristaeus, s. Apollo)

Actaeon

Macris

Polydorus
(see ch. 63)

Agave
(see ch.63)

Semele[3]
(Zeus)

Ino: Leucotha[5]
(Athamas) (see ch. 28)

Dionysus
(Ariadne and others)

Melicertes:
Palaemon

Learchus

Sons

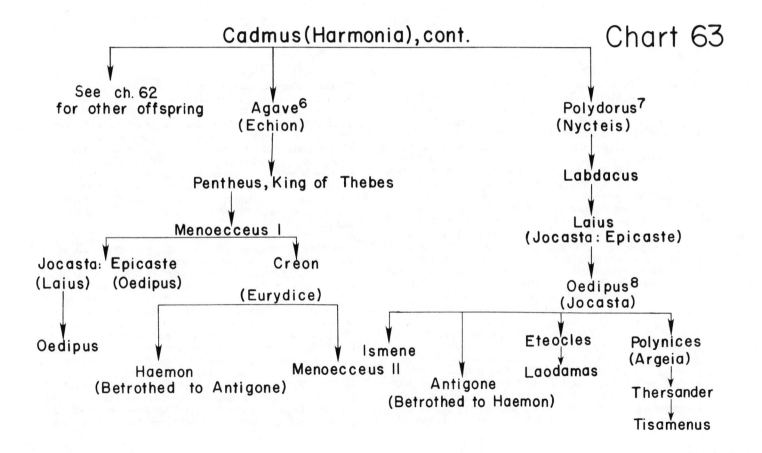

Cadmus(Harmonia),cont.　　Chart 63

See ch. 62 for other offspring

Agave[6] (Echion)

Polydorus[7] (Nycteis)

Pentheus, King of Thebes

Labdacus

Menoecceus I

Laius (Jocasta: Epicaste)

Jocasta: Epicaste (Laius) (Oedipus)

Creon (Eurydice)

Oedipus[8] (Jocasta)

Oedipus

Haemon (Betrothed to Antigone)

Menoecceus II

Ismene

Antigone (Betrothed to Haemon)

Eteocles

Laodamas

Polynices (Argeia)

Thersander

Tisamenus

NOTES FOR CHARTS 62 AND 63

[1]Cadmus son of Agenor and Telepassa, and legendary founder of Thebes, although one myth has it that Thebes was the oldest city in the world, built by King Ogyges, a son of Gaea, before the Great Flood. The walls of Thebes are usually said to have been built by Amphion and Zethus, who usurped the throne during the minority of Laius, son of Labdacus. Euripides, however, in The Bacchae, refers to the walls of Thebes, and the time of this drama is before the death of Pentheus and the succession of Polydorus to the kingdom.

When his mother died, Cadmus buried her in Thrace and then came to Delphi to consult Apollo's oracle concerning his search for Europa. Here he was told to forget about Europa, and to found a city by following a cow to where she should lie down and rest. This Cadmus proceeded to carry out, and after walking a great distance, the cow finally lay down at the site that was to become Thebes. Wishing to sacrifice the cow to Athena, Cadmus sent to draw water from the spring of Ares. A fierce dragon sprang out and killed most of the men. Cadmus then killed the dragon, and by Athena's advice, extracted and planted half the dragon's teeth. The other half Athena is said to have given to Aeetes, king of Colchis. When the dragon's teeth were planted, there arose from the ground a race of armed men, called Sparti, who fell to fighting and slaying each other. Apollodorus and others say five of these Sparti survived and founded the noble families of Thebes: Echion, Udaeus, Chthonius, Hyperenor, and Pelorus. Cadmus, however, served Ares for eight years to atone for the slaughter of the dragon, after which Athena procured for him the kingdom, and Zeus gave him Harmonia, the daughter of Aphrodite and Ares. All the gods came to the wedding and brought splendid gifts, among which was a robe and a necklace said to have been made by Hephaestus. Some difference of opinion exists as to who gave the necklace, Zeus, Aphrodite, Cadmus, or Europa. In any case, the necklace proved to be fatal to all those who owned it after Harmonia.

By Harmonia, Cadmus was the father of four daughters: Autonoe, Ino, Semele, and Agave, all of whom met tragic deaths; and one or two sons, Polydorus, who succeeded to the kingdom after the death of Agave's son Pentheus, and a much younger son Illyrius. After the tragedies of their four daughters, Cadmus and Harmonia left Thebes and went to the land of the Encheleans, who at the time were engaged in a war against the Illyrians. Cadmus led the Encheleans to victory and then reigned over Illyria. A lesser-known story is that Agave, Cadmus' daughter, married the Illyrian king and killed him to give the throne to her father. At their deaths, Cadmus and Harmonia were transformed into serpents and sent by Zeus to the Elysian Fields. Apollodorus, Ovid, Euripides, and others uniformly say they were turned into serpents, but some disagree as to

whether it was an honor or a punishment. At the conclusion of The Bacchae, Euripides gives Dionysus the
role of sending Cadmus and Harmonia into exile to punish them, and of saying they will be changed into serpents.

[2]Illyrius   the youngest son of Cadmus and Harmonia,
           born after they left Thebes. He was named
for the country Illyria, a region of the Adriatic coast,
north of Epirus. It was regarded as a barbaric land.

[3]Semele   daughter of Cadmus and Harmonia, who was
          mother by Zeus of the god Dionysus. Of
Semele there is only one myth, and that relating to her
death. Of her son Dionysus there is perhaps more
mythology than of any other god. Hera, learning of
Semele's affair with Zeus, put it into the girl's head to
ask her lover to appear to her in his true form. Reluctantly, Zeus granted her wish, since he had sworn
to grant one wish she should make. He thus appeared
in all the splendor of the celestial being, and Semele
was instantly consumed by the lightning flash of the god.
The child was snatched from the fire and sewed into
Zeus' thigh, from whence it was born in due time.
Eventually, her son Dionysus descended into Hades and
returned with his mother to Mount Olympus, where she
was known as the goddess Thyone.
      The mythology of Dionysus is far too extensive
anc complex to pursue at length here. The following
sources should be consulted for even a minimum under-
standing of this god:

    (1) Apollodorus for an extended account of the
         wanderings of Dionysus on earth, his dis-
         covery of the grape-vine, and its wide dis-
         persement. This work also contains numer-
         ous instances of those whom Dionysus drove
         mad, and the tragic events that followed.

    (2) Euripides' The Bacchae is the tragedy of
         Pentheus, who doubted that Dionysus was a
         god and died as a result of this disbelief.

    (3) Ovid tells the story of Semele's destruction
         and of Zeus' saving the child, who was
         Dionysus.

    (4) Aristophanes' The Frogs is a literary and po-
         litical comedy in which Dionysus, dressed
         somewhat like Heracles, descends into Hades
         in order to bring back Euripides, the great
         poet-dramatist, whom, he says, Athens needs
         to restore her honor and glory.

    (5) As the god in whose rituals drama had its
         origin, all histories of drama or discussions
         of Greek Tragedy contain information on
         Dionysus.

    (6) As to the relation of Dionysus and the Mys-
         tery Cults, such books as Walter F. Otto's
         Dionysus: Myth and Cult are interesting,
         but may be highly speculative.

[4]Autonoe   daughter of Cadmus and Harmonia, married
            Aristaeus, a son of Apollo and Cyrene, by
whom she was the mother of a son, Actaeon, and a
daughter, Macris. After the death of Actaeon, who was
torn to pieces by his own hounds, his parents left
Thebes. One account says Aristaeus went to the Minoan
Islands and elsewhere, spreading his agricultural knowledge and particularly his knowledge of the value of bees.
Pausanias says Autonoe went to the village of Ereneia,
near Megara, where she died and was buried. In the
Argonautica, Macris is said to have fled to the island
of the Phaeacians and to have lived in a cave there.

When Jason and Medea landed on this island, it was in this cave that they spent their wedding night together.

⁵Ino (or Leucotha)   daughter of Cadmus and Harmonia, married Athamas, and was the mother of two sons, Melicertes and Learchus, both of whom perished miserably.   Driven to madness by Hera, because they had tried to conceal the child Dionysus, Ino and Athamas killed their own sons.   Athamas shot Learchus, thinking he was a deer, and Ino killed Melicertes and then leaped with him in her arms into the sea.   Ino became Leucotha, and Melicertes became Palaemon, both sea deities who came to the rescue of sailors in distress.   It was Leucotha who saved Odysseus in the Odyssey by lending him a veil that buoyed him up until he reached the island of the Phaeacians.

⁶Agave   daughter of Cadmus and Harmonia, married Echion, one of the five survivors of the men who sprang up when Cadmus sowed the dragon's teeth. Agave and Echion bore a son, Pentheus, who succeeded Cadmus on the throne of Thebes.   The story of Pentheus is related in Euripides' tragedy The Bacchae, in which Agave is driven to madness and kills her son because she and her other two sisters, Ino and Autonoe, have maligned Semele, also their sister, and doubted the godhood of Dionysus.   Pentheus is also destroyed because he refused to honor Dionysus as a god and forbade his subjects to worship the god.   After the death of Pentheus, Agave fled to Illyria and married King Lycotherses, whom one myth says she killed in order to give the throne to her father.   Polydorus, the son of Cadmus, then succeeded to the kingdom of Thebes.

There is no direct evidence that Menoeceus was the son of Pentheus, merely that he descended through Pentheus from the Sparti and Cadmus.   It is generally said that he was the father of Jocasta (or Epicaste) and

the Creon who figured in the Oedipus stories.   Apollodorus leaves the impression that this same Creon was the father of the Megara who married Heracles, but another source, the Oxford Classical Dictionary, points out that Creon is "a stop-gap name, meaning 'prince' or 'ruler,'" and that the father of Megara, an earlier ruler of Thebes, is sometimes confused with the brother of Jocasta.   Euripides, however, in The Madness of Heracles, says that Creon, father of Megara, was the son of Menoecceus descended from the Sparti.   At the time of Euripides' play, Creon has been killed by Lycus, who has usurped the kingdom under pretense of acting as regent for the child Laius.   The Creon of the Oedipus plays by Sophocles would be much younger, since he is alive even after the death of Oedipus.

As to the offspring of Creon, there is some conflict of opinion.   The son Haemon is portrayed by Sophocles as the betrothed of Antigone, who kills himself when his father condemns Antigone to die.   Apollodorus says that Haemon was killed by the Sphinx when he failed to answer the riddle that Oedipus later answered.   The son Menoecceus is referred to as having died in the war of the Seven Against Thebes in Sophocles' Antigone.   In Euripides' tragedy The Phoenician Women, Tiresias says that Thebes will stand only if Creon sacrifices the son "who is born of the lineage of the Dragon's Teeth, and is a virgin man."   Creon cannot kill his son, but Menoecceus, knowing the prophet to be true, throws himself from one of the walls of Thebes and dies for the cause.

⁷Polydorus   son of Cadmus and Harmonia, who for some reason did not succeed to the throne when his father stepped down.   The rule of Pentheus, however, was brief, and then Polydorus reigned.   He married Nycteis, daughter of Nycteus, who was either the son of Chthonius, one of the Sparti, or the son of

Hyrieus, a son of Poseidon. By Nycteis, Polydorus was father of Labdacus, who was quite young when Polydorus died. Nycteus, the maternal grandfather of Labdacus, then ruled as regent. Labdacus in turn had a son, Laius, who was one year old when his father died. Apollodorus says Labdacus "perished after Pentheus because he was like-minded with him," but there is no other source that says he died in this violent manner. During the reign of Laius, Lycus, the brother of Nycteus, seized the throne and reigned twenty years. He was killed by Amphion and Zethus, sons of Zeus and Antiope, another daughter of Nycteus. Laius fled to the court of Pelops, where he remained until the deaths of Amphion and Zethus. He then returned home to Thebes where he married Jocasta, or Epicaste, as Homer calls her.

Laius was warned that he should bear no child, for if he did that child would kill him. Eventually, however, Laius and Jocasta had a son whom they exposed on Mount Cithaeron, thinking to escape their fates. Many years later, the King and his hunting party were killed by a young stranger at a place "where three roads meet." Subsequently, it was revealed that this young stranger was Oedipus, the King's son, who had not perished on Mount Cithaeron. Laius, therefore, died unaware that he had met the fate predicted years ago by the oracle.

[8]Oedipus   only son of Laius and Jocasta, who instead of dying when his parents exposed him on Mount Cithaeron, was saved by a shepherd and given to Polybus and Merope, the king and queen of Corinth. Oedipus grew to manhood as their son, and then was told by Apollo's oracle at Delphi that he would kill his father and marry his mother. Thinking to avoid this horror, he left Corinth forever. Not far from Delphi, he met a man in a chariot who, with a few of his followers, ordered Oedipus off the road and lashed him across the back with his whip. A brawl of some magnitude ensued, and the man in the chariot and all his followers except one were left dead. Oedipus continued to Thebes, where he found the city in a desperate turmoil, plagued by the Sphinx, who was eating the Thebans one at a time as they failed to answer her riddle: What goes on four legs in the morning; two at noon; and three at night? It was reported that King Laius had been killed, but at the time no one sought his murderer. Creon gave out the proclamation that anyone who should rid the land of the Sphinx would win the hand of Jocasta, Laius' widow, and a share of the kingdom. Oedipus sought the Sphinx and answered her riddle: Man. The Sphinx then jumped from the wall and died, and Oedipus became the hero-king of Thebes and husband to the queen. By Oedipus, Jocasta was the mother of two daughters, Antigone and Ismene, and two sons, Eteocles and Polynices. For a time thereafter Thebes was at peace, and Oedipus was much honored as their king and savior. As Sophocles begins what is perhaps the single best-known Greek play, Oedipus the King, Thebes is once again bitterly suffering a plague. Apollo's oracle has pronounced that Thebes harbors the murderer of Laius and will not be free of this pestilence until he is found and brought to justice. Oedipus launches into a vigorous investigation, only to learn the truth about himself: he is not the true son of Polybus and Merope, he is the murderer of Laius, the man in the chariot at a place "where three roads meet." He has killed his own father, and he is married to his mother. Jocasta, when she learns the truth of these matters, hangs herself, and Oedipus blinds himself, mercilessly gouging out his own eyes in order that he may never look upon those whom he has so wronged.

What happened to Oedipus after this is somewhat confused. Euripides says, in The Phoenician Women, that his sons, Eteocles and Polynices, kept him imprisoned in Thebes, and that he was not driven out of the city until after the war of the Seven Against Thebes. In this play, Jocasta is alive until she kills herself at the sight of her two dead sons, who have killed each other in the war. At the conclusion of The Phoenician Women, Oedipus, on his way to exile, accompanied by the daughter Antigone, says he will die in the small town of Colonus near Athens.

Sophocles' play Oedipus at Colonus is the most familiar version of the myth of Oedipus' death. In this play, Oedipus has remained in Thebes for some years, until finally Creon sent him out, fearing that his presence polluted the city. Although Sophocles' Oedipus the King ends with Oedipus begging for exile, by the time of the exile itself Oedipus had apparently changed his mind and wanted to remain in Thebes, cursing his sons for not lifting a hand to help him stay in his beloved city. As Oedipus at Colonus begins, Oedipus and Antigone have come into a grove sacred to the Eumenides, at Colonus, a small town outside Athens. It is here that he has come to die, and the earth where he is buried will become blessed. Before he dies, however, he is approached by Creon, who tries to force Oedipus back to die on Theban soil; this fails, and Polynices, the eldest son of Oedipus, comes begging his father to aid him in the war he is about to make against Thebes. Oedipus will have no part in the affair and repeats the curse, that the two brothers may die by each other's hand. As the end is approaching, King Theseus of Athens comes and leads Oedipus away to a spot that will forever remain secret. Later, a messenger reports that Oedipus has died, quietly and mysteriously passing from life to death at the very height of an enormous thunderstorm that Zeus has sent. The two daughters, Ismene and Antigone, then return to Thebes at the conclusion of Sophocles' play.

As for the four ill-fated children of Oedipus and Jocasta, their stories are quickly told. The two sons of Oedipus did not honor the agreement to rule Thebes alternately. At the end of his rule, Eteocles refused to give up the throne, and banished Polynices, who fled to Argos, where he married Argeia, a daughter of Adrastus, and persuaded his father-in-law to raise an army and march with him against Thebes. In this war of the Seven Against Thebes, Polynices and Eteocles killed each other at the Seventh Gate of Thebes. In subsequent action, the body of Polynices is denied the rite of burial because he marched against his homeland. In Sophocles' tragedy Antigone, the burial of Polynices is sought by his sister Antigone, who is prepared to die if necessary in order to carry out her plan. She is finally entombed alive by her uncle, Creon, and commits suicide. Creon's son Haemon, betrothed to Antigone, also dies with her by his own hand. Ismene is portrayed by Sophocles as afraid to take part in defying Creon's order on the burial of Polynices. After this she has no further role in mythology.

The last generation of the house of Cadmus is accounted for by Apollodorus and Pausanias. At the death of Eteocles, the young son Laodamas became king of Thebes, but Creon served as regent until he was grown. In the war of the Sons of the Seven, the Epigoni, Laodamas led the Thebans in their defense of the city and killed Aegialeus, the son of Adrastus, and was himself killed by Alcmaeon, the son of Amphiaraus. Thersander, the son of Polynices and Argeia, had persuaded Alcmaeon to lead the attack against Thebes; and with the overwhelming victory of the Epigoni, Thersander became king. He was in turn succeeded by his son Tisamenus. The war of the Epigoni is said to have occurred just as the Trojan war was getting started, and some of the Theban heroes went directly to join Agamemnon's forces.

The Wars Against Thebes[1]

Chart 64

Defenders:[2]

Melanippus, s. Astacus

Polyphontes, s. Autophonus

Megareus, s. Creon
or Apollo

Hyperbius, s. Oenops

Actor, s. Oenops

Lasthenes, unknown parentage

Eteocles, s. Oedipus

Gates:[3]

Proetid

Electrae

Neistre

Athena Onca or
Onciadian

Boreas

Homoloean

Seventh or
Hypsistan, Highest

Note: Order of gates does
not correspond with
order of warriors.

**The Seven Against Thebes[4] and
Sons of the Seven:[5]**

Adrastus of Argos, Leader —→ Aegialeus

Tydeus, s. Oeneus ———→ Diomedes
Capaneus, s. Hipponous —→ Sthenelus
Eteoclus, s. Iphis —→ Had no son
Hippomedon, s. Aristomachus or
Talaus └——→ Polydorus

Parthenopaeus, s. Melanion
and Atalanta └——→ Promachus

Amphiaraus, soothsayer, s.
Oicles └——→ Alcmaeon, Leader
and
Amphilochus

Polynices, s. Oedipus
└————→ Thersander

NOTES FOR CHART 64

[1]Wars Against Thebes   consist of the war of the Seven Against Thebes and the war of the Sons of the Seven, the Epigoni, which took place a generation later. The first war was initiated by Polynices, son of Oedipus, who wanted to take the kingdom from his brother Eteocles. The chieftains of this war were mustered and led by Adrastus of Argos. In this war, the Thebans were victorious, even though Eteocles, their king and leader, died at the hands of his brother Polynices, himself killed by Eteocles. All of the Argive leaders except Adrastus died, and the matter of their burial caused considerable anguish and subsequent tragedy. Burial of the Seven Against Thebes was denied until the wives and mothers of the fallen men went to Athens and enlisted the aid of Theseus in forcing the Thebans to give up the bodies. This conflict and its resolution is the basis for Euripides' The Suppliant Women and Sophocles' Antigone.

The second war against Thebes was led by Alcmaeon, the son of the Argive seer Amphiaraus, and fought by the sons of the Seven Against Thebes. In this war the only invading chieftain who died was Aegialeus, son of Adrastus. The Thebans, acting on the advice of the blind soothsayer Teiresias, knew they could not hold the city and so prepared to surrender. A great many escaped and fled to Illyria. Thersander, son of Polynices, became king of what was left of the devastated city. The other Argives returned home, and many of them later went with Diomedes to the Trojan War. The Thebans understandably sent no men or ships to Troy.

[2]Defenders of Thebes   The list given here is from Aeschylus' play The Seven Against Thebes. (1) Melanippus killed two of the invaders, Tydeus and Mecisteus, a son of Talaus and therefore a brother of Adrastus. Melanippus was killed by Amphiaraus, or by the dying Tydeus, who ate his brains. (2) Polyphontes was killed as he was leading, with Maeon, the ambush of Tydeus. (3) Megareus, a son of "Creon's seed" is named only by Aeschylus in The Seven Against Thebes, in which Eteocles says Megareus will defend the Neistre Portals against Eteoclus. (4) Hyperbius, son of Oenops, is named only by Aeschylus as one of the defenders of Thebes. (5) Actor, another son of Oenops, is named only by Aeschylus as one of the defenders of Thebes. (6) Lasthenes is named only by Aeschylus as a defender of Thebes. (7) Eteocles, son of Oedipus, is named by all writers as the king-defender of Thebes against his brother Polynices.

The only complete list of the defenders of the Seven Gates is that given by Aeschylus; however, Apollodorus names three others in his account: "In another fierce battle the sons of Astacus did doughty deeds; for Ismarus slew Hippomedon, Leades slew Eteoclus, and Amphidicus slew Parthenopaeus. And Melanippus, the remaining one of the sons of Astacus, wounded Tydeus in the belly." In Euripides' The Phoenician Women, based primarily on this war against Thebes, Parthenopaeus is clearly identified as the son of Atalanta and Melanion, and is killed by Periclymenus, a son of Poseidon. Apollodorus says that Periclymenus also pursued Amphiaraus and would have killed him, but "Zeus cleft the earth by throwing a thunderbolt, and Amphiaraus vanished with his chariot and charioteer ... and Zeus made him immortal."

[3]Gates   or portals, in the wall around Thebes are always specified as Seven, but the names are not uniformly given. Aeschylus, Euripides, and Apollodorus each name these gates and assign an Argive chieftain to assault it. Pausanias, however, in the second century A. D., names the Gates without reference to the warriors. In his lengthy and detailed Guide to Greece he says:

> In the circuit of the ancient Wall of Thebes there were Seven Gates, and they are still there now. I found gates were named after Electra, sister of Cadmus, and the Proetian gates after a local man Proetus whose generation and ancestry were difficult to discover. The Neistan gates were named after the last lyre-string, the Netes, which they say Amphion invented at these gates. But I have heard once that the son of Amphion's brother Zethus was called Neis and the gates were named after him. The Spring gates are named ... and by the High gates is the sanctuary of Zeus All-highest. They call the next gates Ogygian, and the last are the Homoloides. This is how the Homoloides got their name. When they were beaten by the Argives, most of Thebes stole away with Laodamas: some of them could

not face the journey to Illyria, so they turned aside into Thessaly and took possession of Homole, which had the best land and the most plentiful streams in the Thessalian mountains. When Thersander, son of Polynices, called them home they named the gates they came home through after Homole the "Homoloides."

[4]Seven Against Thebes   the Argive warriors who joined   Polynices in his war against Eteocles. Aeschylus, in The Seven Against Thebes, gives the following warriors and the Gates they assaulted:

> Tydeus, the Proetid Gate
> Capaneus, the Electrae Portals
> Eteoclus, the Neistae Portals
> Hippomedon, the Gate near Athena Onca
> Parthenopaeus, the Gates of Boreas
> Amphiaraus, the Homoloean Gates
> Polynices, the Seventh Gate

Apollodorus names the following:

> Adrastus, the Homoloean Gate
> Capaneus, the Ogygian Gate
> Amphiaraus, the Proetid Gate
> Hippomedon, the Oncaidian Gate (Athena Onca)
> Parthenopaeus, the Electran Gate
> Polynices, the Hypsistan Gate (the "Highest")
> Tydeus, the Crenidian Gate (the "Fountain" or Spring)

Euripides gives still another catalog in The Phoenician Women:

> Parthenopaeus, the Neistian Gate
> Amphiaraus, Proetus' Gate

Chart 64   241

Hippomedon, the Ogygian Gates
Tydeus, the Gate of Homole
Polynices, the Fountain Gate
Capaneus, the Electran Gate
Adrastus, the Seventh Gate

In The Suppliant Women, however, Euripides gives a
slightly different catalog of warriors in the funeral ora-
tion spoken by Adrastus, the sole survivor of the war.
This list is the same as that given by Aeschylus in
The Seven Against Thebes:

Capaneus
Eteoclus
Hippomedon
Parthenopaeus
Tydeus
Amphiaraus
Polynices

In this play, one of the choruses is composed of the Sons
of the Seven, who pay tribute to their dead fathers and
pledge themselves to avenging their deaths.   No names
are given in this chorus.

[5]Epigoni: Sons of the Seven   the sons of the Seven,
                                  who marched against the
city and avenged their fathers' death by nearly leveling
the place.   The war of the Epigoni was written about by
several ancient authors: an epic poem called Epigoni,
and tragedies by both Aeschylus and Sophocles, also
called Epigoni.   None of these works are extant, the
earliest surviving account being that of Apollodorus, who
names the following

Alcmaeon and Amphilochus, sons of Amphiaraus
Aegialeus, son of Adrastus

Diomedes, son of Tydeus
Promachus, son of Parthenopaeus
Sthenelus, son of Capaneus
Thersander, son of Polynices
Euryalus, son of Mecisteus

Other heroes involved in the war were Polydorus, son
of Hippomedon; Cyanippus, another son or grandson of
Adrastus; and two other sons of Polynices, named Adrastus and Timeas, according to Pausanias.

BIBLIOGRAPHICAL NOTES

SUBJECT INDEX TO THE GODS

INDEX TO GENEALOGY CHARTS

BIBLIOGRAPHICAL NOTES

The scope of this listing does not aim at completeness. No attempt has been made to evaluate the works or the translations, and only that which the undergraduate is likely to read has been included.

Mythology and English Literature

Bush, Douglas. Mythology and the Renaissance Tradition in English Poetry. New York: Pageant, 1957.

Bush, Douglas. Mythology and the Romantic Tradition in English Poetry. New York: Pageant, 1957.

Gayley, Charles Mills. The Classic Myths in English Literature. Boston: Ginn, 1900. Reprint, 1968.

Guerber, H. A. Myths of Greece and Rome: Narrated with Special Reference to Literature and Art. New York: American Book Company, 1893.

Norton, Dan S., and Peters Rushton. Classical Myths in English Literature. New York: Rinehart, 1952.

Books of Mythology

Bulfinch, Thomas. The Age of Fable. New York: Harper Reprint, 1966.

Campbell, Joseph. The Masks of God. 4 vols. New York: Viking, 1970.

Colum, Padraic. Myths of the World: Orpheus. New York: Universal Library, 1972.

Fox, William S. Greek and Roman Mythology. New York: Cooper Publishers, 1964.

Frazer, Sir James. The Golden Bough. 12 vols. London, 1907-1915.

Frazer, Sir James. The New Golden Bough. 1 vol. Edited by Theodor H. Gaster. New York: Mentor Books, 1964.

Grant, Michael. Myths of the Greeks and Romans. Cleveland: World, 1965.

Graves, Robert. The Greek Myths. 2 vols. Baltimore: Penguin, 1955.

Gray, Louis, ed. The Mythology of All Races. 13 vols. Boston, 1916-1932.

Hamilton, Edith. Mythology. Mentor, 1969.

Harrison, Jane. Mythology. New York: Harbinger, 1963.

Hendricks, Rhoda. Classical Gods and Heroes. New York: William Morrow, 1974.

Larousse. Encyclopedia of Mythology. New York: Putnam, 1959.

Morford, Mark P. O., and Robert J. Lenardon. Classical Mythology. New York: McKay, 1971.

Nilsson, Martin P. Mycenaean Origin of Greek Mythology. New York: Norton, 1963.

Rose, Herbert J. Gods and Heroes of the Greeks. Cleveland: World, 1958.

Rose, Herbert J. Handbook of Greek Mythology. New York: Dutton, 1959.

Dictionaries

Feder, Lillian. Apollo Handbook of Classical Literature. New York: Crowell, 1964.

Hammond, N. G. L., and H. H. Scullard, eds. Oxford Classical Dictionary. Oxford University Press, 1970.

Hathorn, Richmond Y. Crowell's Handbook to Classical Drama. New York: Crowell, 1967.

Tripp, Edward. Crowell's Handbook of Classical Mythology. New York: Crowell, 1970.

Wright, F. A., ed. Lempriere's Classical Dictionary of Proper Names Mentioned in Ancient Authors. First published in 1788; new revision in 1949; reprint, 1963. London: Routledge and Kegan Paul.

Zimmerman, J. E. Dictionary of Classical Mythology. Bantam, 1964.

Greek and Roman Authors

AESCHYLUS son of Euphorion, was born in 525 B. C. at Eleusis, a town some fourteen miles from Athens. He died in 456 B. C. in Gela, Sicily. Of the nearly one hundred plays he wrote, only seven are extant: The Suppliants (daughters of Danaus), The Seven Against Thebes (war waged by the sons of Oedipus), Prometheus Bound, The Oresteia (trilogy on the murder of Agamemnon), and The Persians (only extant historical tragedy, based on the Greek victory at Salamis in 480 B. C.).

APOLLODORUS of Athens, was born about 180 B. C. and died after 146 B. C. , the date on which he left Alexandria. He is generally regarded as the author of the mythological work The Library, although the only extant version of this work derives from the first or second century A. D. Usually called an "uncritical" summary of Greek mythological heroes, The Library is nonetheless an invaluable work in the area of genealogy.

Among translations of this work is that of Sir James G. Frazer with ample footnotes and commentary (2 vols. , Loeb Library).

APOLLONIUS OF RHODES   was born in the third century B. C. , about 295, prob-
ably in Alexandria.   He served as Director of the Alexandrian Library during some portion of his life, and is
believed to have written the Argonautica early in life.
After this work was badly received, he retired to Rhodes,
where he may have revised the poem as we now have it.
Whatever shortcomings the Argonautica may have, it is
valuable as the longest and most complete extant study
of the Jason and Medea story.   An unfinished version of
the story was composed around A. D. 90 by the Roman
writer Valerius Flaccus.

Translations of both works are included in the
Loeb Classical Library.   The Argonautica of Apollonius
is translated by R. C. Seaton; the work by Valerius
Flaccus is translated by J. H. Mozley.   Other translations of the Argonautica are those made by Edward P.
Coleridge (Heritage Press Edition) and E. V. Rieu (Penguin Classics).

ARISTOPHANES   may have been born as early as 457
B. C. or as late as 445 B. C.   He
died around 385 B. C.   Eleven of his plays are extant
(he is believed to have written at least thirty-two others) as well as over a thousand fragments.   Called the
greatest poet of Old Comedy, he is perhaps best liked
for the Lysistrata, The Birds, and The Frogs.

Among translations of his work are the complete
plays by Benjamin Bickley Rogers (3 vols. , Loeb Library) and Five Comedies of Aristophanes, also the
Rogers translation (Doubleday Anchor Books).

EURIPIDES   was born in Phyla, east of Hymettus, in
480 or 485 B. C. and died in 406 B. C. at
the court of Archelaus in Macedonia, where he had lived
two years in some form of exile.   Of the ninety-two
plays he is thought to have written, either seventeen or

eighteen tragedies are extant, the play Rhesus as it now
exists being in some doubt as to authorship.   In addition to the tragedies, one satyr play is extant, The Cyclops, the only surviving example of this genre.   His
extant tragedies, excluding Rhesus, are: Alcestis,
Medea, Hippolytus, The Sons of Heracles, Andromache,
Hecuba, The Madness of Heracles, The Suppliants
(mothers and wives of the fallen Argive leaders in the
War of the Seven Against Thebes), Ion, The Trojan
Women, Iphigenia in Tauris, Electra, Helen, The Phoenician Women (based on the Oedipus myth, but having
little similarity to the usual stories of Oedipus), Orestes, Iphigenia in Aulis, and The Bacchae (Dionysus and
the tragedy of Pentheus, king of Thebes).

Translations of Euripides include those by A. S.
Way (2 vols. , Everyman's Library; and 4 vols. , Loeb
Library); David Grene and Richmond Lattimore (5 vols. ,
University of Chicago Press); Ten Plays by Euripides,
translated by Moses Hadas and John McLean (Bantam
Books); and The Complete Greek Drama, by W. J.
Oates and Eugene O'Neill, Jr. (2 vols. , Random House).

HESIOD   has often been disputed with Homer as the
earliest extant Greek poet.   It is now generally agreed that he came later than Homer, and that
his life period could not have been much before or after
700 B. C.   His best-known work is the Theogony, which
begins with the creation of the primeval deities, Gaea,
Uranus, the Titans, etc. , and ends with the marriage
of Zeus.   The Catalogue of Women, of which numerous
fragments survive, and Works and Days are other mythological source material.   The Shield of Heracles is a
relatively short narrative poem based on Heracles' fight
with Cycnus, the son of Ares.   The title is derived from
the long description of Heracles' shield, which has much
in common with Achilles' shield, described by Homer in
Book XVIII of the Iliad.

Translations of Hesiod's works have been made by Hugh G. Evelyn-White (Loeb Library); the Theogony, in prose, by Norman Brown (Bobbs-Merrill); and the Theogony, in poetry, by Richmond Lattimore (University of Michigan Press).

HOMER according to Herodotus, lived four hundred years before his own time, or about 850 B. C. , and at least seven cities claimed the honor of being his birthplace. It is sometimes said that Homer, like the poet Demodocus in the Odyssey, was blind. The question of Homer's existence and authorship of the Iliad and Odyssey was first raised by a few Alexandrian scholars who suggested that two different poets had composed the two epics. The so-called "Homeric question" had some vogue in the eighteenth and nineteenth centuries, but is generally discredited in modern scholarship. In either case, however, any study of the epic form must begin with the Iliad and the Odyssey, which in effect define this genre, and which are universally regarded as two of the world's greatest poems.

Translations of the Iliad and the Odyssey are far too numerous to list, but among the more easily obtained are those by Richmond Lattimore (University of Chicago Press and Harper & Row); A. T. Murray (4 vols. , Loeb Library); and E. V. Rieu (Penguin Classics). The Odyssey has also been recently translated into English verse by Robert Fitzgerald (Doubleday, 1961) and by Albert Cook (Norton, 1967).

HOMERIC HYMNS are thirty-three invocations to the various gods. The question of authorship was disputed as early as the fifth century B. C. by Herodotus and other ancient writers; today none of the hymns are regarded as written by Homer, but rather by followers of Homer in the seventh and sixth centuries B. C.

Translations of this work have been made by Hugh G. Evelyn-White (Loeb Library); Andrew Lang, in prose (Longmans, Green, and Company); as well as other earlier writers in English verse.

OVID the Roman poet, lived from 43 B. C. to A. D. 17. His family intended an official career for him, but his only real interest was in poetry. In A. D. 8, when he was considered the leading poet in Rome, he was suddenly banished by Emperor Augustus, to spend the remainder of his life at Tomis on the west coast of the Black Sea. The reason for this banishment is variously given, but the exact cause has never been established. Whatever it was seems to have been an affront to Augustus, for the Emperor never forgave him. Although Ovid is the author of several works--the Amores, the Ars Amatoria, the Heroides, the Fasti--the Metamorphoses is the work on which he hoped his fame would rest; and it is this work that has become the great storehouse of mythology for subsequent centuries.

Translations of Ovid's Metamorphoses have been made by Frank J. Miller (2 vols. , Loeb Library); Mary M. Innes (Penguin); and Rolfe Humphries (University of Indiana Press). In 1961, the Heritage Press reprinted the version supervised by Sir Samuel Garth and translated by such well-known English poets as John Dryden, Alexander Pope, Joseph Addison, and others, first published in 1717.

PAUSANIAS is identified as a Greek traveler and geographer who lived in the second century A. D. Nothing is known of his life, but his monumental work, Description of Greece in ten books, is totally extant. This work, although very long and frequently too ingenuous in its construction of missing links in some mythological stories, is invaluable to the student of Greek mythology.

Translations of this work have been made by Sir James Frazer (6 vols., 1898); W. H. S. Jones and H. A. Ormerod (5 vols., Loeb Library); and Peter Levi, S. J. (2 vols., Penguin).

PINDAR   Greek lyric poet, was born in 518 B. C. and died at the age of eighty in 438 B. C. Originally his works were collected in seventeen volumes, of which about one-fourth are now extant, mainly the epinicia--the choral odes written in honor of the victors in the Great Athletic Games at Olympia, Delphi, Nemea, Corinth, Pythia, etc.

The Odes of Pindar have been translated by Sir John E. Sandys (Loeb Library); Carl A. P. Ruck and William H. Matheson (University of Michigan Press); H. T. Wade-Gery and C. M. Bowra (Nonesuch Press); and C. M. Bowra (Penguin).

PLAUTUS   Roman comic playwright, was born about 255 B. C. and died in 184 B. C. As a young man, he possibly worked as a carpenter around the theater and may have been an actor; later he became famous as a writer and devoted all his time to writing for the theater. Of the hundred or more plays that have been attributed to him, some are thought to be the work of his imitators and followers. Of the twenty plays that are extant, Amphitryon has been the most popular over the centuries, the story of Heracles' birth having perennial interest.

The comedies of Plautus have been translated by Paul Nixon (5 vols., Loeb Library) and Frank O. Copley (Bobbs-Merrill).

QUINTUS OF SMYRNA   believed to have lived in the third or fourth century A. D. at Smyrna, is the author of a poem, the Posthomerica, that gives an account of all the events in the Trojan War from the death of Hector to the Fall of Troy. Although the style of this poet is artificial and strained, and he rightly deserved to be called "the pale Homer of the fourth century," the work is valuable and interesting because it accounts for many episodes in the Trojan War that are referred to only briefly by Homer in the Odyssey and by Virgil in the Aeneid.

Quintus' work has been translated by A. S. Way (Loeb Library), and most recently into prose by Frederick M. Combellack as The War at Troy: What Homer Didn't Tell (University of Oklahoma Press, 1968).

SENECA   son of Seneca the Elder, was born about 4 B. C. and died by suicide at the command of Emperor Nero in A. D. 65. His extant works, drama and philosophical writings, are contained in nine volumes. Nine of his tragedies, all based on Greek mythological subjects, are extant: Thyestes, Phaedra, The Trojan Women, Oedipus, Medea, Agamemnon, The Phoenician Women, The Madness of Hercules, and Hercules on Oeta. Octavia, dealing with Nero's divorce from Octavia, is sometimes said not to be Seneca's play.

Seneca's plays have been translated by E. F. Watling (Penguin); Frank J. Miller (2 vols., Loeb Library); and Moses Hadas (Bobbs-Merrill).

SOPHOCLES   Greek tragic dramatist, was born about 496 B. C. at Colonus, near Athens, and died in 406 B. C. Born of a financially prominent family, Sophocles was well educated and had all the advantages that wealth could give. It is perhaps one of literature's greatest ironies that the man who has best depicted the tragedy and suffering of human beings was himself one of the wealthiest, most attractive, and successful of human beings. In his day, he won more competitions than did Aeschylus or Euripides, and since then his tragedies have been best loved. Of the one-

hundred and twenty or more plays that he wrote, only seven tragedies remain complete: Ajax, Antigone, Oedipus the King, Electra, The Trachinean Women (based on the death of Heracles), Philoctetes, and Oedipus at Colonus.
Translations of Sophocles' plays are too numerous to list, but among this number are those by F. Storr (2 vols., Loeb Library); Sir Richard Claverhouse Jebb (Bantam Books); David Grene and Richmond Lattimore (2 vols., University of Chicago Press); and Sir George Young (Everyman's Library).

TERENCE   Roman comic dramatist, was born as a slave in 195 B. C. and died in 159 B. C. The six plays he wrote are all extant.   Based as they are on the New Comedy of Menander and Apollodorus, they do not utilize any traditional mythological themes.
The plays of Terence have been translated by John Sargeaunt (2 vols., Loeb Library) and Frank O. Copley (Bobbs-Merrill).

VIRGIL   generally accorded the rank of greatest of Roman poets, was born in 70 B. C. and died in 19 B. C., thus living during the Golden Age of Rome and Emperor Augustus.   His works consist principally of the Eclogues, the Georgics, and the Aeneid.   Before he died, he requested that the Aeneid be burned, feeling that its imperfections far out-weighed its merits.   Fortunately, Augustus refused to see this request granted, and two years after the poet's death, the epic was published with minor revisions.
Virgil's works have been translated by H. R. Fairclough (2 vol., Loeb Library).   Among the numerous translations of the Aeneid are those by C. Day Lewis, in verse (Doubleday Anchor Book); W. F. Jackson Knight, in prose (Penguin); Frank O. Copley, in verse (Bobbs-Merrill); Rolfe Humphries, in verse (The

Scribner Library); and John Dryden, in verse, issued by the Heritage Press, and now available in a new paperback format (Macmillan Company).

SUBJECT INDEX TO THE GODS

If function is identical, or nearly so, in Roman and Greek mythologies, both names are given. For example, Ares and Mars are not identical: Ares in Greek mythology is the god of war and has no relation to agriculture, whereas Mars is the earliest principal god of agriculture in Roman mythology, and is later referred to as the god of war. The following is a composite list based on the various works given in the bibliographical notes.

Abundance

Demeter (Gr.)
Pomona and Vertumus (Rom.)
Saturn (Rom.)

Agriculture

Demeter (Gr.)
Iasion (Gr.)
Plutus, s. Demeter and Iasion (Gr.)
Ceres and Liber (Rom.)
Faunus (Rom.)
Mars (Rom.)
Saturn and Ops (Rom.)
Jupiter (Rom.)
Janus, also called Consivius (Rom.)

All-High

Zeus (Gr.)
Jupiter, Jove (Rom.)

Archery

Apollo (Gr. and Rom.)
Artemis (Gr.)
Diana (Rom.)

Architecture

Athena (Gr.)
Minerva (Rom.)

Arms

    Ares (Gr.)
    Mars (Rom.)
    Athena (Gr.)

Arms, success in bearing (see also Victory)

    Nike (Gr.)
    Victoria (Rom.)

Assembly

    Athena (Gr.)

Astronomy

    Urania, one of the Muses (Gr.)

Battle (see also Arms; Warrior)

    Ares (Gr.)
    Mars, after Ceres and Liber assimilated his agricul-
       tural functions (Rom.)
    Bellona, sister of Mars (Rom.)
    Janus, also called Quirinus or Martialis (Rom.)

Beginnings

    Janus (Rom.)

Birth and fertility (see also Abundance; Fertility; Vegetation)

    Juno (Rom.)

Birth, pains and deliverance in

    The Illithyias, two daughters of Hera, later assimi-
       lated into one, Ilithyia (Gr.)
    Artemis (Gr.)

Bloom of Life (see also Youth)

    Thalia, one of the Graces (Gr.)

Boundaries, property lines

    Terminus (Rom.)
    Silvanus (Rom.)

Brilliance, brightness

    Aglaia, one of the Graces (Gr.)
    Phaethon, son of Helios (Gr.)

Building, colonizing

    Apollo (Gr.)

Comedy (see also Revelry)

> Thalia, one of the Muses (Gr.)
> Comus (Rom.)

Commerce, trade

> Minerva (Rom.)

Commerce and profit

> Hermes (Gr.)
> Minerva (Rom.)

Contests, runners

> Hermes (Gr.)
> Mercury (Rom.)

Copulation

> Priapus (Gr.)
> Lutinus (Rom.)

Corn, wheat, barley (see also Cereals)

> Demeter (Gr.)
> Ceres (Rom.)
> Iasion, a son of Demeter (Gr.)
> Kore, Persephone (Gr.)
> Triptolemus, son of Celeus of Eleusis, became a
>   demigod at his death

Counselor-at-Law (see also Justice)

> Athena (Gr.)
> Themis (Gr.)
> Dike (Gr.)
> Astraea (Rom.)

Criticism (adverse), mockery

> Momus (Gr.)

Cultivation (see also Agriculture)

> Demeter (Gr.)
> Iasion, demigod (Gr.)
> Triptolemus, demigod (Gr.)
> Ceres (Rom.)
> Mars (Rom.)

Dance (see also Lyric Poetry)

> Terpsichore, one of the Muses (Gr.)

Dawn

> Eos (Gr.)
> Aurora (Rom.)
> Aura, daughter of Aurora (Rom.)

Day

> Hemera (Gr.)

Dead, the Dead

    Hades: Ades (Gr.)
    Persephone (Gr.)
    Hecate (Gr.)
    Hermes (Gr.)
    Pluto (Rom.)
    Dis Pater (Rom.)
    Proserpine (Rom.)

Death

    Thanatos (Gr.)
    Orcus (Rom.)

Departure and return

    Janus (Rom.)

Destiny (see also Fate)

    Clotho, Lachesis, and Atropos: the Fates, three
      daughters of Erebus and Nyx (Gr.)

Discord, strife (see also Combat)

    Eris (Gr.)
    Ate (Gr.)
    Enyo (Gr.)
    Discordia (Rom.)

Disease, plague

    Apollo (Gr.)

Divination (see also Prophecy)

    Apollo (Gr. and Rom.)

Dog or hounds

    Artemis (Gr.)
    Diana (Rom.)

Doorways

    Janus (Rom.)

Doves

    Aphrodite (Gr.)
    Venus (Rom.)

Dreams (see also Sleep)

    Hermes (Gr.)

Eagle

    Zeus (Gr.)

Earth

    Gaea (Gr.)
    Rhea (Gr.)
    Demeter (Gr.)
    Ceres (Rom.)
    Cybele, also called Dindymene (Gr. and Rom.)
    Tellus, also called Terra (Rom.)

Earthquakes

    Poseidon (Gr.)

Earth's riches (see also Abundance)

    Ops (Rom.)
    Plutus (Gr.)
    Demeter (Gr.)
    Ceres (Rom.)

Eloquence (see also Epic poetry)

    Calliope, one of the Muses (Gr.)

Enchantment and spells (see also Magic; Witchcraft)

    Circe (Gr.)
    Hecate (Gr.)
    The Sirens: Leucosia, Ligeia, and Parthenope (Gr.)

Enterprises (see also Beginnings)

    Praxidice (Gr.)
    Janus (Rom.)

Epic poetry (see also Eloquence)

    Calliope (Gr.)

Excellence

    Arete, a daughter of Zeus (Gr.)

Faith, trust, word of honor

    Fides (Rom.)
    Zeus (Gr.)
    Jupiter (Rom.)

Family (see also Hearth)

    Lares and Penates (Rom.)
    Hera (Gr.)
    Juno (Rom.)

Fate (see also Destiny; Chance)

    Fortuna (Rom.)
    Keres, Dooms (Gr.)
    Parcae, Fates (Rom.)
    Moirai, Fates (Gr.)

Fecundity (see also Fertility)

    Liber Pater (Rom.)

Fecundity, vegetation

    Poseidon (Gr.)
    Dionysus (Gr.)

Fertility, of soil

    Liber Pater (Rom.)
    Demeter (Gr.)
    Ceres (Rom.)
    Dionysus (Gr.)

Fertility, in men and women

    Aphrodite (Gr.)
    Venus (Rom.)
    Dionysus (Gr.)

Fertility, in animals

    Faunus and Fauna, his wife or daughter (Rom.)
    Hermes (Gr.)
    Pan (Gr.)

Fire (see also Hearth)

    Hephaestus (Gr.)
    Vulcan, also called Mulciber (Rom.)

    Hestia (Gr.)
    Vesta (Rom.)
    Prometheus (Gr.)

Flocks, protectors of

    Pales (Rom.)
    Hermes (Gr.)
    Apollo (Gr.)

Flowers

    Flora (Rom.)
    Thallo, one of the Horae (Gr.)

Flute

    Euterpe, one of the Muses (Gr.)

Foresight

    Prometheus (Gr.)

Forests and mountains

    Silvanus (Rom.)
    Artemis (Gr.)
    Diana (Rom.)
    Satyrs (Gr. and Rom.)
    Pan (Gr.)

Fortune (see also Chance)

    Tyche (Gr.)
    Fortuna (Rom.)

Fruitfulness (see also Fertility)

    Aphrodite (Gr.)
    Venus (Rom.)
    Flora (Rom.)
    Fauna (Rom.)
    Dionysus (Gr.)

Fruit trees

    Flora (Rom.)
    Carpo, one of the Horae (Gr.)
    Pomona and Vertumus (Rom.)

Funerals

    Libitina (Rom.)

Gaity (see also Revelry; Criticism)

    Comus (Rom.)
    Momus (Gr.)
    Bacchus (Gr. and Rom.)

Gates

    Janus (Rom.)

Goats

    Satyrs (Gr. and Rom.) and Pan (Gr. and Rom.)
    Dionysus (Gr.)

Grain (see also Cereals)

    Ceres (Rom.)
    Demeter (Gr.)

Guests

    Zeus (Gr.)

Harbors

    Portunus (Rom.)
    Castor and Pollux, Polydeuces (Gr. and Rom.)

Harvests

    Ops (Rom.)
    Ceres (Rom.)
    Rhea (Gr.)
    Demeter (Gr.)

Health

    Athena (Gr.)
    Apollo (Gr. and Rom.)
    Asclepius (Gr.)
    Aesculapius (Rom.)

Hygia (Gr.)
Panacea (Rom.)
Telesphorus (Rom.)

Hearth, fire of hearth

Hestia (Gr.)
Vesta (Rom.)

Heralds

Hermes (Gr.)
Mercury (Rom.)

Heroes, the brave and valorous

Athena (Gr.)
Minerva (Rom.)

Heroic hymns (see also Epic poetry)

Calliope, one of the Muses (Gr.)
Polymnia, one of the Muses (Gr.)

Hind

Artemis (Gr.)

Hindsight

Epimetheus (Gr.)

History

Clio, one of the Muses (Gr.)

Horse

Poseidon (Gr.)
Neptune (Rom.)

Hospitality (see also Guests)

Deus Fidius (Rom.)
Zeus (Gr.)

Household (see also Hearth)

Lares and Penates (Rom.)

Hunger, famine

Limos, daughter of Eris (Gr.)

Hunt (see also Chase)

Artemis (Gr.)
Diana (Rom.)

Industry

Athena (Gr.)
Minerva (Rom.)

Inescapable, the

    Atropos, one of the Fates (Gr.)

Inevitable, the

    Nemesis (Gr.)

Initiative

    Janus (Rom.)
    Bonus Eventus (Rom.)

Invisible, the

    Hades: Ades (Gr.)
    Hermes (Gr.)
    Pluto (Rom.)

Joy

    Euphrosyne, one of the Graces (Gr.)

Justice, legal

    Dike, one of the Horae (Gr.)
    Themis (Gr.)
    Athena (Gr.)
    Minerva (Rom.)
    Astraea, Astrea (Rom.)

Justice, good faith, and honor

    Jupiter (Rom.)
    Zeus (Gr.)

Land, clearing of land

    Silvanus (Rom.)

Laurel

    Apollo (Gr. and Rom.)

Law, physical and moral

    Themis (Gr.)

Legislation

    Eunomia, one of the Horae (Gr.)

Life (see also Birth)

    The Fates: Clotho, Lachesis, and Atropos (Gr.)

Light (see also Dawn)

    Coeus and Phoebe, Titans (Gr.)
    Hyperion and Thea, Titans (Gr.)
    Eos (Gr.)
    Aurora (Rom.)

Aether, daughter of Nyx (Gr.)
Leto (Gr.)
Latona (Rom.)
Apollo (Gr. and Rom.)

Lightning (see also Thunder)

Steropes, giant cyclops (Gr.)

Lions

Cybele (Gr. and Rom.)
Selene (Gr.)

Love

Aphrodite (Gr.)
Eros (Gr.)
Venus (Rom.)
Cupid (Rom.)

Love, degraded

Circe (Gr.)

Love, idealized

Aphrodite (Gr.)
Venus (Rom.)

Love poetry

Erato, one of the Muses (Gr.)

Lyric poetry (see also Dance)

Terpsichore, one of the Muses (Gr.)

Magic (see also Enchantment)

Circe (Gr.)
Hecate (Gr.)
Medea, mortal devotee of Hecate (Gr.)

Manuring, of fields

Saturn (Rom.)

Marine Life

Glaucus (Gr.)

Mariners and navigators (see also Harbors)

Castor and Pollux, Polydeuces (Gr. and Rom.)
Ino and Melicertes, became Leucothea and Palaemon
   (Gr.)

Marriage and maternity (see also Childbirth)

Hera (Gr.)
Juno (Rom.)

Medicine (see also Health)

Asclepius (Gr.)
Aesculapius (Rom.)

Memory

Mnemosyne, one of the Titans (Gr.)

Merchants

Mercury (Rom.)

Messengers, of the gods

Hermes (Gr.)
Iris (Gr.)
Mercury (Rom.)

Messengers (see also Heralds)

Hermes (Gr.)
Mercury (Rom.)

Mice

Apollo (Gr.)

Moon

Selene (Gr.)

Luna (Rom.)
Artemis (Gr.)
Diana (Rom.)
Hecate, also called Trivia (Gr.)

Music

Apollo (Gr. and Rom.)
The Muses (Gr. and Rom.)
Orpheus (Gr.)

Night

Nyx (Gr.)

Oaths

Zeus (Gr.)
Jupiter (Rom.)
Styx, river in the Underworld (Gr.)
Semo Sancus (Rom.)

Owl

Athena (Gr.)

Peace

Eirene, one of the Horae (Gr.)

Peacock

  Hera (Gr.)
  Juno (Rom.)

Persuasion

  Peitho, Pitho (Gr.)
  Swada, Suadela (Rom.)

Pomegranate

  Persephone (Gr.)
  Proserpine (Rom.)

Population, expansion of population

  Populonia Juno (Rom.)

Prayers

  Litae, daughters of Zeus (Gr.)

Procreation (see also Fertility)

  Tellas Mater (Rom.)

Prophecy (see also Foresight)

  Apollo (Gr. and Rom.)
  Prometheus (Gr.)

Carmenta, a nymph (Rom.)
Proteus (Gr.)

Prostitutes

  Aphrodite (Gr.)

Protector of crops

  Demeter (Gr.)
  Apollo (Gr.)
  Mars, early mythology (Rom.)

Rainbow

  Iris (Gr.)

Retribution

  Nemesis (Gr.)

Riches, wealth

  Plutus, son of Demeter and Iasion (Gr.)

Rivers, Ocean (see also Sea; Water)

  Oceanus and Tethys, Titans (Gr.)
  Poseidon and Amphitrite (Gr.)
  River gods (Gr.)
  Nymphs (Gr. and Rom.)

Oceanids (Gr.)
Neptune (Rom.)
Triton (Rom.)

Roar of the sea

Triton (Gr. and Rom.)

Sailors (see also Mariners)

Castor and Pollux, Polydeuces (Gr. and Rom.)
Glaucus (Gr.)
Ino and Melicertes, called Leucothea and Palaemon
 (Gr.)
Poseidon (Gr.)
Neptune (Rom.)
Mater Matuta (Rom.)

Schools, education

Athena (Gr.)
Minerva (Rom.)

Sculptors

Athena (Gr.)

Sea, water of the sea

Pontus (Gr.)
Oceanus (Gr.)
Poseidon (Gr.)

Neptune (Rom.)
Nereus and the Nereids (Gr.)

Seasons

The Horae: Dike, Eirene, and Eunomia, daughters
 of Zeus and Themis (Gr.)

She-bear

Artemis (Gr.)

Shepherds and Flocks

Apollo (Gr.)
Pan (Gr.)
Mars, early mythology (Rom.)

Silence

Calypso (Gr.)
Angerona (Rom.)

Sky, heavens

Uranus (Gr.)
Cronus (Gr.)
Zeus and Hera (Gr.)
Coelus (Rom.)
Saturn (Rom.)
Jupiter and Juno (Rom.)

Sleep and dreams

Hypnos (Gr.)
Morpheus (Rom.)

Soil and growth of seeds

Mars, early mythology (Rom.)
Demeter (Gr.)
Ceres (Rom.)
Rhea (Gr.)
Tellus Mater (Rom.)

Song (see also Music)

Muses (Gr. and Rom.)
Linus, at least five figures by this name; not a god
but the son of a god, usually one of the Muses
and Apollo (Gr.)

Souls, conductor of to Hades

Hermes (Gr.)
Charon (Gr. and Rom.)

Sowing

Consus (Rom.)

Spinner, thread of life

Clotho, one of the Fates (Gr.)

Spinners and weavers

Athena (Gr.)

Spring, season of the year

Dionysus (Gr.)
Mars, early mythology (Rom.)
Carpo, one of the Horae (Gr.)
Flora (Rom.)

Springs (see also Water)

Maia (Gr.)
Nymphs and Sileni (Gr. and Rom.)
Juturna (Rom.)

Starry sky

Astraeus, son of Crius and Eurybia (Gr.)
Asteria, daughter of Coeus and Phoebe (Gr.)

Sudden death

Apollo (Gr.)
Artemis (Gr.)

Sun

Hyperion (Gr.)
Helios (Gr.)
Apollo (Gr. and Rom.)

Vulcan (Rom.)
Sol (Rom.)

Sunlight (see also Sun)

Apollo (Gr. and Rom.)

Swan (also Vulture, Crow, Cock, Hawk Wolf, and Serpent)

Apollo (Gr.)

Tempests

The Harpies, three daughters of Phorcys and Ceto (Gr.)

Thieves

Hermes (Gr.)

Thunder

Brontes, giant cyclops (Gr.)

Thunderbolt

Arges, giant cyclops (Gr.)
Zeus (Gr.)
Athena (Gr.)
Jupiter (Rom.)

Vulcan (Rom.)
Minerva (Rom.)

Tragedy

Melpomene, one of the Muses (Gr.)
Dionysus (Gr.)

Travelers

Hermes (Gr.)
Mercury (Rom.)

Truth

Apollo (Gr. and Rom.)
Alethia, daughter of Zeus (Gr.)
Veritas (Rom.)

Twilight

Hermes (Gr.)

Undertakers (see also Funerals)

Libitina (Rom.)

Underworld (see also the Dead)

Hades: Ades (Gr.)
Dis, called Pluto (Rom.)

Subject Index to the Gods

West Wind: Zephyrus (Gr.)
            Caurus, also called Favonius (Rom.)
North Wind: Boreas, also called Thrascias (Gr.)
            Aquilo (Rom.)
Lesser Winds:
            Southwest: Afer, Africus
            Southeast: Apeliotes, Auster, Lips
            Northwest: Corus
            Northeast: Calcias
Destructive Wind: Typhon, also called Typhoeus (Gr.)

Wine (see also Vine-growers)

Bacchus (Gr. and Rom.)
Silenus (Gr. and Rom.)
Dionysus (Gr.)

Wisdom

Pallas Athena (Gr.)
Minerva (Rom.)
Metis (Gr.)
Zeus (Gr.)
Jupiter (Rom.)

Witchcraft

Circe (Gr.)
Hecate (Gr.)

Women, married

Hera (Gr.)

Juno (Rom.)
Artemis (Gr.)

Women, unmarried

Artemis (Gr.)

Women, working

Athena (Gr.)

Women, diseases and deaths of

Artemis (Gr.)

Woods and pastures

Pan (Gr. and Rom.)

Youth

Hebe (Gr.)
Heracles, Hercules, after his death as a mortal (Gr. and Rom.)
Juventas (Rom.)

INDEX TO GENEALOGY CHARTS

Agrius -- son of Odysseus and Circe, 30, 42

Agrius -- son of Porthaon and Euryte; brother of Oeneus, 32

Ajax -- son of Telamon; hero of the Trojan War, 18, 48

Ajax -- son of Oileus; killed at Troy, 48

Albion -- son of Poseidon and Amphitrite, 8

Alcaeus -- son of Heracles by Omphale, 59

Alcaeus -- son of Perseus and Andromeda; married Astydamia, daughter of Pelops; father of Amphitryon, 45, 58

Alcaeus -- son of Androgeus, a son of Minos II, 61

Alcathous -- son of Pelops and Hippodamia, 45

Alcathous -- son of Aesytes of Troy; married Hippodamia, daughter of Anchises, 22, 24

Alcestis -- daughter of Pelias and Anaxibia; married Admetus, 34, 36, 38

Alcidice -- first wife of Salmoneus; mother of Tyro, 34

Alcimede -- daughter of Phylacus and Clymene; married Aeson and became the mother of Jason, 30, 35

Alcimenes -- son of Jason and Medea, 35

Alcinous -- descendant of Phaex, a son of Poseidon and Corcyra, 9, 17

Alcippe -- daughter of Ares by Aglaurus; married Metion, 7, 49, 51

Alcippe -- wife of Evenus; mother of Marpessa, 32

Alcmaeon -- son of Amphiaraus and Eriphyle; one of the Epigoni, 36, 64

Alcmena -- daughter of Electryon and Anaxo; wife of Amphitryon; mother of Heracles by Zeus, 11, 45, 58

Alcyone -- daughter of Atlas and Pleione; one of the Pleiades; by Poseidon the mother of Arethusa, 9, 20

Alcyone -- daughter of Aeolus; wife of Ceyx, 29, 43

Alcyone -- daughter of Sthenelus and Nicippe, 58

Alector -- son of Anaxagorus, the father of Iphis, 57

Aletes -- son of Aegisthus and Clytemnestra; later murdered by Orestes, 46

Alethia -- daughter of Zeus; the goddess of Truth, 10

Alexiares -- son of Heracles and Hebe, 6, 59

Alope -- daughter of Cercyon; by Poseidon the mother of Hippocoon, 8

Alphesiboea -- daughter of Bias and Pero, 36

Alpheus -- river god; son of Oceanus and Tethys; married Arethusa, an Oceanid, 14, 15

Balius -- immortal horse; son of Zephyrus, the West Wind, and Podarge, one of the Harpies; twin brother of Xanthus, 4, 43

Batea -- daughter of ancient Teucer; wife of Dardanus; sister of Arisbe, also a wife of Dardanus, 22

Batea -- wife of Oebalus; mother of Hippocoon, 41

Bellerophon -- son of Glaucas, a son of Sisyphus, 27

Belus -- son of Libya and Poseidon; king of Egypt, 53, 54

Bias -- son of Priam, 25

Bias -- son of Amythaon and Idomene; brother of Melampus, 34, 36

Boreas -- the North Wind; son of Eos and Astraeus; married Orithyia, a princess of Athens, 43, 51

Boreas -- one of the seven gates of Thebes, 64

Briareus: Aegaeon -- one of the hundred-handed Giants, sons of Uranus and Gaea, 1

Brontes -- one of the Cyclops, sons of Uranus and Gaea, 1

Broteus -- son of Tantalus, 44

Bucolian -- son of Laomedon and Calybe, 23

Butes -- son of Teleon; one of the Argonauts; brother of Eribates, also an Argonaut, 39

Butes -- son of Boreas, the North Wind, 43

Butes -- son of Pandion I; priest of Athena and Poseidon, 50

Butes -- son of Amycus, a son of Poseidon; father of Eryx by Aphrodite, 8, 10

Cacus -- son of Hephaestus (or Vulcan) and Medusa, the Gorgon; was killed by Heracles, 5

Cadmus -- son of Agenor and Telepassa; married Harmonia, the daughter of Ares and Aphrodite; founder of Thebes, 7, 60, 62

Caenis: Caeneus -- daughter of Elatus; was given power by her lover, Poseidon, to change her sex, 8

Caicus -- river god; son of Oceanus and Tethys, 14

Calais -- son of Boreas and Orithyia; brother of Zetes; both brothers were Argonauts, 39, 43

Callianassa -- one of the Nereids, 5

Callianeira -- one of the Nereids, 5

Callidice -- queen of Thesprotia; married Odysseus after his return to Ithaca during some of his later travels, 30

Callileon -- son of Thyestes; infant murdered by Atreus, 46

Calliope -- one of the Muses, daughters of Zeus and

Celaeno -- one of the Harpies, daughters of Thaumas and Electra, 4

Celaeno -- daughter of Atlas and Pleione; one of the seven Pleiades; mother of Delphus and Cycnus by Apollo, 13, 20

Cenchreus: Cychreus -- son of Salamis, a daughter of Asopus, by Poseidon, 17

Centaurs -- half-man, half-horse descendants of Centaurus, the son of Ixion and the "Cloud," Hera disguised as a cloud, 7

Cephalus -- son of Diomede and Deion; husband of Procris, 30, 51

Cephalus -- son of Herse and Hermes; loved by Eos, or Eos loved Cephalus, the son of Deion, 21, 43, 49

Cepheus -- king of Ethiopia; son of Belus; father of Andromeda, 54

Cepheus -- son of Lycurgus; participant in the Calydonian Boar Hunt, 33

Cepheus -- son of Aleus; sailed with the Argonauts, 39

Cephissus -- river god, 15

Cerberus -- son of Typhon and Echidna; three-headed monster dog who guarded the entrance to the Underworld, 5

Cerceis -- one of the Oceanids, 14

Ceto -- daughter of Pontus and Gaea; married her brother Phorcys, 4, 5

Ceyx -- son of Phosphor; married Alcyone, a daughter of Aeolus, 29, 43

Chalciope -- daughter of Aeetes and Idyia; married Phrixus, the son of Athamas, 28, 42

Chalciope -- daughter of Eurypylus; wife of Heracles, 59

Chalcis -- daughter of Asopus and Metope, 17

Chalcomedusa -- wife of Arcesius, 30

Chaos -- the primordial elements from which the universe was created, 1

Charis -- one of the Graces, 15

Charites -- the Graces, 15

Charon -- son of Erebus and Nyx, 1

Charybdis -- daughter of Poseidon and Gaea, 4

Chimera -- daughter of Typhon and Echidna, 5

Chione -- daughter of Boreas and Orithyia; mother of Eumolpus by Poseidon, 9, 43

Chione: Philonis -- daughter of Daedalion; by Apollo the mother of Philammon, and by Hermes the mother of Autolycus, 13, 21, 43

Chiron -- most famous and noble of the Centaurs, 7

Clymene -- daughter of Catreus; married Nauplius; sister of Aerope who married Atreus, 54, 61

Clymene -- wife of Pheres, 34

Clymene -- wife of Phylacus, a son of Deioneus, 30

Clymenus -- son of Oeneus and Althaea of Calydon, 32

Clytemnestra -- daughter of Leda and Tyndareus; wife of Agamemnon and later wife of Aegisthus, 40, 46, 47

Clytie -- daughter of Oceanus and Tethys; loved Helios, 14, 42

Clytius -- son of Laomedon, 23

Clytius -- son of Eurytus; one of the Argonauts, 39

Clytius -- son of Alcmaeon and Arsinoe, 36

Coeus -- one of the Titans, sons of Uranus and Gaea; married Phoebe, his sister, 2, 12

Coon -- eldest son of Antenor, 24

Copreus -- son of Pelops, 45

Corcyra -- daughter of Asopus and Metope; carried off by Poseidon, 9, 17

Coronis -- one of the Hyades, daughter of Atlas, 19

Coronis -- daughter of Phlegyas, a son of Ares; mother of Asclepius by Apollo, 7, 12

Coronus -- son of Caenus; one of the Argonauts, 39

Corybantes -- also called Curetes, sons of Apollo and one of the Muses, 3, 13

Corybas -- son of Iasion, 22

Corythus -- son of Oenone and Paris, 25

Cottus -- one of the hundred-handed Giants, sons of Uranus and Gaea, 1

Cranae -- daughter of Cranaus; married Amphictyon, son of Deucalion, 49

Cranaechme -- daughter of Cranaus, 49

Cranaus -- son of Gaea; second king of Athens, 49

Cratais -- another name for Hecate, 4, 12

Creon of Corinth -- son of Sisyphus; his daughter Glauce or Creusa betrothed to Jason, 27, 35

Creon of Thebes -- son of Menoecceus; brother to Jocasta, 63

Creontides -- son of Heracles and Megara, the daughter of an earlier Creon of Thebes, 59

Cretan Bull -- father of the Minotaur by Pasifae, 42, 61

Creté -- daughter of Deucalion II, 61

Creté: Creta -- daughter of Asterius of Crete; married Helios; possibly the mother of Pasifae by Helios, 42, 60

Dares -- Trojan priest, 24

Dascylus -- son of Lycus; one of the Argonauts, 39

Deianira -- daughter of Oeneus and Althaea; wife of Heracles, 32, 59

Deicoon -- son of Heracles and Megara, 59

Deidamia -- daughter of Lycomedes; wife of Achilles, 8, 18

Deileon -- son of Deimachus; one of the Argonauts, 39

Deimos -- fear, terror; son of Ares, 7

Deion: Deioneus -- son of Aeolus; husband of Diomede, 26, 29

Deiopites -- son of Priam, 25

Deiphobus -- son of Priam; second Trojan husband of Helen, 25, 40

Deiphyle -- daughter of Adrastus; wife of Tydeus, 32, 64

Delight -- child of Eros and Psyche, 7

Delphus -- son of Apollo or Poseidon and Celaeno, the Pleiade, 13, 20

Delphus -- son of Thyria and Apollo, 15

Demeter -- daughter of Cronus and Rhea; by Zeus the mother of Persephone; by Poseidon the mother of Arion, a horse; also the goddess consort of the Trojan Iasion, 6, 10, 22

Democoon -- son of Priam, 25

Demolean -- son of Antenor of Troy, 24

Demonice -- daughter of Agenor and Epicaste, 32

Demophon -- son of Theseus and Phaedra, 52

Deucalion -- son of Prometheus; survivor of the Great Flood of mythology, 19, 26

Deucalion II -- son of Minos II and Pasifae, 61

Dexamene -- one of the Nereids, 5

Dexithea -- wife of Minos II, 61

Dia -- daughter of Deioneus; wife of Ixion; mother of Pirithous by Zeus, 7, 11, 30

Dictys -- son of Magnes and Nais, 26

Dictys -- son of Magnes, a son of Aeolus; may be the same as above, 29

Dike -- daughter of Zeus and Themis; one of the Horae, 2

Dino -- daughter of Phorcys and Ceto; one of the Graeae, the gray ones, 5

Diomede -- daughter of Creusa and Xuthus; wife of Deion, 26, 29, 51

Diomedes -- son of Tydeus and Deiphyle; one of the Epigoni; hero of the Trojan War, 32, 48, 64

Electra -- one of the Oceanids; wife of Thaumas, 4, 14

Electrae -- one of the seven gates of Thebes, 64

Electryon -- son of Perseus and Andromeda; father of Alcmena by Anaxo, 45, 58

Electryone -- daughter of Helios and Rhode, 42

Eleuther -- son of Apollo and Aethusa, 9, 13

Emathion -- son of Tithonus and Eos; brother of Memnon, 23, 43

Emulation -- son of Pallas and Styx, 4, 14

Enarete -- wife of Aeolus, the son of Hellen, 27

Endeis -- daughter of Sciron, a son of Poseidon; wife of Aeacus, 18

Endymion -- son of Calyce and Zeus or Aethlius; loved by the Moon goddess Selene, 29, 31, 42

Enipeus -- river god in whose likeness Poseidon made love to Tyro, mother of Neleus and Pelias, 16

Enudus -- son of Ancaeus, a son of Poseidon and Astypalaea, 8

Enyo -- daughter of Phorcys and Ceto; one of the Graeae, 5

Enyo -- see Eris, 1, 4

Eos: Aurora -- the Dawn goddess; daughter of Hyperion and Thea, 4, 23, 36, 42, 49

Epaphus -- son of Io and Zeus, 11, 53

Epicaste: Jocasta -- wife and mother of Oedipus, 63

Epicaste -- daughter of Augeas; wife of Heracles, 59

Epicaste -- daughter of Calydon and Aeolia, 31

Epidaurus -- son of Pelops; eponym for a city north of Argolis, 45

Epigoni -- sons of the Seven Against Thebes, 64

Epimetheus -- son of Iapetus and Clymene, 19

Epione -- wife of Asclepius; mother of Machaon, Podalirius, and others, 12

Erato -- one of the Muses, 2

Erebus -- son of Chaos; brother of Nyx, whom he married, 1

Erechtheus -- son of Pandion I; sixth King of Athens, 50

Erginus -- son of Poseidon; one of the Argonauts, 39

Eribates -- son of Teleon; one of the Argonauts, 39

Erichthonias -- son of Batea and Dardanus, 22

Erichthonias -- son of Hephaestus; fourth king of Athens, 49

Eridanus -- river god; son of Oceanus and Tethys, 14

Hades: Ades -- son of Cronus and Rhea; ruler of the Underworld, 6

Haemon -- son of Creon and Eurydice; betrothed to Antigone, the daughter of Oedipus, 63

Haemus -- son of Boreas, 43

Haliacmon -- river god; son of Oceanus and Tethys, 14

Halie -- one of the Nereids, 5

Halirrhothias -- son of Poseidon; ravished Alcippe, a daughter of Ares, 7, 8

Harmon -- Trojan ally, 24

Harmonia -- daughter of Ares and Aphrodite; married Cadmus, 7, 60, 62

Harpies -- three daughters of Thaumas and Electra: Aello, Celaeno, and Podarge, 4

Harpina -- daughter of Asopus and Metope, 17

Hebe -- daughter of Zeus and Hera; wife to Heracles after his death, 6, 59

Hecate -- daughter of Perses and Asteria, 4, 5, 12

Hecatoncheires -- three sons of Uranus and Gaea, the Hundred-handed Giants: Cottus, Briareus, and Gyges, 1

Hector -- son of Priam and Hecuba, 24, 25

Hecuba -- daughter of Dymas, or daughter of Sangarius

and Metope; principal wife of Priam, 16, 24, 25

Helen -- daughter of Zeus and Leda; wife of Menelaus; abducted from Sparta by Paris of Troy, 10, 25, 40, 47

Helenus -- son of Priam; a prophet, 25

Heleus -- son of Perseus and Andromeda, 58

Heliades -- offspring of Helios by Clymene and Rhode, 42

Helicaon -- son of Antenor of Troy, 24

Helios -- the Sun god; son of Hyperion and Thea; married Perseis, daughter of Oceanus and Tethys; also bore offspring by Rhode, daughter of Poseidon, Clymene, and others, 8, 14, 42

Helle -- daughter of Nephele and Athamas, 28

Hellen -- son of Deucalion and Pyrrha, 26

Hellenes -- descendants of Hellen, 26

Hemera: Day -- daughter of Erebus and Nyx, 1

Hephaestus -- son of Zeus and Hera, 6

Heptaphorus -- river god; son of Oceanus and Tethys, 14

Hera -- wife and sister of Zeus; daughter of Cronus and Rhea, 6

Iolus -- son of Iphicles, 58

Ion -- son of Apollo or Xuthus and Creusa of Athens; possibly the eponym of the Ionians, 13, 26, 51

Iphiannassa -- daughter of Proetus and Stheneboa; second wife of Bias, 36, 57

Iphiannassa -- wife of Endymion, 31

Iphicles -- son of Alcmena and Amphitryon; half-brother of Heracles; hunter of the Calydonian Boar, 33, 58

Iphiclus -- son of Thestius; one of the Argonauts, 32, 39

Iphiclus -- son of Phylacus and Clymene; one of the Argonauts, 30, 39

Iphidamas -- son of Antenor, 24

Iphigenia -- daughter of Agamemnon and Clytemnestra, 47

Iphinoe -- daughter of Proetus and Stheneboa; died at an early age, 57

Iphis -- son of Alector; father of Evadne and Eteoclus, 57

Iphitus -- son of Eurytus; one of the Argonauts, 39

Iphitus -- son of Naubolis, a son of Ornytus; one of the Argonauts, 39

Iphthime -- daughter of Icarius and Periboea; wife of Eumelus, 38, 40

Iris -- goddess of the Rainbow; daughter of Thaumas and Electra, 4

Ismene -- daughter of Asopus and Metope; married Argus, 17

Ismene -- daughter of Oedipus and Jocasta, 63

Ismenus -- son of Niobe and Amphion; killed by Apollo, 44

Ismenus -- son of Apollo and Melia, 13, 15

Ismenus -- son of Asopus and Metope, 17

Ister -- river god; son of Oceanus and Tethys, 14

Isus -- son of Priam, 25

Ithona -- wife of Minos I; mother of Lycastus, 60

Itylus: Itys -- son of Tereus and Procne, 50

Ixion -- son of Phlegyas, a son of Ares and Chryse, 7

Jason -- son of Polymele and Aeson or the son of Alcimede and Aeson; leader of the Argonauts and participant in the Calydonian Boar Hunt, 21, 27, 30, 33, 35

Jocasta: Epicaste -- daughter of Menoecceus I; married Laius; was mother and wife to Oedipus, 63

Medusa -- daughter of Sthenelus and Nicippe, 58

Megapenthes -- son of Menelaus and a slave mistress, 47

Megapenthes -- son of Proetus and Stheneboa, 57

Megara -- daughter of an early Creon of Thebes; wife of Heracles, 59

Megareus -- son of Creon or Apollo; defender of Thebes with Eteocles, 64

Meges -- son of Phyleus; went to the Trojan War, 48

Melampus -- son of Amythaon and Idomene, 36

Melanion: Hippomenes -- husband of Atalanta, 28

Melanippi -- daughter of Aeolus; by Poseidon the mother of two children, 29

Melanippus -- son of Priam, 25

Melanippus -- son of Hicetaon of Troy, 23

Melanippus -- son of Astacus; defender of Thebes with Eteocles, 64

Melas -- son of Porthaon and Euryte, 32

Melas -- son of Phrixus and Chalciope, 28, 42

Meleager -- son of Oeneus and Althaea; married Cleopatra and also loved Atalanta of Calydon; went with Jason and the Argonauts, and later was the hero of the Calydonian Boar Hunt, 28, 32, 33, 39

Melia -- one of the Oceanids; mother of Ismenus by Apollo, 13, 15

Melia -- mother of Amycus by Poseidon, 8

Melia -- wife of Inachus, 53

Melicertes: Palaemon -- son of Ino and Athamas, 28, 62

Melite -- one of the Nereids, 5

Melobosis -- one of the Oceanids, 14

Melpomene -- one of the Muses, 2

Memnon -- son of Tithonus and Eos; was killed in the Trojan War, 23, 43, 48

Memphis -- wife of Epaphus, the son of Io and Zeus, 11, 53

Menelaus -- son of Atreus and Aerope; went to the Trojan War over the abduction of Helen, 47, 48

Menestheus -- son of Peteus, the son of Orneus; went to the Trojan War from Athens, 48, 50

Menesto -- one of the Oceanids, 14

Menoecceus I -- son of Pentheus, 63

Menoecceus II -- son of Creon and Eurydice, 63

Menoetius -- son of Actor, the son of Myrmidon and Peisidice; one of the Argonauts; by Sthenele or Polymele, the father of Patroclus, 17, 29, 39

Index to Genealogy Charts

Ram with the Golden Fleece -- son of Poseidon by Theophane, the daughter of Bisaltes, 8

Rhadamanthus -- son of Europa and Zeus; husband of Alcmena after the death of Amphitryon, 11, 58, 60

Rhea -- Titan daughter of Uranus and Gaea; married her brother Cronus, 2, 6

Rhesus -- son of Strymon and Euterpe, or one of the other Muses, 3, 14

Rhexenor -- son of Nausithous; father of Arete, 9

Rhode -- daughter of Poseidon; wife of Helios, by whom she was the mother of the Heliades, 8, 42

Rhodea -- one of the Oceanids, 14

Rhodius -- river god; son of Oceanus and Tethys, 14

Rhodope -- wife of Haemus, the son of Boreas, 43

River gods -- sons of Oceanus and Tethys, 14

Rumor -- daughter of Gaea, 1

Salamis -- daughter of Asopus and Metope, 17

Salmoneus -- son of Aeolus; father of Tyro, 27, 34

Samia -- daughter of Maender; married Ancaeus, a son of Poseidon, 8

Samus -- son of Ancaeus and Samia, 8

Sangarius -- river god; possibly the father of Hecuba, 14, 16, 25

Sarpedon -- son of Europa and Zeus, 11, 60

Scamander: Xanthus -- river god of Troy; father of Callirrhoe, who married Tros, a King of Troy, 16, 22

Schoeneus -- son of Themisto and Athamas; possibly the father of Atalanta, 28

Scylla -- daughter of Phorcys and Hecate, 5, 12

Scylla -- daughter of Nisus, 52

Scythes -- son of Heracles and Echidna, 59

Scythian Kings -- descendants of Scythes, the son of Heracles, 59

Sea-Hags: Graeae -- daughters of Phorcys and Ceto, 5

Selene -- Moon-goddess, daughter of Hyperion and Thea; loved Endymion, 31, 42

Semele -- daughter of Cadmus and Harmonia; mother of Dionysus by Zeus, 11, 62

Sicyon -- son of Pelops, 45

Sidero -- second wife of Salmoneus, 34

Silenus -- son of Pan, or possibly a brother of Pan, 21

Stymphalus -- son of the river god Ladon, 16

Styx -- one of the Oceanids; married Pallas, the son of Crius and Eurybia, 4, 14

Syrinx -- daughter of the river god Ladon; loved by Pan, 16, 21

Syrus -- son of Sinope and Apollo, 17

Talaria: Hilaria -- daughter of Leucippus; sister of Phoebe, 41

Talaus -- son of Bias and Pero; father of Adrastus, Eriphyle, and others; one of the Argonauts, 36, 39

Talus: Perdix -- son of Polycaste; nephew of Daedalus, 50

Tanagra -- daughter of Aeolus, 29

Tantalus -- son of Zeus and Pluto, one of the Oceanids, 11, 14, 44

Tantalus II -- son of Thyestes; first husband of Clytemnestra, 40, 46

Tantalus -- son of Niobe and Amphion; killed by Apollo, 44

Taphius -- son of Hippothoe, 58

Tartarus -- creation of Gaea, 1

Taygeta -- one of the Pleiades, 20

Tecmessa -- war bride of Ajax, the son of Telamon, 18

Tecton -- son of Harmon of Troy, 24

Telamon -- son of Aeacus and Endeis; married Periboea, the mother of Ajax; father of Teucer by Hesione, a Trojan princess; one of the Argonauts, and hunter of the Calydonian Boar, 18, 23, 33, 39, 45

Telastus -- son of Priam, 25

Telchines -- nine daughters of Pontus and Thalassa, 4

Teledamas -- son of Agamemnon and Cassandra, 47

Telegonus -- son of Circe and Odysseus; said to have married Penelope after the death of Odysseus, 30, 40, 42

Telegonus -- a King of Egypt; married Io in her later life, 53

Telemus -- Cyclops son of Thoosa and Poseidon, 5, 9

Telepassa: Argiope -- wife of Agenor, 53, 60

Telephus -- son of Heracles and Auge, 59

Telesto -- one of the Oceanids, 14

Telphusa -- daughter of the river god Ladon, 16

Temenus -- son of Pelasgus, 17